Walking in
Their Footsteps

Walking in Their Footsteps

by Fr. Daniel Taillez, O.M.I.

Queenship

PUBLISHING COMPANY
P.O. Box 42028 Santa Barbara, CA 93140-2028
(800) 647-9882 • (805) 957-4893 • Fax: (805) 957-1631

Library of Congress Number # 98-66434

Published by:
  Queenship Publishing
  P.O. Box 42028
  Santa Barbara, CA 93140-2028
  (800) 647-9882 • (805) 957-4893 • Fax: (805) 957-1631

Printed in the United States of America

ISBN: 1-57918-069-8

CONTENTS

PREFACE

Twelve years ago, I began to imagine how Mary would have remembered what had happened that night in Bethlehem. While I was writing that first "meditation," *"He thought of us, first!,"* my mind was on a couple of very good friends. Down through the years, I've remembered each of them often. The first of them was a classmate, ordained with me something over thirty years ago. In the 70s, he left the ministry and got married. Over the years, we've kept in touch. The second was born in Laos, where I'd been working as an Oblate Missionary until 1975 when we were summarily removed from our Mission. He is a Catholic, although over the years, his connection with the Church has become quite tenuous, quite peripheral. I continue to stay in touch with him, too.

Over the years, with both of them in mind, I've continually posed to myself two questions: "Is there some particular word of comfort and encouragement that might 'speak' to them in their present situation?" And: "What can be done to reach out to them, to reassure them that the Lord's awesome peace can be theirs ... whatever be the roads they've traveled?"

My two good friends — and for that matter, each one of us, wherever we might find ourselves on our own pilgrimage — are called to measure-up to that Message of Liberation, to make our own turning-to-the-Lord more conscious and more real. We are all called to know something of the enthusiasm of the writers of the

Gospels, of Paul and James, of Peter and the other Apostles. And we are called to make that enthusiasm our own!

In fact, God has provided the means to accomplish this. We have all the books of the New Testament, we have well over eighty generations of believers, we have all of our celebrations, and — above all! — we have the ever-living, ever enlightening presence of the Consoler.

Is there anything else? Perhaps, we wish — sometimes — that we'd lived in the midst of those first-generation Christian communities. There, we'd have been able to hear Matthew or Luke, Mark and John, and Paul, and the others. We'd have known the hardships that each of them had come to know as they'd gradually come to the surrender of themselves into Christ's hands, as they'd gradually seen something new and different ... something so new and so different that it enabled them to live and die for it. Walking in their footsteps, we too would have been overwhelmed by the humility of our God, of our merciful Savior.

Perhaps these simple reflections will evoke something in us which will take us to Capernaum or to Jerusalem, to Ephesus or to Rome. Letting go of our present-day anxieties and doubts, of our earthly convictions and our so-much needed securities, we'd join them in making — day by day Jesus' commitment to the Father visible, tangible, real. Ever so gradually, the Lord's peace and serenity would penetrate, and shine through each facet of our own life, as a sunbeam lighting the way as we pursue our own pilgrimage.

That one day when Jesus was talking with Matthew in Capernaum. It was only after a lengthy and warm conversation that Jesus dared to make the request: "Come, follow Me!" And, it was no different for Peter or James, or for Mary who spent much time listening to persons like Mark, or Nicholas, or Rebecca. It always takes time to sort-out our feelings and our hesitations in coming to believe, really and radically. It takes much time to accept a new way of seeing things, to come to that empathy which alone would help them cross over from mere interest to faith in the New Way, the Way that renews and refreshes the world. As but one example: James was completely present to Nicholas, who was so steeped-in and proud of the religious traditions of his people. It was only through, and after his long conversation with James that he could be ready to accept the newness and uniqueness of the Gospel.

Peter could readily identify with the renowned Senator, Gaius. He, in fact, could put himself into Gaius' shoes. And then Peter could explain how it was that his "hope" had sustained and strengthened him during the course of those past twenty-five years.

May that time of grateful listening become the "style" of each of us, at this time in our lives. For, only thus will we be able to earn the attentiveness of our sisters and brothers, and then to let the Good News bear fruit in them, too! The illustrations have been drawn by Doug Bekke, Minneapolis MN; they bring the message home.

It has been a long and tedious effort for Fr. Robert B. Wellisch (University of St. Thomas, in St. Paul) to make the first corrections; without him these meditations couldn't be the way they are now. Fr. Bob, thanks so much for your exacting work.

A special word of gratitude to Fr. Joseph Paris, O.M.I., a fellow Oblate, who reviewed these reflections. When I translated them from my French into English, they could scarcely have been understood; they were like a baby who needs suitable clothes before the Christening-reception! And it was this that Fr. Joe has done. He undertook the lengthy and demanding task of reshaping them. Without his thorough and careful work, I'm afraid that they'd hardly have "spoken" to you.

Fr. Daniel Taillez, O.M.I.
St. Paul MN
August 4, 1997

FOREWORD

Walking in Their Footsteps is a series of imaginary conversations among people we have met in the New Testament and between them and others created entirely by Father Daniel Taillez, OMI. The author is a missionary who has served the Church in his native France, in Laos, in Haiti and in the United States. He has walked in many places, always in the footsteps of the apostles. Everywhere he's walked he has also talked of the Lord the apostles knew and loved.

Missionaries think differently. Their conversation is never just with the person they're talking to; it includes Jesus and His friends throughout the ages. The Church is created through sacred conversation: the Father sends His Eternal Word who introduces us to His Father and tells us to call Him ours. While God needs only one Word, we need many. For two thousand years those who follow Jesus have spoken of Him in thousands of languages using many thousands of words. Great artists portray this sacred conversation which creates the Church by gathering on canvas or walls saints from many cultures and across many ages around Jesus in the arms of His mother, the Virgin Mary. She makes Him available to us and fosters the conversation in her quiet way. Each of the saints picks it up in his or her distinctive voice.

Fr. Taillez's voice is that of an Oblate of Mary Immaculate, one who has let himself become Mary's servant in order to speak more authentically of her Son. The conversations he sets out in this book aim to engage the reader personally. They are designed to bring the reader into a sacred conversation. Father Taillez's original and personal insights into the Gospel can jog his readers along their own paths into a Kingdom which is always both a gift enjoyed now and a gift still to be proclaimed.

Francis Cardinal George, OMI
Archbishop of Chicago

I

He Thought of Us First

During the past couple of days, I've been wondering just what Mary would have said were She to have reminisced with Luke, around the year 45 or 50, about everything that had happened at Bethlehem. Luke is there, "drawing Her out," evoking memories. For her part, Mary speaks very quietly, and very simply, retelling as best as She can remember. She says:

"You know, Luke, I'll never be able to forget those moments in Bethlehem! You just can't forget those shepherds as they came into the stable, out of the darkness of the night. I don't know... maybe the most striking thing was their surprise: "What, a baby? Here? In this stable? With an ox and a donkey? What is this anyway...?

"They looked long and hard at the Baby; and they came and picked Him up. I remember, when they did, I just shuddered... I was afraid for my Baby! After all, they'd come from nowhere, dressed just about the way you'd expect shepherds to dress ... not very clean, and so tattered and torn! As a matter of fact, I don't think that they'd even washed before coming! That stable fairly reeked of their sheep, not to mention the ox and the donkey. The stench, it was just there, saturating everything ... and need I say, pretty overpowering!

"And amidst all of this, the one thing that really stands out in my memory is the smile on their faces as they took turns holding the Baby, passing Him from one to the other. It seemed that they just became radiant as they held ... and beheld ... my Baby! Their eyes, their whole face just glowed with happiness! The happiness of having God and holding Him right there, in their arms. Never again, in all my days, have I ever seen such radiant smiles as I saw on the faces of those shepherds. It was something overwhelming ... certainly strong enough that I completely forgot the "aroma" ... and the stable! I even forgot that it was night, that it was so cold. The shepherds being there ... it warmed my heart, and enkindled light there in that dark, dank stable.

"And during all this time, they were jabbering, excitedly, among themselves: "What a break! ... to be here, the first ones to see, and to hold the Savior!" "...in our own arms, and hearts!" "...It IS real... and it's really US! ... just "nobodies" like us!" "God must really love the simple people... *He thought of us first!"*

"They stayed ... they stayed with us all through that night. It was just the Baby, and Joseph and me ... and those shepherds! We just kept talking with one another; we were all pretty excited. Neither Joseph nor I wanted to stop. And the shepherds, well, they couldn't! Even now, I can somehow feel the warmth and the excitement of their happiness. It seemed that they just couldn't get over the fact that they were the first to see Him, the first to cradle Him, the first to hold Him so very tenderly and caress Him.

"And you know, Luke, when I take the time to remember this now, I just tell myself: 'The Good News of Salvation' is — first and foremost! — for the 'little people!' It is to them that the love of God has to be announced first. And as I remember it over these many years, there's one thought that keeps coming back to me: there'll never be a life, never be anyone destitute, or degraded, anyone who is really hurting, on whom God's smile will not blossom. That unfailing serenity of God, His inexhaustible peace, His never-ending kindness ... they're just there for anyone, for all of us who hunger for it! No one is 'left out!' **No one is excluded!** Every last one of us can 'glow.' I certainly saw it shining in the eyes of those shepherds.

"Luke, from now on, there will not be anyone to say these words, 'That message of peace and joy is not for me All that is for the others, not for me! I don't deserve such attention I am not worthy to see God take care of me anymore!' No, from now on, nobody, I mean nobody will ever say these words anymore; that kind of despair is over. By-gones are by-gones. God's light and peace are for each and everyone of us.

"Just think about it! Isn't this the very heart of Jesus' message spoken to each one who is born again in Him? This great joy of knowing that we are loved by God, *no matter what ... whatever be our past...* This irrepressible peace, which can well-up and overflow the human heart ... *whatever be our past!* ... God can breathe life into delicately perfumed flowers in the heart of every one of His children. Luke, haven't we all known that — really! — God is not like us! He makes a flood-tide flow out of parched, lifeless ground. Just where we'd expect bitterness and confusion, weariness and despair, God can germinate and call into growth kindness and hope, confidence, and the most peaceful surrender to Him.

"And, thanks to my Baby, every single human being — and I truly believe that: *'every single one!'* — can come to glow with the splendor and the joy of being close to God. Thanks to Jesus, the open-hearted welcome God holds out will never be an empty gesture, a hollow word. Thanks to Jesus, the goodness of God is always there, renewing everything, restoring everything. His goodness brings happiness and a deeper and more pervasive happiness than we'd ever dreamed... the happiness of becoming — or maybe, becoming again! — Friends of God! ...and this, *whatever be the past!*

"In that little, dark stable, in spite of the cold, and with all those smells, I came to have a clear idea of the truth of this. Those shepherds with their tattered clothes, and their dirt ... came with open hearts. And it was this that nourished me with God, and with His goodness to all the people on this earth! ALLELUIA!"

December 31, 1985

Walking in Their Footsteps

2

A Fairly Long Conversation

When I try to imagine just what happened in that little town of Capernaum that day when Jesus called Matthew, I come up with something like this:

I guess that Jesus would have been there, talking with Matthew — the Tax-Man — for some time, there in the local Tax Office; it'd only be after a fairly long and friendly conversation that Jesus would dare to make his request: **FOLLOW ME**! *(Mt 9:9) And it wasn't easy! It would have taken a bit of time ... and effort ... and a bit more diplomacy! After all, Matthew was being asked to give-up a lucrative career to "follow" an itinerant preacher; and those others who were already "following" Jesus, they just weren't quite "his kind!"*

Maybe this might have been the way that Jesus managed to "get" Matthew. When He came to the Tax-Office, there wasn't anyone else around. Perhaps, it was just past mid-afternoon, and Matthew was almost finished with the books for that day. Maybe this would be the scenario:

JESUS: Hello! I've been hearing quite a little-bit about you, Matthew; and I was in the neighborhood. I just thought I'd stop by to meet you. How're things going? How're things going for you?

MATTHEW: Just great! Things have never been better!

JESUS: Wonderful! You must be one of the luckiest men around, or I'm missing my guess!

MATTHEW: Oh, so-so! You know, once you've got it made, you shouldn't have to worry about anything. You can wear what you want ... and nothing is really "too expensive"; if you want to throw a party, or have a dinner, you have no trouble getting the big-shots to come ... they know they'll be well taken-care of ... the food, the drinks. So, at the end of the party, everyone goes back home quite "tipsy!" Yeah, I guess I am pretty lucky... You know, in this kind of work, I can feel pretty safe from the ups and downs of the local economy. When I take time to think about it, I'd have to consider myself as one most singularly blessed, wouldn't you say?

JESUS: I guess that you would hardly have to worry about your tomorrows ... or, for that matter, for your next years! And, I'd have to guess, too, that there are plenty around here who might be more than a little envious, jealous. Like you said, you are mighty lucky! ... but deep down, Matthew, in your heart, are you really happy?

MATTHEW: Yes and no! I guess I'm like most: not completely happy ... you know, even for me, there are so many things that I'd like to have, that I think I need. So, when they look at me and see me as supremely contented, I'm afraid they're wrong!

JESUS: What're you saying, Matthew?

MATTHEW: I need some friends! I mean, it's just terribly lonely! I need some real friends. You know, there are plenty of hangers-on, but real friends ... where are they?

JESUS: But with your success, your money, there must be a lot of people who like you...

MATTHEW: Maybe so ... but I sure'd have a hard time finding them! I'd be ready to say that they just aren't any! ... not as I see it! You know, you can be well-off, like I am; you can have all you want, but *you just can't buy friendship and love: they're just not* *for sale!* Really, here in Capernaum, most everyone — deep down — really detests me, hates me because I do this work for the Romans. And as for myself, I'm considered as, and I consider myself as the toughest tax-collector around. Nobody gets by, no one escapes my "attention" ... so they all pay-up, no exceptions! Once you start letting one or the other off, you might as well get out of a job like this. They all come in and repeat, time after time, that I have no mercy. But, what choice do I have? So they come to hate me. There's not a single Jewish citizen of Capernaum that'd think of me, or call me a "friend." They all respect me — I do have the where-with-all — but still, when I'm at home at night, I think of myself as the unhappiest of them all!

JESUS: You know, Matthew, I've met, and I've talked with lots of people over these past months, but you've put it all in a nutshell as well as, or better than any of them.

MATTHEW: Hey, thank you! Maybe I've finally found someone who understands how things are. You know, often enough, I think to myself: 'How come *you have everything* you need, everything you want ... and at the same time, *you are nothing at all?*'

JESUS: Well, you've just said that you know that money can't buy friendship, or real respect, or love. I feel the same way. And when we try to act as if it might, what we find is emptiness, uselessness, meaninglessness.

MATTHEW: Finally! You're about the first one who's ever put himself in my shoes... But, how do I get myself out of this kind of situation? I need happiness just as much as anyone else, you know.

JESUS: If you would come and listen to me, I have something to say ... something that comes from heaven. You'll hear that mercy is the first thing God expects from us. In fact, it's only when you truly love people that God's peace and happiness can be yours.

MATTHEW: Well, to come along, to be one of your followers ... doesn't sound all that great! ... but then, it isn't all that bad either. It could be ... it just could be that I could "buy into" it.

JESUS: Matthew, I'm going to say just three things... Maybe you will "buy into it," as you put it... *The first is this:* you've just complained about the emptiness of your life, that it is as if you are a nothing. And, what I say is this: "What does a man gain, if he wins the whole world and ruins his life?" (Mt 16:26). Can you answer that?

MATTHEW: Well ... no! While I appear as among the richest here in Capernaum, deep down in my own heart, I am the poorest. It's as if my life is empty, a failure, that it just doesn't add up! But, you said you have three things to say?

JESUS: I do ... *the second is this:* "Man does not live by bread alone, but by every word that comes from the mouth of God." (Mt 4:4) And, I'm not talking about the bread you pick-up at the bakery! I'm talking about your money, your reputation, anything you can count. Tell me: does any of it ... does all of it give you enough to make you genuinely happy?

MATTHEW: No, not really! I've thought about it often enough ... and I've just thought aloud: my riches, my properties, my position, everything I have, none of it really fulfills my hunger for happiness, none of it gives any precise focus to my hope of making something out of my life. Maybe, someday God will show me a way out of this miserable situation. Now, let's see: you said "Man does not live..." Almost every day these past months, I've never thought that deeply. Maybe there *is* a way to save me from myself ... by merely listening to God's word, and by living accordingly... As you might imagine, over these months, I haven't given God much time or space in my life! I wonder ... why didn't I ever think about that before? But, you said you had three things...

JESUS: You seem to be so successful, so prosperous, so well-off ... but deep in your heart ... you've said it yourself, you're heart-sick! And this? Simply because you have no respect, no compassion, no real love for anyone. Yes, your heart *is* sick. As you look at the rest of your life, you can find recovery in only one way ... and that is, to live on love. For God says (and *this is my third word*)

"What I want is mercy, not sacrifice." (Mt 9:13). So, you see, Matthew, if you would begin again to love God, and to show mercy to others, don't you think that your life would have a finer focus, a better direction?

MATTHEW: Yes, it would! If I could only begin to love, maybe I could be inflamed with it ... and for sure, everything would be so very different. Yes ... and it would give a direction, a purpose to life, to me. As you said, nothing counts more than genuine mercy. The vision your words provide have already begun to heal my heart of its emptiness, to make me aware of the depth of my selfishness. You know, Jesus, you've saved me from myself. Do you have any other words that'd do what these have? What would I have to do that'd help me become poor in spirit?

JESUS: *FOLLOW ME!*

January 7, 1989

Walking in Their Footsteps

3

Immediately They Left, and Returned to Jerusalem

This just might be part of Cleopas' and his friend's conversation while they were returning to Jerusalem (Luke 24:13-35)

CLEOPAS: He really did rise! He has to be the Son of God! ... (Sing: "For his love is ever lasting!) He ... He *rose* ... from the dead! Our Messiah, our Liberator, the Savior of humankind ... it *was* He ... it wasn't just a look-alike! (Sing: "For his love is ever lasting!)

HIS FRIEND: This is too much ... how could you ever imagine such a thing? We've got to tell them ... we've got to tell everyone! We've got to talk to the other disciples. They have to believe us ... but then, will they?

CLEOPAS: We've got to tell them, all right ... and not only them, but everyone!

HIS FRIEND: This will certainly be light overcoming their darkness, joy overcoming their grief and sorrow. They'll smile on God ... as God as evidently smiled on all of us. God is with us ... He's so powerful ... and so close to all of us...!

CLEOPAS: Now, let's try to put it all together ... just what we've got ... For me, the first thing is that from now on, Jesus will always be with us, walking with us, just like he did with us on the road. Nothing will ever be able to separate us from His tremendous love, from His unbounded mercy. (Sing: Blessed be God, forever. Amen!)

HIS FRIEND: But, really, isn't that what He has been doing for these past three years. In the beginning, we were all caught-up in it, trying to see who would be closest to Him ... trying to be first! Remember when they asked Him who would be first in His Kingdom? And, do you remember how we were looking forward to a rebellion, to getting rid of the Romans? When He told us about forgiving... that "seventy-times-seven?" Really, that *was* a bit much! And Jesus, He was so calm through it all... neither angry with us, nor terribly disappointed! Little by little, He brought us around to thinking in new ways. He always seemed to be ready... and so good at putting Himself into our shoes. He really had a way of bringing us around ... so gently, but so surely...!

CLEOPAS: And do you remember how — at the beginning — everyone who knew us, all our relatives, and our friends, just about everyone we knew or who knew us thought we were nuts, that it was just a dream to follow Him ... that following Him had no tomorrow. And, really, there were those times when we too felt deep down that it could never add up! Thank God, we never acted on those thoughts! He was so close to us, and He did make sense, so much sense! Day after day, His gentleness, His simplicity, His "bigness" and His unshakable confidence in us, despite our doubts and hesitations and reservations ... it all fit together ... it finally overcame everything that was against Him and His way. When I think back and remember, well, it was just a tremendous experience to be with Him, to be like brothers with Him. (cfr. Mt 17:4; Hebr 2:11)

HIS FRIEND: Yeah, and in spite of everything, I've never regretted that I stayed. I just knew in the marrow of my bones that He could, and would take care of us. And, with time, and His untiring efforts, something new took root in us, it was almost like a "new creation." When I think back, He was really transforming us ...

almost like being reborn — not just once, but time and time again. And He always seemed to understand us even better than we understood ourselves. And, you know ... when I think about it, He really did love me! ... so very much more than I ever deserved. And, He loved tirelessly ... just think of what we were, before...

CLEOPAS: And this afternoon, He did it again! Even when we — with our blinded eyes — couldn't see Him, He was there. And He knew our disappointment, our hopelessness ... our unbelief, our anger! And He just walked along with us ... He knew we didn't recognize Him ... we just didn't expect anything! He really wanted to hear what was going on with us... As I think back to what we were talking about while we were walking along, He must have a great sense of humor. He pretended to know nothing at all about what was bothering us and when He asked: "What are you talking about, back and forth?" ... And when we'd relived everything that'd happened in Jerusalem these past few days, He just heard us out, listened so patiently, so attentively to everything we said. He never interrupted our outpouring of disappointment, our recital of grief ... how everything had simply disintegrated right in front of our eyes, everything...!

HIS FRIEND: And, not even a hint of disappointment with us and how we were feeling. I guess that, really, He could have been even more disappointed with us than we were with all that had happened. You know: I think that He sensed our pain, even more than we did! He listened to every word ... never even hinting that our lack of faith could have made Him sick with disappointment. He listened to all our "whys," and He didn't seem to be that disturbed with our anger either. He was just there, listening, and understanding. I felt that His heart was right where mine was ... almost as if He'd put the heavier part of the Cross back onto His own shoulders. And, I really felt good ... having someone so close, so attentive, listening, understanding. I can't think of anyone, or any other time that I felt myself in such close and warm communion, in the presence of such tender and respectful love.

CLEOPAS: And, that's just His way... I can't imagine that He'd deal with any one less gently, less understandingly than that! Who could ever suffer, who would ever be able to pour-out his pain and suffering and He would not listen as attentively, as lovingly as He heard us out this afternoon? Who could ever claim to "be alone" with his or her anguish now? Nobody ... because Jesus, the ever present, the compassionate friend and brother, the respectful Master is there, walking along with us. Our struggles and our efforts to live out His Gospel, He'll carry all of them in His heart, right along with us. His unbounded mercy will be just as close as He was this afternoon on the Emmaus Road.

HIS FRIEND: And, there's something else we have to remember... Jesus was put to death for us, for our sins, and He rose from the dead to justify us. From now on, He is Lord, He is our Savior (Rom 4:25; Acts 4:12). (Sing: Blessed be God forever. Amen, Alleluia!)

CLEOPAS: You know, I never did find it easy to really *believe* that Jesus is the Lamb of God who takes away the sins of the world.

HIS FRIEND: When we were back there on the road, when He asked us what we'd been thinking about, and talking about: "Weren't you kind of thinking something like: 'The Lord, our God, He is everywhere, but not there ... not on that Cross...?'"

CLEOPAS: Yeah, it was precisely what we'd said a thousand times. How often have we heard those words of Isaiah: "A man despised, the lowest of men, a man of sorrows, familiar with suffering; one from whom we turned-away. Like a lamb that is taken away to be slaughtered..." (Is 53)

HIS FRIEND: And, when He said "Of course, on Golgotha, you weren't there to jeer and ridicule like those passing by who said, almost in chorus, 'He saved others, but He cannot save Himself. He trusted in God! Now let God save Him if He wants... For He did claim to be the Son of God...'" But Jesus just continued, "...you didn't join them ... even though in your hearts you couldn't imagine that God would be there, when someone is suffering so much! Really, it was just too much!"

CLEOPAS: Yeah, it sure was! We'd lost faith ... but, remember how gentle He was when He reminded us of the Centurion's faith. He said: "That pagan, that Roman, he saw the way I was suffering, and dying. He was struck by my deep peace, by my steadfast trust in the Father. He heard the words: "Father, into Your hands I commit my spirit." He'd overheard my prayer: "Father, forgive them..." That Centurion had never seen a dying man with such grandeur, overcoming all his fears. So (Jesus said) the Centurion had concluded: "Without God, this, any of this ... all of this, would be impossible! God does help this holy man! Truly, this is the Son of God!" (Mk 15:39)

HIS FRIEND: And, when Jesus added: "...and, realize that the Centurion alone believed that Jesus is the Son of God ... at the very time when you, those with whom Jesus had lived, among whom He'd walked and talked for most of three years, you were just beside yourselves, aimless!" And then ... did you notice how gently Jesus spoke, and that inimitable smile when He said: "Don't you think that you should be ashamed of yourselves?"

CLEOPAS: Yeah, we sure should be! For so long we'd believed that Jesus was the Son of God — just like Peter (Mt 16:16) and Martha (Jn 11:2) — that He was the fulfillment of God's promises. But, faced with the incomprehensible fact of the crucifixion, we just quit believing!

HIS FRIEND: And, remember how point-by-point He explained that He, the Son of God, had offered Himself to God, so as to cleanse us from all our sins? He quoted Isaiah's own words when He said: "By his wounds, we are healed . He was bearing the faults of many, and He was praying through it all, for us sinners." (Is 53)

CLEOPAS: Really, on the Cross He chose to identify Himself with the serpent Moses raised-up in the desert, and "all the afflicted who looked on it were healed." (Nm 21:4-9; Jn 3:14)

HIS FRIEND: He died, He most certainly did die, but He rose. From now on, His purifying Blood, His Spirit, and His love are there, will *always* be there, to cleanse us from our sins, to quench our thirst for purity and healing, to flood our hearts with "His fountains of living water." (Jn 7:38)

CLEOPAS: And "He rose to life to justify us" (cfr Rom 4:25); He's alive now! He can die no more! He really "passed-over" to the Father (Jn 13:1). Jesus explained that just like the Jews, who'd left their slavery in Egypt and become free, just as they'd thrown away their chains, left their slavery, and become in a very particular way God's own people ... well, the same thing was happening for us!

HIS FRIEND: I was awfully slow to recognize that He *had* risen to new life, that "death now had no power over Him." (Rom 6:9) "He is the first to rise from the dead." (Acts 26:23) "He's the first to be reborn from the dead." (Col 1:18).

CLEOPAS: And, then He explained that "all His brothers and sisters in the whole world, who call upon the Lord's Name, will be saved." (Acts 2:21). We can all walk the path He walked; we'll all share in His life, His power, His strength, His humility, His peace, His joy at being God's own sons and daughters

HIS FRIEND: Yeah, "He passed from this world to His Father." (Jn 13:1). From now on, He is our Way, our ladder. Through Him, every one of us can return to the Father's house ... like prodigal children. Each one of us belongs to God again, if we so choose; we can love Him more than ever, because we've been empowered by the touch of the Holy Spirit.

CLEOPAS: But, there's still something else: He promised to be close to us forever! He told us that as we gather in His name, whenever we gather to recall His offering on the Cross and His victory through His resurrection.

HIS FRIEND: Do you remember ... when we went into the Inn and invited Him to stay with us... how He sat at table with us, took the bread and said, "Take this, and eat it, this is My Body, given for you."

CLEOPAS: And at that instant, our eyes were opened, we finally "saw!"

HIS FRIEND: How could we ever forget? In that simple meal, just like the Hebrews have been doing for generations. They remember their deliverance from the slavery of Egypt in the Passover Meal; in that commemoration, God was continually reminding them that He is the One who can save people from their bondages, from all their sins and failures, even from their lack of faith. He is the One, alive still, Who is always watching over, taking care of His children. He is always there ... He'll never quit watching, and caring for every one of us.

CLEOPAS: From now on, our meal — when we gather to remember Jesus' death and victory — will be the real Passover. We'll always have the Victim with us, a Victim Who purifies us from our sins, and that wine which gives deep and lasting joy. Our meal — which recalls His passover to the Father — will be "the Cross for us, each day." Through His meal, He'll let us be part of His own offering made in love and it'll be so real, so empowering in our lives. Day by day, we'll be able to renew our offering to the Father with His offering, our surrender with His surrender! Through His meal, He'll be with us, be at our side, "drawing each of us to Himself." (cfr. Jn 12:32)

HIS FRIEND: It just overwhelms me that our God could be so humble ... Through His meal, He lets His victory become ours. He overcomes our own lack of faith, He renews our bonding to the Father ... Emmanuel, today, tomorrow, and for ever, always so close, always so — available, always there... just for us.

CLEOPAS: Hurry up. We've got something awesome to tell the Apostles! There's no one on this earth...there'll never be anyone who doesn't need to hear...

October 11, 1989

Walking in Their Footsteps

4

He Took Everything From Me... And Yet, I've Got Everything

Some time after Jesus' Resurrection, Mary Magdalene ran into an old friend, one who is still "working the streets." What would they have to say to one another? Let's just guess...

HER FRIEND: I haven't seen you for quite a while... Where've you been? (Very surprised) ... where's all your stuff, your jewelry, your perfume, your outfit? ... The stuff that always made you the prettiest of all? You... you know, there are plenty of men who are pretty disappointed...! What happened? were you mugged, or what?

MARY MAGDALENE: Well, yes ... in a way! There was someone who came and really ripped me off! You know, there's just nothing left, nothing at all!

HER FRIEND: Oh, gee! And you were always so nice ... one of the nicest ones! And, I guess I don't have to tell you, the most popular! With the tricks you turned, you had money for whatever you needed or wanted; really, more than you knew what to do with. Did someone turn you in to the police? Maybe, it'd be good if all of us just got together and nailed whoever it was...

MARY MAGDALENE: The one who took away everything, He is the one who enriched me in a way that I'd would never have imagined ... and He did it in the very act of taking it away!

HER FRIEND: Hey, what's that all about? You're saying that He took everything, and at the same time, made you as rich as the Queen of Sheba? Hey ... have you lost your marbles, or what?

MARY MAGDALENE: Well, maybe you could say that! Among other things, I did lose my senses ... and, really, I don't regret losing everything, not really!

HER FRIEND: OK, let's quit talking in riddles, old girl! Let's cut out the mystery. Just tell it like it is! Let's cut away from all this mystery bit! Just tell me: what's going on with you during these past months?

MARY MAGDALENE: My "secret" ... well it's this: I met a man who changed my life completely! When I look at myself ... or think about myself, I'm just not the same as the one we both knew...

HER FRIEND: Your man ... is it someone I might know?

MARY MAGDALENE: Oh yeah! It's Jesus of Nazareth, the one they're calling the Prophet. I went to see Him and listen to Him. He forgave me... He healed me. And now He's ... well, He's my friend, really! I never knew that I could love anyone like this ... I guess that I'd never known love at all ... but, Him, I do love! You just can't know how I love Him! And that love! His love makes me the richest woman in the whole world, much richer than your Queen of Sheba...

HER FRIEND: Now, let me get this straight ... You're talking about that Jesus who fed that great big crowd, the one who healed the lepers ... the one — isn't He the one? — the one who was crucified? You say that He healed you? Were you sick? I hadn't seen you in a while, but I didn't know you'd been sick.

MARY MAGDALENE: Yes, as a matter of fact, that's just what He did. His healing wasn't from some sickness, but from what was all twisted-up in my heart, in my head ... what was so rotten! Deep inside me, there was just nothing good anymore, nothing really "human." It was almost like a really nice house, or a splendid mausoleum ... nicely furnished but "full of dead men's bones and rot on the inside" (Mt 23:27). I don't know how to describe it; you just have to know it yourself. The most horrendous leper who ever lived on the face of this planet ... I was even worse ... before Jesus came, and healed me ... by His forgiveness.

HER FRIEND: You know, Mary, there are those days when I really hate myself, hate the "johns," hate the streets ... I just have to close my eyes and the eyes of my heart to all the shadows and darkness of my life. I feel, deep down, like a termite infested house, it might look good enough, but there is just nothing solid there!

MARY MAGDALENE: Let me finish ... I went and saw, and heard Jesus. Whether or not you can believe it, He looked at me, and saw so much deeper than what everyone else was seeing ... beyond the jewelry, the clothes, the perfume. He saw the rottenness ... the sin; everything about me that disgusted even me! He, Jesus, saw all of that. And I cried; I cried more than I've ever cried; I cried my heart out at His feet. He looked and saw the deep side of my heart. And, with the kind of assurance I've never seen in anyone but Him, He calmly said to me: "Your sins, all of them, they're forgiven. Go in peace, Mary, and sin no more!" (Lk 7:38-49; Jn 8:1-11) And, when He spoke, He spoke with such power, with so much authority ... it had to be, just like He was saying!

HER FRIEND: Are you trying to tell me that with those words, He wiped away your whole past life? He wiped away all the shame? He gave you a new heart ... and new hope? Isn't this what you're really saying?

MARY MAGDALENE: That's just how I feel. I went to see and to hear — and my heart was harder and colder than a stone, my life wasn't worth a plugged-penny — and He healed me, inside and out. A totally new heart, warm and soft, as clear as spring water, that's what He gave me ... besides a new hopefulness ... and new eyes! That's what I meant when I said that I feel like I'm the happiest person alive, the most satisfied, richer than Solomon, Pilate or Caesar. What I was before? It's as if I had only a single dime to my name. And now, it's as if I were a millionaire. To have Jesus, to love Him, that's my treasure. Now, I have everything, I've got everything that my heart hungers and hopes for!

HER FRIEND: And, you have no regrets? The jewelry, the perfume? the clothes?

MARY MAGDALENE: Not really... When I think back ... I'm just so happy now that I did get rid of all that!

HER FRIEND: Come on now, Mary! Don't try to tell me that you don't look back ... and miss it ... some of it...

MARY MAGDALENE: No! Really, I don't! When I think about it ... any of it ... all of it ... I don't miss it at all. I'm just too happy with what I have to miss it!

HER FRIEND: Mary ... I've known you too long ... and too well! You should know better than to try to lie to me ... but right now ... well...

MARY MAGDALENE: Yes, I do know only too well! But then, I remember how wasted all those years were, how I spent so much ... time, money, energy ... on the kinds of things that I don't need now ... and I'm humiliated! Really, they strike me as nothing more than cheap trinkets, a heap of garbage! (Phil 3,8) For so long, I've been so terribly, so desperately wrong. I had made myself the center of everything; it's as if I was enslaved, chained, bound. To go back to that? Not on your life! You see, to love Jesus, it's ... it's like heaven on earth. There's just nothing to compare it to ... there's nothing that'd make me change my mind about the one I call "Rabbouni — Good Master." (Jn 20:16)

HER FRIEND: Now, wait a minute, Mary. If I understand what you're saying, you mean that by loving Jesus, you're just trying to repay something of what He has given to you?

MARY MAGDALENE: Well, not exactly! When you say "what He has given me" ... are you thinking of something in the past? That's not really the way I see it. His words — spoken with such assurance, with such deep conviction — they're not "in the past." Every single day of my life, they're there ... as if He were saying them to me again, right now! Every single day, His love comes to purify, to renew, to free me ... each day He is there to keep me on the Way, His way... His words — spoken another day — echo and re-echo in my mind, in my heart continually. Remember: His love isn't something in the past ... or from the past ... it's in my heart, right now! It's always with me, sustaining me, encouraging me, guiding me. And it's there — each day — more real to me than the ground we're standing on, much more warming than the sun up there in the sky.

HER FRIEND: So ... what do you have to give Him?

MARY MAGDALENE: It's just too much to even consider! I could never give back a love as intense, as tender and gentle as the love He's given me. You see, I'm sort of like a young girl who comes to realize all that her parents have done over so many years to provide her with the opportunity for a good education. Her appreciation, her respect, her obedience ... it'll never be enough to make-up for all that her parents did for her. And, my love for Jesus is like that! He "who died for us, to put to death our sins. He who was raised from the dead, living forever so that we might live of His life" ...no one life, nothing we could ever do would be enough to give back even a hundredth of what He has given to us.

You see? Believing in Him isn't a question of "getting" something from Him, asking Him for something, for some help, or for His Spirit who remakes us in His image. To believe in Him, is to love Him ... simply to love out of gratitude. And then ... when you're grateful — just like I am, now! — you just walk in His way, follow His teaching, obey His word ... as the only way we have to show our gratitude for His patience with us, His love for us, His gentleness toward us. It's so little in comparison to His love which goes so far beyond what our poor human hearts could ever dream, or imagine!

And, I'd be the happiest person alive if I could just spend the rest of my life trying to make-up for all that I've been! I'm simply overcome with the thought that nothing I'll ever be able to do will compensate, pay Him back "love for love"!

HER FRIEND: That's all well and good ... but what about all the others? Those who have seen Him, or heard Him? and what about those who'll come after us ... what about them? What about all those people — like me! — who've fallen so low ... is there any hope? ... Hope for us to be healed too? We've walked in our own way ... pretty far from God's way ... When I think just of myself, I can't help thinking that I'm "lost" to myself, as well as to God; is there any hope that I ... and all the others just like me ... maybe a little better, or maybe a little worse ... is there any hope that one day we might find something like your freedom?

MARY MAGDALENE: I don't look at it that way... we all have to remember that for God, no one is "too far away" ... no one is "lost." There is no way, no wound that His touch cannot heal."

HER FRIEND: How can you say that?

MARY MAGDALENE: Because of all that has happened to me! The same things can happen ... and *will* happen! ... to anyone who turns to Him, until that day when He returns in glory.

How may sleepless nights I've spent thinking about nothing but my sin ... and telling myself that no one, absolutely nobody could ever take away this burden of guilt. But I was 100% wrong! He, my beloved Lord, He came ... He who is so much greater than my sin, or my heart ... He knew that I was being eaten-up with remorse, He knew that my own heart was my accuser. (1 Jn 3:20) And in the end? All my sins weighed less that a spider's web. A single word from Him: "Your sins are forgiven," they were gone. My past life? It's as if none of it ever existed.

And, don't let yourself forget: The Lord is powerful enough, His compassion is rich enough to forgive all our sins.. .to heal all our desires, our worries, our frustrations. Just think: IF the Lord is not greater than our sins, than our sinful heart ... how could we ever think of Him as "the Master," as "the Lord," as "Almighty?"

HER FRIEND: Well, I guess we couldn't! He is "the Almighty" ... there's nothing that He can't overpower. So ... all our remorse, that vast ocean of misery in which we lose ourselves... none of it ... not one bit of it can prevent Him from coming and healing us ... and our hearts. That is Good News... He can come to us, and reign ... guide and guard our lives ... dot every "i" and cross every "t"...

MARY MAGDALENE: You just have to trust! Despair is your worst enemy! He can ... and He will take care of you, just like He did me! You know: I rightly deserved to be damned; He could have turned me away, just like that! And, had He done so, I would have had no complaint. All I could have said was "serves me right!" As our Elders put it: "An eye for an eye." That'd be my story! But, no! That's just not His way... He, Rabbouni, my "Good Master," just listened to His bounty. He used His almighty mercy so as to heal me and save me and engrave in me a pure and noble heart, and an all-consuming love ... simply because He is pure and noble ... and His love is all consuming.

HER FRIEND: (Smiling) Mary, I said that you struck me as being "out of your mind!" Now, I think that you've sensed something, that you've got something ... something I'd really like to have ... Your love for Jesus has enriched you with "the right thing" (Lk 10:42). To be like you, to walk where you're walking that's what real happiness is about! And, to live up to that love out of gratitude... that just seems to be the deepest hope, the fiercest hunger of my heart. I don't know how to thank you ... I don't know what to say ... or do!

MARY MAGDALENE: Just thank the Lord. And be glad that so many who've come to believe will be nourished by that same "big secret." Each of us ... really, all of us have to come to accept that we are loved, infinitely, by the Lord. We need only be convinced that His mercy is without limit. He loves me ... and you ... and every single person across the whole world, as if we were the only one!

July 2, 1990

5

What We Have Seen, and Contemplated

After the Resurrection, Mary returned to Nazareth. Having to pass through Samaria (where those outcast Samaritans lived, rejected by Judaism as heretics) One evening, Mary talked for quite a while with Rebecca. It soon became evident that Mary was the mother of the Prophet, Jesus of Nazareth. Could we imagine, together, what they might have said to one another that evening?

REBECCA: Around here, and all through the countryside, we heard what happened to Him. They killed him, crucified Him as if He were a criminal. If God were with Him, such would surely never have happened!

MARY: I was there, on Calvary. And, for a while even I might have thought that it all made no sense. My heart was revolted by it all. God seemed then to be so distant... His silence was crushing. His seeming absence tore my heart to shreds.

REBECCA: If I might dare to ask: how can you even speak of God now? He ... He must have been busy with something else when you really needed Him. One thing for sure: That God who they say is everywhere, certainly wasn't there at Calvary!

MARY: And, that's exactly how it seemed to me, too. My only anchor then was to recall and recite Psalms in my heart, Psalms that persistently cry out their "Whys" to the Lord. They know well that the All-Merciful will hear them. And they know, deeply, that He will not remain indifferent to them or to their questions, in those times of desperate need.

REBECCA: How can you keep saying that He listens to us? You don't really believe that He would hear and heed all our sufferings, our cries do you? I don't doubt that He is all-powerful; He can deal with all our miseries, with all our "Whys" ... but this seems so pitiful to me. God is more likely just viewing them from afar, untouched, unconcerned.

MARY: Yes, He is the Almighty! But, as Jesus repeated so often, He is above all a Father. He is *our* father and *our* mother. And, simply because He is, whatever hurts us, or wounds us... He is there. He is close, taking these to Himself. All of our confusion, our darkness and doubt, our despair, all of our crosses, when we present these to Him, He cares for us ... He cares about them, and about us!

"He will never look-down on any of this; if we couldn't tell Him everything, tell me, where could we turn?" (P. Talec) (Mary remains quiet for a while). His children ... that's what we are in His eyes ... Tell me, Rebecca, do you have any children? When they are afraid ... or when they hurt themselves ... do you turn a deaf ear?

REBECCA: Of course not! Really, I am their mother most of all at those times! If they're afraid of strangers, they run to me, they hide behind me. I am their **SHIELD, THEIR REFUGE.** Nothing can harm them there, close to me. And, come what may, they know instinctively that I'll be there, that I'll guard them, protect them. For them, I'm all-powerful, all-sheltering, I'm their security, their comfort, their fortress, their support. When they come running to me, so quickly they stop crying ... and it isn't long before they're smiling again, bright-eyed as ever!

And, I guess that that's because I can never be "neutral" no matter what might happen to them. What concerns them, concerns me even more; when they're afraid, when they run into all kinds of problems — big and just big-to-them — we face things together, and they aren't so terrifying then. And, if I were ever to conceive of seeing these things "from a distance," I'm afraid that I'd have to deny what is deepest, what is most "mother" in me!

MARY: So, for Jesus, the beloved child of God, things don't change! During His terrible, horrifying sufferings and agony, He turns to His Father. He finds refuge with Him. Jesus is completely sure of God, in whom He has put His entire trust. Jesus knows that the Father's love remains unshakable, as firm as a rock, even when things get out of control, when He is faced with a situation that is completely unexpected. He is calmly convinced that His passion and death is *the path of love,* the best, the only way for Him to be His Father's Son. Jesus is completely convinced that He is "on the right side, on the side of salvation." (Heb 6:9). Feeling the closeness of His Father, Who remained with Him through it all (and here, Mary began to sing softly...) "I have all that I need..." (Ps 23)

REBECCA: I'm beginning to see what you are saying ... After His three years of service to His people, Jesus — on the Cross — recognizes that He has failed, utterly. One by one, His disciples have abandoned Him; everyone would grant that He is the most despised, the most dishonored, the one banished and condemned. So, what else could He do except give up? After all, isn't it only too true: such was His destiny? You say that — through it all — Jesus still believed in God. So, if He retained even a shadow of faith, He is still ready to "see if God — by chance — could still come to assist Him."

Really, that's about the most that we could expect from someone whose life was a failure, who has no standing in the eyes of men. That's about the most anyone would imagine...!

MARY: Well now, that "nothing else" (that I cannot even imagine!) that is just what Jesus accomplished! I was right there, on Calvary. For Jesus to give in to the "forces of destiny" is just unthinkable, completely out of the question. To hope to see if — by chance — God could still do something to help Him ... I can't even imagine that, either! If He had acted, or even thought like that, "these thoughts of His wouldn't have been God's thoughts, but men's." (Mt 16:23)

I was right there, at the foot of the Cross. I was struck, captivated, fascinated by the peace which shone on His face, in His eyes ... even in the midst of such horrifying suffering. It was like a sunbeam shining through the darkness. Love was claiming one more victory! Faith was claiming one more triumph in Jesus, during those darkest moments, "perfect love was driving out all fear." (cfr. 1 Jn 4:18)

Yet, I have to admit: it's not easy at all to speak of my own feelings right then. You're the very first one that I've spoken with about it ... any of it!

REBECCA: But ... condemned to death! No one can even imagine anyone in such a situation being "at peace." How can any sane man be like that? It'd be a miracle. Say what you will, Mary, I feel that all you're saying is a bit stretched! It's just beyond belief...!

MARY: But, that is exactly what John, some other women, and I have "seen and contemplated" (1 Jn 1:1-2). Our eyes were fixed on Him... we couldn't look elsewhere!

Nailed to the wood, Jesus remained — even then — what He had always been. He remained fixated on His Father. He no longer belongs to Himself, but only to God, His Father. Submission ... dependence, out of love! His feet and His hands are nailed ... unmoving ... firmly fixed ... on God. That's the way it was...

Crucified, Jesus chose to be a "Yes" to the Father's way, to His will. His whole life, everything that matters most, this is what He offered the Father ... it is this that the Father wants. He had submitted His entire will to the Father. Jesus didn't reverse the role, hoping, expecting the Father to submit to Him ... God was first, foremost ... really, Jesus was loving God "with all his heart, with all his soul, with all his strength."

Nailed to that Cross (and after Him, all his brothers and sisters), He places Himself in His place: the most obvious truth... that has led Him, that was at the bottom of His entire life: "I love the Father. That is why I do, always, and in everything, as He commands."

Crucified on that hill... but anchored in God (Heb 6:l9) He clings to God, whether in life or in death. Nothing... absolutely nothing can overpower Him, can turn Him away from His Father.

REBECCA: That image of the anchor strikes me! I have a cousin, a fisherman, over at Capernaum. Once, he was telling me: "You see, when the anchor is firmly fixed, hooked on a rock at the bottom of the sea, a strong wind can come up, and blow against the boat; even when violent and turbulent storms come ... tossing the boat here and there, yet nothing moves it because it is so firmly anchored.

You just said ... on the Cross, Jesus is kind of "anchored in God." But, just what do you mean by that?

MARY: On Golgotha, all those people who are dead-set against Him, they come as a storm, breaking against Him. I can still hear them shouting and yelling: "God is Your Father, or so you say! Where is He now?" "King of the Jews! but where is your palace? Where is your army?" "Perform a miracle! Save yourself!" "Everything you always said, all that you've done has come home now to roost!" Really, a very real storm ... really appalling!

Against it all, and contrary to all of them, Jesus stood His ground. The **rock**, on which He was anchored (that is, His life ... and not only His own life but also the lives and eternity of all His brothers and sisters...) that **rock** is God Himself, His Father. "He keeps holding firmly to the hope he professes." (Heb 10:23) (Mary quietly sings: "You are the faithful God, for ever and ever...") That's why, on the third day, He will rise again, come out of that tomb to reign forever with His Father.

Against it all, and contrary to all of them, Jesus stands His ground, closer now to His Father than ever. Accepting the agony, all the suffering, but He invests it with love. So, He is "made perfect" (Heb 5:9). Remember: "Behold the man!" as Pilate said ... I'm sure that he never dreamt how suited his words were...or would be!

Against them all, and contrary to all of them, He held His head high! Nothing could be strong enough to cut Him adrift from the One who held Him. "He is at my right side, I will not be troubled." (Act 2:25) (Once again, Mary is humming a little song: "Lord, your love is stronger than death...") That's why He returned to His Father. Alive now, He will live forever. And His life, and His glory will be without end!

REBECCA: You know, Mary, what you've just said really touches me. But, there is still something that doesn't quite "fit." You speak of all of this as if it were happening right now. You said: "Jesus stands His ground. His ROCK, it is His Father ... He anchors His life in Him." Think about it! what happened to Jesus (everything that happened!), well it just seems that it has nothing to do with our everyday lives, now. How do you "connect" what He submitted-to (which is, after all, in the past...) how do you "connect" Him with yourself now?

MARY: Rebecca, it isn't easy to find words to say what I truly believe. You know me by now... I'm not just that good at speaking about these things... But, it seems to me that all of us, every man and every woman, we're all caught-up in a very large net. Jesus (on the Cross certainly, but also in His triumph over death) has escaped from it. He is as free as the wind! He is the one who bursts asunder that net. (Ps 117) It is in this light that I see Him as our Way to God.

Right here, right now (for me, certainly, and equally for all His brothers and sisters who will make themselves His disciples) this is Jesus, our Way, our Path, our Strength carrying us and leading us to God, our Father. (1 Pt 3:8)

Each day now, I entrust myself to Him, to His gentle hands. It is there that I am "born again, from above." If I allow Jesus to anchor my life in God, He makes me become what He already is, a child of God, as He is the Beloved of God, the first-born of many... He continues to set us free ... freedom, and rebirth ... at the same time!

He continually makes us "grow-up in all ways" toward God. "He makes me diminish, so that He may increase" in me. He takes hold of my hand when I hold it out to Him. He leads me ... carries me "where He is, where He dwells." He is my connection with God. His trust in God is a light along my way; His peace shines upon every step I take; His heart beats within my breast. His very love has become my life...!

REBECCA: All of this seems so very beautiful, Mary. But in my life, what is going to change? I'll grow older, just like everyone else. Maybe, one day, I'll be sick. Why all that suffering, all that misery, all that loneliness? Why all those stupid failures? Why does everything good have to end? You know, Mary, when I sometimes think about it, I'm really afraid of death!

MARY: For a long time, I had those same fears, those same questions... But after seeing, being right there and contemplating the peace and serenity on my Son's face there on the Cross, it just seems that everything's different. It is as if He were telling me: "That cross which weighs so heavily upon you, that bruises your shoulder, give it to me. I'll carry the heavy part, you just take the lighter end. Together, we'll set out. I'll go first, right in front of you. All you need do is follow..."

"It is hard, very hard to think of anything else when you're suffering. It just limits your vision... Then, let my prayer become your own: 'Father, Daddy ... into Your hands...' I've prayed to Him with loud cries and tears (Heb 5:7), and He has not abandoned me to the world of the dead, but He has shown me the paths that lead to life (Act 2:27f).

"It is, really, so very hard for any one of you to imagine what is going to happen when you close your eyes for the last time. At that moment, just let me take your hand. Then, 'you will stay close to me...and I will be close to you.' (Rev 3:20)

Then, you will open your eyes again, to "have your share of what God has reserved for His people in the Kingdom of Light (Col 1:12).

REBECCA: I'd really like to believe like you do! It would make everything so clear for me, for my life...

MARY: Rebecca, "Don't be afraid! God may be gracious to you as well!" (Luke 1:30)

September 21, 1990

Walking in Their Footsteps

6

But... I Came Out Ahead

Some time after Pentecost, Nicodemus made a most important decision, one of the most significant in his entire life: He was baptized! Those strict precepts that he'd followed and preached so ardently as a Pharisee, all that was now in the past. One day, he meets a friend, himself a Pharisee, named Barnabas. This latter remains quite convinced that he is "faithful." Could you imagine their conversation that day?

BARNABAS: Hey, Nick, I haven't seen you in quite a while! I'm glad to see you... but I'm also — let me speak openly — I'm also disappointed... really, disgusted! I'm really not at all "OK" with what I hear you've done!

NICODEMUS: What's the matter, Barny? Did I do something to you? If so, I'm really sorry... but I don't really know what it is that I might have done...

BARNABAS: Well, you didn't do anything against me, personally. But there is something that I just can't comprehend ... that I can not forgive! You've become a disciple of that Jesus ... and from what I've heard, you've been "baptized." You simply threw out everything you — we — had always believed; you deserted, you've become a traitor. We who have always followed precisely all that has been handed down ... you've rejected all of this ... It's like a soldier going over to the enemy! Everything that we hold dear, everything that has made us stand-out among the followers of the Law of Moses, everything that has continued to constitute us as "faithful Israelites," the "favored by God" ... all of this, you've rejected, just like that! And, you know how much all of us respected and admired you over the years, how much we appreciated, and really loved you for all you've done, and preached. And after all of this, do you blame me for being disappointed with you, and angry?

NICODEMUS: Well, Barnabas, I must say, you do speak frankly, you sure don't hold-back on your punches! And I appreciate that! After all, you're simply being honest, true to yourself, and to what you believe. But, if you have a little time, I'd like to explain all that went into my move. (After a moment of silence between the two). What you see as having been rejected... I did it knowingly, and willingly, believe me! And, I'm deeply convinced, I'm a better, a more honest man for it!

BARNABAS: Better? What about all the precepts that we've received from our Elders? And all the temple-regulations and the moral precepts that have molded our people for generations? All the commandments that we've so carefully interpreted and followed?

These have all made us a holy people, a good people. They've formed us into a people that remains closer to God than any other ... And you still dare to tell me that you're "better," "more honest"? Come on ... that I just can't accept! But, I did want you to know how disappointed I am with you, with what you've done. And, sorry though I am to be so angry, I had to let you know...

NICODEMUS: No need to apologize, Barny ... Really, I'd have been more disappointed had you not spoken as you have! You see: I see myself as a chariot driver, heading for the line. But now, instead of heading North, I'm heading in another direction ... in a 180 degree change of direction!

BARNABAS: Who got you, who pushed you into this? ... this change of heart? Into something so total and so radical as this?

NICODEMUS: And, you know? Left to myself, I'd never have imagined even the possibility of such a change! But — perhaps, you've heard! — I had visited Jesus a number of times. In the course of these visits, I came to see that He was, truly, a teacher sent by God. "No one could do the mighty works He is doing, unless God were with Him." It is He — not someone else — who gradually overpowered me! He proved stronger than I... He convinced me first to question the path I was on, and then to change course...

BARNABAS: Hey, be careful, Nicodemus! You'll soon be voicing all the criticisms, the judgments, the condemnations that Jesus spoke against us! He — I am really convinced — He never saw us as the most righteous, the most just among the righteous of God ... as those beyond the judgment, and certainly beyond the reproach of the simple people!

NICODEMUS: You know, Barny, for a long time now — really, for most of my life ... from the time I was of age — I've been a Pharisee: I thought, I acted and reacted, I conducted myself as one of them. And then, Jesus — with His wise teaching! — came along, and through our conversations convinced me that I was wrong, that I was hitting the bulls-eye but on the wrong target!

Most particularly, I remember these words: "That which is born of the flesh is flesh." I understood this to mean that of the 613 precepts and laws that we preached and practiced so scrupulously, that these were good ... up to a point. That all of these were necessary up to a point. But, we'd come to see them as the do-all and end-all of life itself. We'd come to see them as "making us just," sin-free, one-hundred-percent pleasing to God. We had come to imagine that our holiness could and would be accomplished simply by the strict observance of these precepts, fulfilled by our firmness, our dedication ... our own strength. If you will, our "observances" were the requirement for a "Diploma in Holiness." Let's be honest with ourselves: "We feared God for nought!" (Job 1:9) We had come to think that because of our faithfulness we could get all we wanted or needed from God.

And for all those years, I considered myself as someone truly "good." At that time, the love of God was not in my thoughts, or in my life. God was not my Father. My total purposefulness in life was centered on doing the right things, rightly! When you think about it, I was the center around which my life turned! When I came to the point of really and radically facing myself, I appeared to myself as one wearing a mask: I had the illusion of being completely and irrevocably in the "state of God's good graces"!

BARNABAS: I like your allusion to a "mask." Often enough, I think of myself as doing everything myself too. I'm pleasing to God because I'm pleasing myself, my own laws, my own whims, really! I can't say this publicly, but I feel that I'm not on the path of faithfulness to God, but simply to myself!

NICODEMUS: And Jesus, the one we call "Lord," He so gently, but with such determination let me take off that mask, and for this I shall remain forever grateful. Now, I can stand before God, unashamed, because I feel that I'm now living the truth. And His help gives me the honesty and the strength to overcome whatever might tarnish the image of God within me. Day by day, he opens my eyes to new horizons ... in myself! Constantly I am mindful of those words that come from God: You know well that I am not better than everyone else, that daily I fail ... I fail myself, my deepest hungers, my God. And daily I ask God to remove all my arrogance, my pride; to take away any pretense of being able to stand before Him as a just man...!

BARNABAS: You know, Nick, I'd be willing to bet that you have quite a few more friends now than what it was before...!

NICODEMUS: More? There are so many that I can't begin to count them! Before, all those who were not with me, were against me... and against their God! Every last one of them was a "good for nothing," quite literally! They were too despicable for me to even speak with them; the most I could bring myself to do was to talk to them... of their failings. I looked down my nose at them ... and looked down pretty far! But now, things have changed, they are so different! Each day, I discover new dimensions, new horizons...

BARNABAS: Speaking of those "new dimensions," you make me think of an eagle ... who refuses to be limited to his nest. He can't shut-off his field-of-vision to that tangle of twigs and leaves into which he was born. He is always ready to discover, and to explore new horizons. He flies! He soars! Carried on the wind yet never captured by the wind... he is forever discovering wider horizons... He peers at the snow-clad peaks and the lush valleys, the dazzling whiteness and the plentiful harvests of the valleys. The eagle can't remain "nested," bound to his nest ... it'd just be too small, too narrow, too confining and restrictive. Tell me, Nick, what did you mean when you said that your life had taken-on "new dimensions?"

NICODEMUS: You know, Barny, that "eagle-image" that you propose... I really find that rich in meaning ... that perspective of always searching new horizons. For myself, I imagine that "my nest" was my conviction that I was really good ... in men's eyes, and in God's! Now, the Lord Jesus has opened my eyes ... has given me something of His own eyes ... and it is through them that I see my fellow human beings. Certainly, I can no longer look down on them; I see them as brothers and sisters. Instead of continually judging them, I find myself trying to discover ... and really discovering, that which is unique in their lives. Instead of always "being right," dictating my outlooks and understandings, I try to understand them. Instead of putting everyone else down, I find that I'm much more patient, more tolerant of others ... after all, they DO have a right to be themselves, to be different from me!

So, I find that I'm noticing things about them ... things that I really admire, and I like to mention these to them ... and I've found that they accept this, readily! You should see their faces! And, it doesn't take much, you know. Acknowledging their accomplishments — "I never thought that you could have done that!" or "Your flowers are certainly beautiful! You must have worked long and hard to have a garden like that!"

Everyday, I try to leave the nest, to "fly" higher, and farther. I have to let Jesus, the Christ deepen, and broaden my heart, to expand my tent (Is.) to make room for still more people... with no one left out! Barnabas, this is something very "new" for me ... it has forced a 180 degree turn-about!

And, when I pray, I find that I'm not so fixed on myself and my own concerns. That time is long past for me to say "I thank you, God, that I am not like everybody else..." (Lk 18:11) Now, I simply thank God for the variety of gifts that His Spirit has sown in their hearts ... and lives. And, really, day by day, I'm discovering a whole list of qualities that I'd never dreamt were there!

Every single day, I have to stretch the space in which Christ can expand His work of salvation, at the pace and with the intensity that He chooses. I've still got a long way to go to let Him really "run" my life, to really rule my life, my thoughts, my desires, my hopes! I continue to try to let Him reign as The Master over every moment, and every facet of my life.

BARNABAS: You talk about "domination," about "occupation"! All of that brings to mind those Pagan Romans who have us under their heel!

Our independence has been annihilated; they trample on everything we hold dear. There is nothing that happens which they don't control. We're a conquered nation, an enslaved people, really! It's not easy to endure their oppression. They've shredded our national pride, reduced us to little more than nothing...

And, if I understand you, you're saying that the way Christ acts in you is just about the way the Romans treat us! Am I understanding you correctly?

NICODEMUS: Barnabas, I want you to realize that I suffer the pain of the Roman occupation quite as much as you do! Those Romans... forever calling upon their various gods! Really, I find it as hard to endure as you do!

But, loosen up! When I say "I have to let the Lord, Jesus, dominate, occupy, reign as Master over every facet of my life" ... well, I'm just not talking in political terms! I'm talking ... and thinking, only about my heart, my hopes, my hungers ... that in me which — I guess — most makes me a human being! And so I can say: He is my Master, but He is "gentle and humble in spirit." What He is trying to do in me is to let me be reborn in the Spirit. It is just as He said: "That which is born of the Spirit is spirit!" Could I — could anyone? — ever imagine anything better than that? He is my King;

and I want Him to control my life, every aspect of my life, to form within me that dwelling place that God has dreamt about for so long a time. He asks only that I be malleable in His hands ... as clay in the hands of the Potter (Rom 9:20f)

How could I ever resist His will? He is my Leader; He knows well the path that I will walk to make my life a "success." So, everyday — just like I said — it is as if I'm driving my own chariot, but gradually, with His hand on mine, He can lead me in His way. This is my deepest hope, my deepest desire: that He take hold of the reins of my life! that He be the one in charge of my heart's hungers and hopes! I can only hope that He will have enough elbow-room to accomplish in me and through me all that He wants!

When I pray, this is how I pray: "Lord, make yourself comfortable ... within me! come and overcome what is not patterned after You!" Really, I've never — never! — been happier than now. I feel that my Lord is taking over my life and my life's ambitions. Can their be any greater happiness?

BARNABAS: But, don't you see, Nicodemus? As I'm hearing you — and quickly enough, I'm afraid: old habits die hard! — you'll be right back being "better" than anyone else ... the classical trait of every good Pharisee! You'll pretend that you've hit the mark, arrived at the peak. And, soon enough, you'll be thinking again that you're making God happy!

NICODEMUS: Oh, not at all, Barny! I'm just at the beginning of a long ascent. I'm just at the very beginnings of the dawn of a new life. I'm still taking baby-steps, don't you understand? I'm like a little boy, whose whole future still lies before him...

BARNABAS: Now, you make me think of my own son, Alexander. He's now three years old! And, his whole life is one big discovery! He is as beautiful as an angel. And, being with him ... well, everything is new and fresh! Simply by living, and by exploring, and by discovering ... and especially, by his smile ... he just makes both my wife and myself so very happy. And, being with him, even just watching him, I find myself rediscovering so many things that I've not noticed ... maybe since I myself was his age. When he laughs, whatever it might be that my wife and I are worrying about ... it's gone. The whole of our lives ... all our work and all our efforts. . .they just crystallize in him, and for him! There's nothing we wouldn't do for him!

NICODEMUS: That's precisely it! Maybe you've never heard that word of the Lord, Jesus: "Unless you become like a little child, you will not enter the Kingdom of Heaven!" (Mt 18:3) Everyday now, I have to put on the ways, and the attitudes of a little child in front of his Dad; instead of looking at myself — as I've been doing all these years, and which got me no place — I just seek to look at Him, at our Father in heaven, with the eyes and the love of His child. But, it IS an ongoing challenge, believe me!

Every moment of Jesus' own life was saturated with peace because of His trust and confidence in the Father. Am I — or am I not! — going to develop such confidence in Him?

The Lord, Jesus committed Himself completely to the service of the Father and His Kingdom. Am I — or am I not — going to make such a commitment visible, apparent?

In this decision I have to continually seek to know what Jesus — were He now in my place, in my shoes — would do, and pursue it?

Would Jesus, the Christ, feel "at home" in my life?

Is there, and can I find a "best way" of showing the love of Christ, and especially His tactfulness, His gentleness in dealing with every other human being?

You see, Barny, day be day, it IS up to me to "tune-up," to re-examine myself and my life, my ways of acting ... and reacting! The Lord is demanding ... He gives me little time to rest on my laurels! I've still got a long, long way to go before reaching the finish line.

BARNABAS: So, Nicodemus, to put it on the line, you have no regrets about what you have done?

NICODEMUS: Well, yes! But only one... and that's that I delayed so long before taking this new way!

December 6, 1990

7

It's Just So Hard
to Get Used To

*In Ephesus, endlessly, John — the Evangelist, the Apostle
— conversed with Bartholomew, and deepened his grasp
of all that John himself had witnessed as the privileged
witness of the miracle of love. His conversations were so
vivid that Bartholomew "re-lived" the actual experience,
especially the Last Supper, the Passion and the various
Resurrection appearances of Jesus. However,
Bartholomew, just newly baptized, felt some particular difficulty in relating what had happened in the past (that is,
ten to fifteen years before!) with the Sunday gatherings of
those following The Way, each Lord's Day. Maybe, we could
guess at their conversation?*

BARTHOLOMEW: For you, John, well ... you were there! You
saw when Jesus "left this world and returned to the Father." You've
got it made! To have lived with Jesus, to see Him and hear Him ...
(and, after a short silence...) For me, as long as I live, I'll live in
regret for not having seen or heard Him. I'd just give anything ...
ANYthing to hear His voice...

JOHN: Yeah, during those three years that we walked and talked
together, I was right with Jesus, I could almost say, I was his con-
fidant... "Beginning from the time John preached his baptism until

the day Jesus was taken up into heaven!" I think that I was really close to Him ... really close, I mean ... I was right there. His words, the way He lived and loved, the way He spoke ... they just took me right out of myself ... sort of "with God," "in God's presence." (And, after a silent pause...) and **that still continues now, everyday!** And, not just for me, but for you too... IF you want it!

BARTHOLOMEW: I don't follow you, John! Jerusalem ... Calvary ... they're so far from here, from us...

JOHN: It isn't just "in Jerusalem" that we can hear His voice, and walk in His Way, that we can worship the Father with Him, belong to Him, love Him, be close to Him... Really, it matters little where we live! Nor does it matter what language we speak, what part of the world we live in...

What matters is only this: do we let Christ **change our hearts and put new meaning** into everything we do?

BARTHOLOMEW: Change our hearts? give new meaning? I like what I think I'm hearing ... I like it a lot. It sort of reminds me of the **grains of wheat** that you told me about. Those little grains that become our food, our nourishment. The work that goes into producing those "grains of wheat" — the plowing, the cultivating, the fertilizing, the irrigating ... and finally the harvesting — only then do we have that good wheat which crunches between the teeth! — and the threshing! But **the threshing is not the end, it is only the beginning!** After that, comes the milling through which those grains are transformed into fine flour. Yes, the grains of wheat are still there, but **we can't recognize them.** And the flour — and the other ingredients — mixed and baked ... finally the golden loaves of bread ... those "golden loaves of bread!" And then, the bread becomes our flesh and blood, our bones and muscles and sinew. It allows us to walk and to talk, to breathe, to admire the birds of the air. And we can go on walking and talking ... all because of the nourishment that comes from those tiny grains of wheat.

Then, all sorts of things find their meaning. **What remained hidden** in the wheat-grains, **their real purpose,** is to sustain and build life. They truly are "the fruit of the earth and the work of human hands..." ...here it is that the tiny grains are **transformed** into poetry and song. And those tiny grains give the strength to extend the reach of His love to the whole world.

JOHN: Your example of the "grains of wheat" ... I like it ... I like it a lot! In the milling, they are transformed, their "meaning" expands. They become capable of engendering and sustaining life. Like you said, we can walk and talk, we can think, we can work to make our world better just because of those "tiny grains of wheat!"

Yes ... those "grains of wheat" ... First it is Jesus Himself ... and then — after Him — it comes to include everyone, you, me, all those who believe in Him.

BARTHOLOMEW: Just a minute now, John! You're going a bit too fast for me again. The "grains of wheat" ... I remember what you told me Jesus said: "Unless the grains of wheat, falling to the ground dies to itself, it remains alone. But IF it dies, it bears many more grains..." (Jn 12:24) But, what does that have to do with Jesus? I don't quite see the connection...

JOHN: The grains of wheat have to be ground by the millstone. The grapes, too, have to be crushed by the winepress before the "good wine" that gives joy to the human heart is produced! Now, Bart, as you look at Jesus' life, when was Jesus "ground" by the millstone, pressed by the winepress ... so as to acquire that power to give life?

BARTHOLOMEW: Well, it was when He left this world and returned to His Father. As the prophet Isaiah has said: "the servant of God is *no longer recognizable.* A man of sorrows, He never opened His mouth; He is like a lamb being led to the slaughter. *Crushed with suffering*, He gave Himself up to death."

It was then that Jesus — the finest, most beautiful human being I could ever imagine has become the poorest of the poor. There's just nothing left! Really, He's become less than nothing...

JOHN: Just a minute now, Bart...

You're forgetting those other words of Isaiah, those that give perspective and some understanding of the **"meaning" of His Pas-**

sion. "The Servant of God Himself took our weaknesses and carried away our burdens. All the while, He prayed for sinners. By His sufferings shall my servant justify many."

"Jesus is raised up..." (Jn 12:32) Thus, He approaches the Father, and prays. Doing just the opposite of what Adam had done, Jesus submitted Himself, radically, to the Father. Jesus — the New Adam — was "possessed" completely by the Father to Whom He surrendered His life as an offering of submission, of love. Strengthened by the Spirit, Jesus is infinitely enriched by His unconditioned faith, His serene trust and His unshakable conviction. And this torrent of love simply "carried Him away," bonded Him with the Father, there where the Father is, in His heavenly dwelling place.

"**...Lifted up from the earth,**" and from there, Jesus makes His prayer, His request with loud cries and tears before God, who can save Him from death. Because of His humble submission, His acceptance, God hears Him. (cfr. Heb 5:7)

This **"new Moses,"** Jesus raises and stretches out His hands to the Father, His heart filled with a tender compassion, an ocean of mercy in which He submerges each one of us...

Leader of humankind, Jesus takes-up that desire for salvation — that hunger which lies at the bottom of the heart of each one of us — and **accepts it as His own.** Our thirst for "more life" — the divine life which we can have only from God! — **Jesus takes into His own heart.** "You are my God! In You I place all my trust. Save me by your steadfast love!" (Ps 31) And there, from the Cross, Jesus gathers and expresses our need for deliverance: "I thirst!"

Merciful Shepherd, Jesus pleads that we will be healed: "Father, here I am among those that You have given me... Father. forgive them, they do not know what it is that they are doing!"

BARTHOLOMEW: Which brings back to mind what you've so often said, John: "One of the soldiers took a spear and pierced Jesus' side, and blood and water came forth. This was done so that the Scripture might be fulfilled: 'People will look upon Him whom they have pierced. (Jn 19:34ff) And you, John, you saw that with your own eyes... Why did you emphasize that in your Gospel?

JOHN: Really, I wrote that "so that you also may believe," whole-heartedly, that the Father did hear Jesus' prayer ... so that you would turn to the Crucified Jesus Who is — and Who will forever remain — the fount of living water, the source of relief for anyone who "thirsts," and who believes.

BARTHOLOMEW: Which — in fact — reminds me of another of Jesus' words ... when He stood in the Temple and cried out: "Whosoever is thirsty, let them come to Me and drink!"

It is because I do believe, and because I am so thirsty for God that — nothing in the world will ever make me miss our prayer gatherings, our Lord's Day celebrations. It is there that Christ does quench my thirst and grant me healing. He is there comforting and purifying me. When I hear that Word, my thirst is slaked.

Week by week, — Sunday after Sunday — I am changed! I seem so different now that I hardly recognize myself! When look back to when I first came to believe, and was baptized, well, it's just so different now ... so very different! It's almost as though I had been seriously sick, and am now regaining my health, and my strength. **The healing** of that which is "most" me, of my deepest inner-self — for me, that's the wonder of the love the Savior keeps on accomplishing in me!

Each Sunday ... it's as if I were coming back ... from some-where deep within me the song arises: "Source of Life, of peace, of love, I turn to You day, and night!" It's as if I were standing right there, at the foot of His Cross, with you, John...

JOHN: Now, don't say "as if..." **YOU ARE REALLY RIGHT THERE,** Bart! Simply by faith, you gradually become attuned to His Spirit, who heals and invites and strengthens you to become what Jesus is on the Cross: "a living sacrifice to God, dedicated to His service, pleasing to Him!"

BARTHOLOMEW: Slow down, there! Now you're talking about something else again! You've just said that "little by little we our-selves become a living sacrifice, a holy offering pleasing to God." Isn't that a bit exaggerated? As I've been taught ... and learned ...

there is but one great sacrifice, the one our Lord Jesus offered to the Father! Jesus alone is able to turn to the Father with that fullness of love which is pleasing to our God, our Father! For us ... for our offerings what are we ... what are they anyhow?

JOHN: You're right, Bartholomew, we are small, even insignificant. But — remember? — "Whoever remains in me and I in him, will bear much fruit!" Did you overlook that? Are we — and do we remain — aware of who we are? Day by day, Jesus honors us by inviting us to continue His offering of love... and He returns to carry us safely with Him back to the Father. He "introduces" us to God, "He presents us to our Father!" (1 Pt 3:18)

His passing-over to the Father — His Easter-mystery — Jesus invites and allows us to share. He is raised-up from this earth and continually draws us to Himself (Jn 12:32). He envelops us in His own prayer, into His own adoration before God! He puts us on the Cross with Him, very visible to the Father. His prayer becomes ours. The "Our Father..." becomes a song on our lips. And God — for His part — receives us all ... Jesus — the Head of the Body, — and each one of us, — the members of that Body — to the praise of His glory!

Jesus came and lived on this earth to belong completely to the Father, so as to be nourished and filled with the Spirit. He is the AMEN to God, for His greater glory. And we — with Him and after Him — we become a harmonious song of adoration resounding more clearly and more strongly each day, throughout the world, from more and more people.

You see, Bartholomew, each Sunday when we hear Christ's Word, when we re-present His offering to the Father, we come forth from our tombs so as to come to life again, in Him. We leave this earth to enter God's Kingdom! And there, in His presence, guided and accompanied by Jesus Himself, we stand before God, transformed and offered to the Father, "a living sacrifice of praise, pleasing to God." *We are no longer in Ephesus, or in Jerusalem, in Rome, or in Athens or in Corinth!*

BARTHOLOMEW: And, that is just what I feel — (and I'm sorry that I keep saying that!) But, **each Lord's Day** Christ re-opens my eyes, the eyes of my heart and my soul. He makes me aware — each Sunday! — of His presence; He, the most powerful in the whole world, He lifts me up from my tawdry self... I almost feel as if He carries me as the currents carry a twig in a raging stream. He draws me out of myself ... beyond myself! He bonds me to Himself and takes me into Himself ever so gently, and gradually, despite my own setbacks.

But, and again, I must apologize, John, I keep repeating: you had that singular privilege of being right there at the end of Christ's ministry, there on the Cross! You were right there, you saw the "water and the blood" flowing from His pierced heart. And, you were there too, witnessing His appearances after He rose. For me, here in Ephesus, there's just no "going back," reliving that past. I wasn't, nor can I be there to see and to hear Christ ... like you did!

JOHN: No, there IS no way of going back to the past. And *Christ knows that!* Yet, He does want to give some obvious and visible proofs of His presence, and of His life-giving Love...

BARTHOLOMEW: And, what are they? Is it His Word? or the community of His faithful? I recognize that through all of us — His disciples — Jesus remains alive and present, and His love is made present to each one, and for each one of us...

JOHN: Our friend Matthew remembered that enlightening Word of the Lord "Wherever two or three of you come together in My Name, there will I be in the midst of you!" (Mt 18:20) And each day of our life, the Christ seeks to convince us of this, almost as if He were reminding us, telling us that "even though there are so many differences among you — some know and speak different languages, some are rich and highly respected, some barely manage to survive, some have callused hands and sun-baked foreheads, some are old, or handicapped and others are young and vibrantly alive..."

But among us, more important than everything that we can see and touch and count, He is there, He, the Lord! He unites and gathers all of us, each of us into Himself. He is in us, the "new blood" coursing through our veins. At arms reach, He remains the attentive companion along The Way, watching over and caring for each one of us. And, close as He remains, He gives His Spirit of consolation to dry away our tears. None ever need be fearful of talking about those things of our everyday life. Each one is precious in His eyes, each one unique, irreplaceable. And always being at hand, He is ready to heal, to make whole again. *No one will ever be able to accuse Him of being a "distant God,"* or an absent God ... someone who is "missed" in His absence! The power of His love is always there, empowering, bolstering, supporting us "until He comes"!

So you see, Bartholomew, what you have just said is true: the Lord remains present, as He promised whenever the community of believers gathers. But, beyond even this, He wishes to show His unending attentiveness ... far beyond anything "we could imagine or dream"!

Each Lord's Day, all of us, each of us, finds him- or her-self *back in the Cenacle, and on Calvary ... and at the same time, in heaven.* We lift our hands and hearts to God ... but really, *it is Christ Himself* who takes us and presents us to His — and our — Father as He Himself stands before God. His "Amen" to the glory of God becomes ours. Jesus takes us along with Him as He offers His own sacrifice.

In this sacred meal, through the signs of bread and wine, *each Lord's Day* Christ offers Himself to the Father, and us with Him! He allows us to be included in His offering, a living sacrifice to the glory of God, our Father.

BARTHOLOMEW: You've really lost me now! I just can't understand that ... I just can't ... there's something that just won't "go down!" How can we understand that the simple bread can become the Sacred Body of the Lord, and the wine become His precious Blood? This is just too much!

JOHN: Well, really ... **I can't "make sense" of this either! I can't explain it.** And, I just have to feel that no one, either now or ever, will be able to explain this awesome Love by which our Lord remains so close to us.

All I can really say is **"It is the Lord!"** (Jn 21:8) It is the Lord Himself Who blesses the bread and the wine; it is He who repeats those words "Eat it, this is My Body ... Drink it, it is my blood for the salvation of the world. It is my sacrifice to the Father... and yours as well!"

It is He who — **each Lord's Day** — puts His supreme power at the service of His sisters and brothers, because of His undying love for us. He speaks anew those same words. And, He is present — to us, and to the Father — offering Himself and offering all of us to the Father. Jesus never tires of coming back to be in our midst. He comes to rescue us amidst life's storms ... just like He did that day on Lake Tiberias. That night we hadn't caught a single fish, and He said 'Throw your net out on the right side of the boat, and you'll find some!" So we did, and there were so many fish that we couldn't haul in the net. And, only then did we know that it was He, the Lord. Then, someone cried out **"It is the Lord!"**

You see, Bartholomew, those very same words... **each Sunday!** ... repeat them Sunday after Sunday, dazzled yet radiant with happiness, just like it was there on the Lake!

Each Sunday, The Lord, Jesus, speaks anew His own words: "This is my Body ... this, my Blood!" Then, I believe: Here is the Sacred Body of the Lord! Here, His precious Blood! Here is our divine food coming from heaven ... So many times I repeat **"It is the Lord!"**

I simply believe ... even though I cannot explain how it is that the Lord perform this miracle of His closeness. I don't understand... yet, **it is not because I fail to understand Jesus'** miracle that I could ever dare to say: "It's just nonsense! It just can't happen that way! That's just "too much!" You just couldn't be that close to us!"

Really, who am I? ... Who are we to question, or doubt His almighty power? Who are we to presume to disobey His command?

Once and for all, we just need to accept and recognize this marvelous sign of His loving and life-giving presence in our midst.

Each Sunday we need but cry out: **"It is the Lord!"** ... always so close, always so available, always there ... just for us!

BARTHOLOMEW: The Lord's command: "Do this in memory of me!" ... we can't forget that! As you've said, He is the Lord! We have to listen to Him, to obey Him. And, who among us would dare to refuse Him the honor of helping Him?

JOHN: Yes, **each Sunday** we witness human words saying "This is my Body ... this, my Blood," but it is really Jesus speaking, using a simple human being, one just like any other, so that His words may be pronounced over and over again. Just think: the Lord uses me — a simple fisherman from Galilee, unworthy of doing anything for Him.

It's just like you taking up a pen to write a letter. In that same way, Jesus uses one as insignificant as any other to make His sacrifice present, so that we can share in it and we can live on in His love. It is all part of the Mystery of His closeness!

BARTHOLOMEW: The pen I use in writing, what is that in comparison with the one who holds it in his hand and does the writing? Really, you, I, any of us, we have to remind ourselves that we are only instruments in His hand for the service of His people...

JOHN: Precisely! Jesus wants to remain within our reach, to be at "our level." Emmanuel — "God with us" — until the end of time...

Each Sunday, He wants to lift us up, in His own offering, so that we can live in His Love. He wants to be so close to us that through Him, with Him, and in Him, we can approach the Father. Then ... then, who are we to put any limits on His actions? Who are we to question the way the Lord goes about His mission of saving the world?

Each Sunday, He comes again, so that His Passover may be ours. That Last Supper, His Crucifixion ... they are for us, today! This is our salvation, our very life! It would certainly be presumptuous to give Him any counsel (cfr. Rom 11:34), to tell Him that in this "He is just going too far!" Who are we to question His way of coming to us? Who are we to refuse — because that is what it amounts to! — the gift He chooses to make, the gift of Himself?

BARTHOLOMEW: Now I begin to understand what you mean when you say that you **just can't get used to each Sunday's celebration!**

JOHN: You, me ... all the sisters and brothers in our community, we know well enough that we have so little to offer the Father ...

what do our works and our worries amount to? and our joys and our tears? the smiles on the faces of our children, or our whitened hair? ... What do we have? Well, **we do have Jesus!,** the SON of GOD, to offer. **Each Sunday,** we have the Lord's praise of the Father!

BARTHOLOMEW: John, thanks for taking the time, for making the effort. I'm always richer after our talks. All we can do ... really, all we need to do, is to live in the conviction that the Lord — through His Eucharist — keeps pouring into our hearts "that love by which we will love God for all eternity."

St. Paul, MN
February 16, 1991

Walking in Their Footsteps

8

Instead of Saying

Mark and Peter have been together for quite a while; in fact, they've become very good friends. Even with this, the Gospel has not "impacted" Mark's life, and he feels uncomfortable about this. He has doubts... "Is the Gospel really the way of salvation? Is it really God's gift to His people?"

Can we then imagine a conversation between Peter and Mark, a discussion that took place some time after Pentecost?

MARK: You know, if I were in Jesus' shoes, I sure wouldn't have handled you disciples the way He did! After the Resurrection I'd have found myself a few really dependable men, someone I could count on, really depend on

PETER: Well, we certainly didn't do anything that'd provide Jesus with much assurance, or make Him particularly proud, that's for sure!

MARK: You, His closest friends, His confidants, you disowned Him openly, right in public! **Were I in His shoes,** I'd have had nothing more to do with any of you ... I'd have "cut loose," I'd have turned you out, and that would have been it! I'd have avoided you guys like the plague!

PETER: Yes, we simply neglected completely all the love and tenderness He'd shown us during those three years, we just abandoned Him! We all failed Him! I myself, when I was there warming myself with the others there in Barracks Square ... three times, I said, — swearing besides — "I don't know the man!" In my whole life, I've never done anything so cowardly, so gutless! I just openly disowned Him ... Him, the dearly beloved Son of God!, Emmanuel, God-with-us!

MARK: Right then and there, I'd have dumped you, and the rest right along with you! You just weren't the caliber of disciple I'd have been looking for! You showed yourselves untrustworthy, incompetent, incapable of walking with Him, of walking His way! And, really, you couldn't have complained! How do you see it, really?

PETER: And if He had, we certainly couldn't have complained! After all, who among us doesn't live by the "eye for an eye, a tooth for a tooth!?" When we apply the Laws, or even the rules, we're pretty relentless, we're rigid! We like things to be perfectly clear. That way we have some kind of order, even though people might be forced to act more out of fear...

I remember once when the Scribes and the Pharisees brought a woman before Jesus, one who had been caught in the very act of adultery. They presented their indictment: "She was caught in the act! According to the Law, she deserves one thing, to be stoned to death. And, that's it! We have to do something to uphold the Law, or..." Jesus — as you know — knew the Law! But, quite calmly, and in His own unhurried way, Jesus casually mentioned that they too were sinners. And then He stooped down, and began doodling in the sand, making some kind of marks right in the sand. And, quickly enough, they began to fade away ... beginning with the oldest! He didn't make them "lose face"; in fact, Jesus was busy with something else, something really insignificant, — like doodling! — he didn't even have to look them in the eye!

And it must have been about the same with us. It'd have been perfectly right for Him to have dumped us, and found someone else, someone trustworthy this time! But, — as you know so well

— Jesus "doesn't act as we do, poor men that we are!" (Jdt 8:14-16) Being Emmanuel, God-with-us, He is God, the Holy One, Who comes "not to judge, but to save!" His purpose, after all, was not to reject anyone, but to draw them closer to Himself! (Hos 11:8; Jn 3:17) He came to heal us, and to save us, and for this, He makes use of His omnipotent love, of the depth and height of His love to restore us to His Way, to restore ... to rebuild the courage of those who've lost all hope!

This is — after all — the core of the Gospel! Even when we turn away from God, He does not disown us! (2 Tm 2:13) He sticks with us, come what may! **His watchword just seems to have been:** "Anything! ... just so they keep walking ... with Me!"

MARK: But you, Peter, you disowned Him three times, right there, in public! When the cock crowed, you went out and wept bitterly. Do you think that Jesus took your remorse into consideration? Did He see your tears? Did He know how miserable and ashamed you were?

PETER: (Smiling...) He must have! He had to have known! And maybe, that's why He forgave so generously, why He let me stay! Why He trusts me, still!

MARK: After He came back, after the Resurrection, did He ever mention your denials? about your cowardliness, your unfaithfulness, your weakness?

PETER: Well, I'm sure that He knows about it! How could He not know? And, I'm pretty sure that He must have thought about it too. He must have been crushed by it. But, in fact, He never did mention it to me, or — in so far as I've heard — to anyone else. He never once made any comment ... that's **just not His way...**

MARK: I guess He showed us all what big heartedness really is ... that's how I'd size-up the situation.

PETER: Yeah...! He just isn't one of those who'd come back and "harp"! The past is past; He just doesn't have it in Him to keep bringing it up again and again. He leaves all that behind (cfr Is 38:17) When He pardons, forgives, it's final! I remember what happened that time when we were out on Lake Tiberias, the day we caught so many fish ... He didn't ask me why I'd betrayed Him ... although I really was afraid that He might! He never even mentioned my denials ... He didn't want me to "lose face," to be humiliated in front of the others. He just asked me whether I loved Him. And He asked me not once but three times (You know, I had disowned Him three times!) He asked that same question three times ... when I think about it, I think that He was really pleading for my love.

MARK: If He'd have blamed you, that might have crushed you ... you whom He'd already selected to be the leader of the Twelve. I wouldn't have blamed Him if He had, but...

PETER: Yes, but...! **That's just not His way!** He doesn't re-hash the past. I remember the story He told about the Prodigal Father and his two sons ... how he welcomed the one back who'd come to recognize, and who acknowledged how he'd wronged his Father. And, just like that, He took us back, almost as if He were saying to each one: "You must really be disappointed with yourself! You must really be discouraged! The burden must really weigh heavily upon you...!"

MARK: Not only did He not blame, or find-fault, in fact He showed you ... He showed all of us ... the trust He was putting in you, in us. You must have really felt relieved!

PETER: Relieved? That's not the half of it! Once again, I could be free and alive again, light-hearted, peace-filled! You know, when you think about it, Jesus never classifies any of us as "good for nothing!" or "beyond redemption!"

Time after time, repeatedly, and endlessly, he radiates that unceasing optimism ... **about us!** For me, that's the bottom-line of why He draws us to Himself, and of our dedication to Him, of our love! How often do you see that?

He believes that we can ... and will! ... do better, that we will get our act together and move on ... and up! He never measures out

His trust in terms of what we've "earned," deserved! — or by what we have failed to do!

He believes that this burgeoning love will eventually blossom...

He sees our "best," and He, somehow, makes us see it too, and want it! And, He won't let us forget about it either! Whatever it is in our lives that is good, honorable, admirable, whatever it is that is pleasing to our God and Father, Jesus is right there to "name" it, and to help us become more conscious of it, over and over until finally we "get used" to it being our own "bottom-line!" That's how He sees us ... and how He wants us to see ourselves!

He just has the knack of seeing what is best in every single one of us, and of seeing only that. He certainly doesn't measure our "best" against our "worst" to see which one out-weighs the other! He looks at the "best," and contentedly waits for it to blossom, to bear fruit!

For me, it is this that makes His Way, His Word so powerful, so over-powering!

MARK: Yes, but besides that, Jesus treats everyone the same ... there are no favorites! He doesn't ever consider us Jews as "special," or different! Everyone ... absolutely everyone He meets is welcome! He knows how to respond to all of God's "winks," those little signs of His presence!

PETER: Well, for me, I'll tell you one thing: I certainly never have found it as easy to "warm-up" to people as He does. It takes me a while; it has been, and still is, a struggle, but I think that I'm gradually "learning" that God's Spirit is at work well beyond the blood-lines of the People of Israel. I just wasn't ready for such an all-encompassing, openness of mind and heart...

MARK: I can still remember how Jesus welcomed that Roman Centurion who'd come asking... His concern was so heartfelt, and so apparent. He was really anxious about that slave. When I think how I feel about those Romans, about those oppressors, and who, besides, are so open in their opposition to any thought of the One True God, the Creator, our Father...

And yet, that Roman had the guts to come to Jesus; he'd seen in Him some kind of extraordinary "Messenger" of God. And, he wasn't shy about making his request, about asking a favor from God. If anyone didn't "qualify," surely it was he! Really, I don't know what possessed him to dare to come up and ask like that!

If I'd been in Jesus' shoes, I can assure you: he'd have gotten nothing ... not even a hearing! And, it wouldn't have taken me long to decide, either!

PETER: Yet, Jesus knew who that Centurion was...

MARK: Then, why do you think He wasted His time on him...?

PETER: Simply because He was not "satisfied with looking at outward appearances; He looked deeply, at the heart!" (1 Sam 16:7) He knew how to look, to probe and find the deep-down hopes and hungers that the Centurion bore, and to know them better than what the Centurion — or we! — would see! Jesus just doesn't care about all those divisions and separations that we've created, and learned to live with, especially among us Israelites who consider ourselves as "set apart" — Jesus just ignores those divisions!

And, He also overlooks our ways of judging others. He forces us to question all those things which go into our judgments. For Him, the attitude by which we "catalog" people, put them into some sort of index-file under "good" or "bad," "black" or "white," with no shades in between ... for Him, that just doesn't exist!

MARK: Maybe ... just maybe, it IS better that way...?

PETER: "Maybe," you say? Just consider, Mark, how we had always tried to "monopolize" God; we imagined that He was ours, exclusively! that He cared only for Israel, as if He'd make His sun to shine only on us! Come on...!

And while we've been talking, I've been thinking: That Centurion had been friendly toward our people; he'd even built a synagogue for us (Lk 7:1-10); and besides, he acknowledged that Jesus came from God, and spoke with the authority of God himself: "Just say the word and my servant will be cured!"

Hearing that, Jesus — filled with joy, exultant with gratitude — fairly shouted: "I tell you solemnly, nowhere in Israel have I found faith such as this!"

But again, I'd have to say it again: **it hasn't been easy for me** to learn this! God, our God, He is there, present even among those people. Such an outlook, such a conviction demands a lot from us, demands a deep, and radical change! I personally feel that this is nothing short of revolutionizing everything we've always learned ... and believed ... and taught!

MARK: All I can do is to remember that simple prayer we heard so many times: "I bless you, Father, Lord of heaven and earth, for hiding these things from the learned and the clever and revealing them to mere children!" (Mt 11:25)

PETER: Those without much learning, without too much schooling ... and those too, who've only heard a smattering, here-and-there, some little smidgen of everything He said and taught, even those "outsiders" ... every single one of them can seek God, even if that God is not all that well-defined, that clear in their minds and hearts. And these people, no less than we, can "thirst" for God. I have a feeling that such a desire really makes God present to them. And, with that, what else do you need?

Here, **Jesus sees Himself in those people,** in all those people. And they — for their part — find their peace and consolation in that mere regard, in that gentle, loving, understanding smile with which the Father turns to Him, and in Him to them! Their happiness comes as they realize that they are loved by Him Who gives life. I ... we are *His* children; He guides me ... us with a tender, loving touch! He lifts me ... us up, like one would lift a baby — and cuddles me, close to His cheek (Hosea 11:4) It makes me ... us so very much more than "just a number!" I am *His* child! He carries my picture engraved on His heart ... and He finds His total happiness in watching me, in watching over me, continuously!

The peaceful, loving surrender into the hands of the Father, that tranquil sense of being His, of belonging to Him, that assurance of the all-merciful presence of the Father ... that is the secret of Jesus' happiness. And, **Jesus sees to it that all of this is mirrored in each one of us "unlearned" ones!**

With such as these gathered about Him, Jesus, glowing with joy, can cry out and say: "Father, watch over them carefully! They do look so much like Me! And there are still others who are not yet convinced, saved. Gather them in, Father; they are Yours, just as I am Yours!"

And, with all of them gathered around Him, they are like one large family ... the very same blood courses through their veins! Day after day, Jesus puts Himself on an equal footing with them as they present themselves before the Father!

And, when Jesus rejoins the Father — during that prayer of praise that never ceases to be in His heart and on His lips — He finds no need for elegant phrases or long speeches. Knowing as He does that those He has gathered are of one heart, united intimately with Him, they are all "poor in spirit!," that all the Father looks for from Him ... from them ... is a word of affection: "ABBA/ FATHER!" It is this closeness, this tenderness that binds us, that bonds us to Him!

MARK: You know, Peter, two or three times now I've said **"if I were in Jesus' shoes,"** and then went on to say something about "choosing dependable, worthwhile people," and of starting all over when they'd failed Him, of turning away from those who'd disowned Him like You did, Peter..." And I also thought how I would have curtly dismissed that Centurion, and sent him away empty-handed... But now, after hearing what you've said, I guess I'll have to change my tune ... to say ... to make this my prayer:

"Come and put Yourself in my shoes! Give me something of what You are. Let Your glance transform my ways of seeing others ... help me to see them through Your eyes, and with Your love. Envelop my heart with all that makes You mankind's greatest treasure. As others see me ... as God sees me ... may I be 'all simplicity, and all littleness,' just like You! (Paul Claudel)." There is just so much that has to change and it will, if I pray like this, don't you think?

PETER: Yes, I see what you're getting at! For you, for me, for everyone who walks His Way, who'll ever walk His Way, that'll be the Great Challenge: to react with mercy, and not judgment. Just as this was the way that Jesus instinctively reacted, we'll have to make it the way that we too act, and react! It'll take people like us — simple, uneducated, unpolished people like us to mirror His Way, to make it apparent, to make it real! We can make those who have yet seen to see; to help those who haven't heard Him hear Him and His Gospel. And this, wherever we are, wherever we go! We're the "instruments of God," undaunted ... and absolutely unwilling to become discouraged...!

MARK: And, you know, Peter, Jesus' readiness to give Himself unrelentingly, this really impresses me! And it hits hard! He's just there, making His gentle response, whatever be the situation! He chooses the twelve and **He loves them without condition, without limits!** He takes them as they are, and helps them become what they aren't, yet! For Him, those friends are everything! Even after He'd died, and then rose, He still trusted them ... it seems that His trust became even greater! He is so very good —guess that it's just lots of practice! — at closing an eye to their unfaithfulness, their weakness, their cowardliness, their betrayal! He certainly deals with them so much more gently than ever they deserved! So, the great task remains: **to make His openness apparent, visible!** We must never let ourselves FIND-OUT what hate looks like! We have to always be the first to love, to forgive, to reconcile, to trust! We have to become beacons of hope, lifting hearts, guiding them toward the joy which will let them feel that — in the deepest recesses of their being — they are understood, and loved!

PETER: I think that we just have to do whatever it takes to never forget Jesus' openness to everyone, and to everything. He doesn't bother about all the "small print," or the footnotes, about what it is that makes us different from one another... He just looks for, and finds what it is in us that the Father finds LOVABLE, and sees only that. He acts on His conviction that the Spirit "breathes where He will" (Jn 3:8) **That Centurion Just "knew" that he would be understood and accepted** for what was good, and hope-filled, and noble in him, like his trust in God, even though it wasn't all that "correct." And then, THROUGH that spontaneous and sincere acknowledgment, Jesus made him grow ... **in his own eyes!**

IT'S UP TO US to make the hidden goodness and richness and generosity of Jesus' love to be seen, to make it visible, tangible, experiential. We have to be ready — always! — to listen to others, not just to their lips, but to their hearts... We have to get "good at" listening to what is beneath the words, to "put ourselves in their shoes," and appreciate, even to admire what it is within them that thrills and excites them!

IT'S UP TO US to acknowledge, and to value all that is true, all that is good! We have to get rid of our ways of "judging," especially when we consider all our own prejudices, the biases, the narrow-mindedness that goes into them...

MARK: You know, Peter, the "mission" Jesus entrusted to us is sure scary! I just have to wonder whether I'll ever manage...

PETER: And, who among us "deserves," is "worthy" of such a mission? to think that we — in our day-to-day lives — are called to pass along this same magnanimity, this broad-mindedness, the same generosity and gentleness which shone through Jesus? And as for me, who would dare even mention the word "unworthiness" when I'm around?

What can we do...? I guess that each of us — as best we can! — just have to treasure more deeply His love for us, His caring for us. If we do, and as we do, His unconditioned love and the serenity of His peace, His complete surrender into the hands of God, and His meekness, His humility which are the joy of the Father, will gradually come to glow in us and radiate from us to each one we meet. What more CAN we hope for?

St. Paul MN
July 15, 1991

9

Nothing, Absolutely Nothing is Wasted!

Sometime around the years 58-60 A.D., Paul, the Apostle, was taking a "forced vacation!" He was imprisoned in Caesarea! The book of the Acts of the Apostles, and the Second Letter to the Corinthians suggest that Jesus appeared to Paul, in his prison-dungeon (cfr Acts 18:9; 2 Cor 12:9-10)

Let's try to imagine how those encounters — or "apparitions" might have taken place. What was it that they might have said to one another?

PAUL: You know, it's going on thirty years since you returned to the Father, and since then, very little has changed: why hasn't the power of the Holy Spirit moved more quickly and more powerfully to overcome the adversary, to abolish his hold on the world and the world's peoples? Why is it that God's Kingdom isn't taking-hold? Why is it that the ignorance, the care-LESS-ness, the rejection of any thought of giving oneself to Him is so common? I know that there are some small communities of Christians here and there, but how long are we going to have to wait for the promised salvation of all peoples?

JESUS: Well, Paul, you're right about all the obstacles and barriers that the Gospel has met with in various places. But, exactly, what's on your mind?

PAUL: There are plenty of places, and plenty of obstacles! Just one example, in Rome some Christians themselves are causing divisions, and upsetting peoples' faith, going against what they received from the beginning. And those who do this are not serving anything or anyone but their own interests, themselves with all their nice words and flattering speech, they are misleading innocent people!" (Rom 16:17f) And, in Crete, "they claim that they know God, but their actions deny any such knowledge! Whole families are being upset by teachings that shouldn't be, and all of this for just one motive: money!" (cfr. Ti 1:16, 1:11)

Lord, just think of those people who refuse to give themselves to You; look at so many of our converts, those "pseudo-Christians," false because their hearts are still far from You, and from Your Way! It all just makes me sick!

JESUS: Paul, be real careful not to get over that "sickness," that restlessness, so deeply rooted in your heart!

PAUL: But... what do you mean? I don't understand...!

JESUS: That obsession with the salvation of your brothers (smiling...) excuse me, of OUR brothers!, that's what has to continue to empower you, to keep you going, to excite you, to energize you and to show you the way that you're to go. What makes each day supremely important is to attain the reconciliation of so *many* of the brothers and sisters with God. "Be conscientious about what you're doing and what you're teaching! and continue to do this because in so doing you will save yourself and those who listen to you" (1 Tm 4:16)

Don't let-up in your dedication and in your efforts, in your service of God's people: "Make yourself all things to all men, so that they may be saved at any cost!" (cfr. 1 Cor 9:22) Their reconciliation with God, well, you and I are co-responsible for that! What we're about is of no small import, you know!

PAUL: How well I know! Every single day I "give thanks to God, our Father," for having entrusted me with this challenge, this mission. He has empowered us, simple human beings, with a divine task of being responsible "for God's hidden plan." "In God's Name, we are His ambassadors, His ministers..." The disappointing part is that there are so many who just refuse to open their hearts to this Message of Salvation, and they get locked into their own narrow way of living life. They could care less about changing at all!

JESUS: Do you have anyone in particular in mind?

PAUL: Well, do you remember how they responded in Athens, when — in Your Name — right there at the Areopagus, I was proclaiming the message of the Resurrection. I was sure that all those people, well-educated, reflective, smart, interested, would never before have thought about the reality of Resurrection, or the very word "metanoia," conversion, of turning things around so that they might begin to live in You, and then — in You — to find their way to the Father. What could we — or they — ever imagine that would be more tremendous than that?

Well, most of them just refused to be interested in that Way, the Way to their own freedom ... the freedom that'd release them from their inner enslavements, that'd make them just and holy people! Yet, as I think back to that day, it was a failure, a staggering defeat. Believe me, Lord, wherever I've gone, and in all that I've done, I've never felt so powerless, so insignificant...!

JESUS: Why, what did they say? How did they act?

PAUL: Well, effectively, they just laughed right in my face! They ridiculed me, as if I were out of my mind; they looked as me as if I were a prime candidate for the asylum! I can still hear their response: "You've talked enough now! We appreciate your efforts, and perhaps, some other time, we'll come by to hear more about this..." (Acts 17:32) It was just a way of getting rid of me, and the Word I spoke; they couldn't have been less interested. I'd been there once ... and for them, I guess that that was just once too often! Their laughing, their ridicule, their disinterest ... I can still feel the sting! In their eyes, I was nothing even less than nothing!

JESUS: But, you had prepared yourself, hadn't you? You'd planned to gradually lead them from within their own searchings for truth, and to demonstrate to them that all that seeking was in vain. Really, what was lacking was an openness of heart! They just weren't ready to hear God's Word. If they had been, they would have been ready for that "increase in being" for which they were hungering, and hoping ... about which they're always talking!

Paul, in your talk there at Athens, you invested the best of yourself; and even then, they turned you off! They weren't ready for what you were telling them, however well, however brilliantly you presented it. And, when they remained uninterested, it seems that you lost courage, didn't you!

Let me put it this way: you came away from there convinced that you had wasted your time and your energy. So much so, that now you're questioning the very grounds of your mission...

PAUL: I've lost my courage, my determination? Well ... yes, I guess that I have! went, convinced that it was God Himself Who had sent us out to "announce the Light of salvation to the Jews and to the Gentiles" (Acts 26:23), and we are rejected ... and we come away, dejected. We're thought-of as the most insignificant of all. And, really, for them ... and for so many we ARE insignificant! We succeed at changing absolutely nothing!

We'd thought that we were chosen by God to beget new life in our brothers and sisters, to help them to grow to full stature, to nourish them so that they could grow into their full dignity as children of God ... and we find that they can be interested in most anything ... everything BUT Your Word! We surely haven't accomplished much ... much of anything!

JESUS: (Smiling) Paul, be at peace! Put your mind at rest! What you've just said about being "less than nothing," about being so insignificant, so small, about your feeling unable to transform anything at all..., well, that is precisely what I expected of you!

PAUL: What? That I can't believe ... that you'd "enjoy" our humiliation, our failure...

JESUS: I don't! I could hardly be your loving Lord if I "enjoyᴄᴜ your failures, your weakness...

PAUL: Then, if I understand what You're saying, what You're expecting from us is the offering of even our limitations, and the admission of our failures, and our consciousness of being so insignificant and powerless, about our ineffectiveness...

I'd have to admit: IF we offered You this, we'd really be offering nothing, we'd be "offering" empty hands! Humbled, simple people like ourselves, rejected, ridiculed, mocked, disbelieved, discredited by those in power, beaten and imprisoned (like I am, right now!), servants who've shown themselves unequal to the mission they've received ... with all of this, are you saying that God finds this acceptable? even pleasing? That He would even bother to take a "second look" at our empty hands?

JESUS: Paul ... Paul ... you're getting excited! Have you forgotten that now — as always — God calls simple, humble people? And that it is all but inevitable that things would get pretty difficult for them sometimes? The very challenge that God has given goes well beyond just human will-power and human effort! Yes, it DOES boggle the mind. But look at Moses, and at David, think of Isaiah, or Jeremiah. Each of them knew only too well his own weaknesses, his own limitations.

And, precisely as they "knew" these, they turned to God,... because they had to! They turned to ... they called upon the One for Whom nothing is impossible. They learned to depend on Him, the Rock that holds firm despite the storm and the wildness of the winds. They put their trust in God, not in their own human work, their own skills!

For it is then that they come to realize that it is God's grace which is working through them to move hearts and minds, the grace which truly and deeply effects those to whom they are sent. Moses, Jeremiah really, all of our forefathers, each of them could rightly speak out and say: "It's by God's grace that I am what I am (...and not only me, but also each of those who has heard me!), and His grace in me has not been wasted!" (1 Cor 15:10; 1 Cor 4:6-7)

Jeremiah ... Moses ... really! **"It is when they were weak that they were strong!"** (cfr. 2 Cor 12:10)

PAUL: You're really making me think ... But that was then; this is now! For me, living in this present-day world...

JESUS: "...living in this present-day world..." Remember Mary, my Mother! She was not living in Jerusalem with the Temple and all the learned men of the Law. She lived way out in the little village of Nazareth...

PAUL: And I remember what they told me Nathaniel once said: "Can anything good come out of Nazareth?" (Jn 1:46)

JESUS: And still, it was her, Mary, whom God chose to call... Maybe my Mother herself thought of herself as a simple, unremarkable girl, unexceptional in any way; and then, one day, the Prince of the realm had chosen her, had picked her out as His very own. That young girl would have been so shocked, so surprised by the fact that the Prince had even known of her, or had noticed her, much less that he had selected her among all others.

And Mary was "content to be 'nothing,'" and she is exalted in realizing that it is God who has made her "everything!" [Emile Zola, *Reve*]

PAUL: I'm trying to follow you, but I'm having a little trouble! How could Mary be "contented — as You say! — in being "nothing" Isn't it just normal, and expected too, that we would find pride in what we have and what we've accomplished, in what we are and are becoming? ... in our possessions, our wealth and our skills, our successes, our reputation?... How could Mary find contentment in being "nothing"?

JESUS: Do you really find that so surprising? Just keep in mind that Mary stands in purest light, in undiminished light. She stands ... she CAN stand before her God! She recognizes, and acknowledges that she possesses nothing as her own, neither her youth, nor her beauty ... nor her faith, nor her ultimate trust in God. Everything she has is hers from God! She has nothing that she thinks of as her own! Just ... just nothing! (cfr. 1 Cor 4:7; 2 Cor 5:18)

What makes her life so singular, so attractive is that she thinks of herself as the simple servant of God. It is her poverty, her simplicity that has permitted God to come and refresh the world with the riches of His love.

Mary, unpretentious, unadorned, recognizes just how powerless she is to accomplish all that God wills. "How can a young girl like me, a virgin, how could I conceive and raise the Savior of the world?..."

Acknowledging her "littleness," **Mary is really the key.** And it is because of Mary that the "heavens opened up" (Isaiah) and God could allow the torrents of His love to rain down on humanity. (Is 45:8)

PAUL: Then You are suggesting that we are to look to Mary as an example, as someone to be imitated in her simplicity, her poverty, her dependence?

JESUS: Not only imitate her, but **become a second Mary ... for Me, for the whole world!** Like she did, you have to learn to find your joy in being "nothing," so that "He who is mighty" might do great things in you, and through you!

PAUL: It seems to me that You want us to be really conscious of just one thing: it is God alone Who gives the grace of faith, Who nurtures its growth in the hearts of those who accept His Word...

JESUS: Yes! It is God alone who gives faith! God alone can beget God! ... or His holiness, or His glory, His purity, His joy... You, Paul — and all the other Apostles, too! — you have been given the privilege of sowing the good seed, the Word of God. And, you do what is given you to do, you sow! And without that sowing, there'd never be a harvest! But when you think it through, the sowing is only the beginning! But it is not you who are at the heart of the seed that is sown, in that seed which will sprout and grow. It is God Who is at the heart, Who makes it all happen! Yes, you do your part, you sow! Someone else — call him Apollo —

waters the seedlings, he cultivates them by encouraging, he fills-out the faith of the believers. And then you, Paul, along with Apollo, and all the others who contribute step-by-step, each has done his part, played his role. But **it is God alone who gives growth!** (cfr. 1 Cor 3:7)

PAUL: And still the fact remains that as we grow older, and prob-ably because old habits die hard, change becomes much more dif-ficult. As I've heard it said so often... "Don't waste your time with so and so; he, or she, is too old to change!"

JESUS: Paul, let me remind you — again! — just "hang loose!" Don't get so worked-up! Don't you remember that once there was a guy named "Saul" ...he knew pretty well just what he was about! He went from one place to the other with violent threats against the disciples... He was heading for Damascus to follow-up on some "leads" there. And, on his way... (cfr. Acts 9)

PAUL: You really wouldn't HAVE to remind me! I remember it VERY well! How could I ever forget? You came! You saved me ... from myself! And, I might add: without that, I'd have undoubtedly continued doing that until my dying day!

JESUS: All your life? What difference would it make? You know, now, that in the Lord's sight, "a day can mean a thousand years, and a thousand years is like a day!" (2 Pt 3:8) So, why worry about others' ages, about how long they've been going their own way, about their graying hair, or about all those acquired habits that time has rooted in them? For me, you know, these are just trifles! Paul, I want you to firmly grasp just one thing: the eternal newness of my Resurrection enables Me "to work in you, to accomplish mar-vels that go well beyond whatever you could ask, or think, or dream about!" (Eph 3:20)

Once and for all, think of me as a "potter" in your life, working unceasingly to shape and create you, to make you make right your heart and your hopes, your deepest hungers.

Someone's age? How could that possibly keep Me from doing what I've set out to accomplish?

PAUL: You know, Jesus, I think of that "potter" quite often! We're like clay in Your hands (cfr. Jer 18:6). The potter can take a "glob" of clay and fashion it into whatever he dreams (cfr. Sir 1 5:7; 33:13); and that is precisely what God accomplishes in us, to bring His plan for us to fulfillment.

JESUS: And, remember: the Prophet Isaiah wrote this: "Woe to anyone who would tell his father, 'Who did you beget?' And woe to anyone who would say to his mother: 'Whom did you bring forth?'" (Is 45:10)

PAUL: Yes, the Word speaks clearly! Who are we to argue with our God, our Father and our Mother, saying to Him: "This one is worth nothing!" Whoever would dare to speak that way, well ... well, he certainly hasn't thought through the merciful and meticulous care that God has for each of His children!

JESUS: Yes, and it is up to each one to believe in God, the God Who day by day, infuses human life into each one ... and Who, moreover, infuses His own divine life into each. He IS our Father and Mother, as you've put it. So, nothing fails, nothing is lost of all that He has created.

It is up to each one to believe in the awesome personality that God continues to create within. So, day after day, you can confront the world, thanks to His Almighty Love. And you can make His endless love — in all its facets — even more obvious. In all of creation, nothing is wasted.

PAUL: Now, just a minute, Lord! You're saying that there are no failures, that nothing in all of creation is wasted ... but the Prophet has also written: "When the vessel that the potter was making of clay was spoiled in his hands, he reworked it into another vessel, as it seemed good for the potter to do." (Jer 18:4) What does this mean to you?

JESUS: It means simply that after a long life, with the cumulative weight and wisdom, the experience of many years, and the acquisition of many habits, there might well be some who could be seen as "spoiled vessels." There is nothing in them that would be pleasing in God's eyes...

PAUL: But, that is just what I was saying a while ago! There are some people for whom we can do nothing! They're just too old, to fixed in their ways; nothing good could ever be drawn out of them. Then, would you say that God has failed in their regard?

JESUS: Just a minute now, Paul! Slow down! Remember what the Prophet says? "The potter reworks the clay! ... which means that God can take anyone into His hands again ... and that He will, unceasingly! And anyone you'd think of as "too old to change," "too fixed in his ways to change..." well even for such as these, God can reshape them, take them into His hands and refashion them, infuse a new heart into them and lift them up. **This reality of Easter** happens whenever it happens! **It is a continuous new beginning!**

To say that "it's just too late, it's all over for him, or for her!" God would never talk that way. The dazzling newness of Spring can show with unexpected, or delayed suddenness, whenever, and wherever! And **God's PENTECOST, it too is happening day after day!** The Spirit of holiness is still sent! And when that Spirit "settles," it completely overwhelms you. It totally penetrates each one. Persons like the ones you were talking about when you were claiming that nothing good could possibly be hoped for from/in him ... The Holy Spirit can come and settle, refreshing the clay for the potter's hands. After a while, I'll become "the most important person in his or her life." I'll become the very reason for his or her coming to live life. I'll become his or her dearest friend, his very treasure. I'll be the one that he or she couldn't have gotten along without: In a very simple, direct word: **"I will be everything for him!"** (Col 3:11) — That one that you are talking about, any day I can make his life different ... other ... divine! I will be within him, coursing through him as his own blood! That intensity of life — it is just what he'd always dreamt about! — it is the spiritual balance that lies at the base of every facet of his personality ... and it brings with it that inner peace for which every man so desperately hungers, that peace-filled manner of "living life" that makes life like a citadel, secure from any enemy! This, and so much more would my Spirit provide, transforming and informing his own spirit! No, Paul, **for God, it is never too late!**

One thing you must always be careful about: never doubt the almighty power of God to influence and effect any of His children! "Indeed, this IS the day of salvation!" (2 Cor 6:2)

PAUL: What you've said is really helpful! I'm really grateful! You've rid my heart of all my growing pessimism. I just hope that from now on, I'll be able to remember this ... when new disappointments and new challenges come my way! I just can't let even the shadow of despair enter to darken my vision! What I came to understand through that tremendous "event" on the road to Damascus (as You just reminded me!), something similar can be the experience of anyone! And, remarkably, it can happen even for those who reject God, who refuse to let the seed of His Word "fall into good ground!" Even those will — one day — come to recognize that "God can become everything for them!" Perhaps, what we most need is simply "to pray for them with greater hope, to let our hearts sing out our hopes as we say:

> "Give us, Lord, a new heart!
> Put a New Spirit in us, O Lord!"

JESUS: I like that song a lot! Maybe, it's because it doesn't say "Give ME...," but "Give US!" It means that when you pray, you must not forget to embrace ALL of those the Father calls "His own!" Each one must be responsible for every other ... responsible for their salvation! You understand this, don't you?

PAUL: Yes ... yes, I do! The unfortunate thing is that — so very often! — I just forget that basic fact: no one is saved alone! We must inevitably draw others along! It's no less true: many depend in one way or another on my prayer...!

JESUS: How right you are, Paul. **No one finds salvation alone!** Just don't forget that when you go to the Father in prayer, you speak on behalf of all your brothers and sisters, you are their spokes-man, their intercessor. You are their advocate, like Abraham — was it was because of his faithful prayer for Sodom and Gomorrah, that he became the "Father of all Believers." And, know too, Paul, that God cannot resist this anxious cry for help.

Through you, and thanks to you, the very holiness of God can become more pervasive, it can "invade" the hearts of so many, and always so many more ... radiating outward like the light from a lamp. A light isn't lit so that it can be "lit!" It is so that it will give light to the whole house.

Through you, and thanks to you My own Sacrifice continues to be offered to the Father. In Me, you pay again and again! — the price of redemption for all humanity. Through your prayer, in the Father's eyes, "you are crucified with me!" (Gal 2:19) Your blood is mingled with mine. Learn to love My Cross, not just for what I did for you, but for what I am doing, and will continue to do for the whole world. In a way, you must bear my Cross each day, wher-ever you might be! You will find — and don't be afraid of this, Paul — you will find that the salvation of even one soul is costly!

PAUL: Lord, what you said about Abraham strikes me ... God does not resist the prayer of the righteous. In a way, He is "victimized" by it! (Cfr. Jas 5:16)

That reminds me of something one of my aunts used to say ... **"Nothing is ever wasted of what you give to God!"** (Marie Theve)

JESUS: Yes, that pretty much puts it all together! Paul, my brother, just remember that "In the Lord, you will never labor in vain!" (1 Cor 15:58)

PAUL: That reminds me of that young kid ... that day when you'd been instructing the people for nearly the whole day, and it was getting late; they had had nothing to eat ... and they had nothing with them. That kid still had five loaves of bread, and two fish. You accepted them ... and after asking God to bless them, you passed them around to everyone ... and they all ate as much as they wanted. And afterwards, the left-overs filled twelve baskets! And, if I remember, there were about five thousand men there that day, to say nothing of the women and children! (Mt 14:21ff)

That day, You were there for those people with such an abundance... Whenever You accept anything from anyone, You give it back ... multiplied a hundredfold! You just can't be stingy! The return You make is always made with such unanticipated generosity ... it exceeds by so much whatever it was that'd first been given to You! And, every day You accomplish such awesome signs and miracles. It is just unbelievable!

JESUS: The "sign" that day when I fed all that vast gathering of people, you should not think of it as something I did, but as something I continue to do. I'm still accomplishing such things ... with your help! Just never forget that when you give to the Lord — and especially when you give yourself to Him! — you are not poorer. You come away so much richer. Five loaves! Two fish! and "all of them ate, as much as they wanted!" There is just no proportion between what you give to God, and what He gives in return!

PAUL: You know, You once said something that has provided me with lots of strength and courage during my journeys: "Be careful! Be especially careful of your teaching! But never lose heart because in doing this you will save both yourself and those who hear you!" (1 Tm 4:16) That spiritual inter-dependency (or "communion of saints"!) is what gives a special flavor to what we're doing...

JESUS: Paul — when I say this, I'm also thinking of many, many brothers and sisters throughout the world, and down through the ages — be convinced that many will be saved just because someone, somewhere, at some time, prayed ... prayed out of love!

One day, you will be astonished, really so very pleasantly surprised by the welcome you receive when you enter the gates of the Father's Kingdom. "Finally, you're here! You know, we've been waiting for you for so long now!" And this will be the "welcome" of ... of how many? What a welcome to God's house and home! Naturally, you'll wonder just who these people are ... you'll look around and probably not recognize a single one of them! Then one or the other will step up and explain: "No, you don't know us! You never lived where we lived, nor did you speak our language then! You lived in a different place, at a different time...! But, we know you! In fact:

- By all your efforts to make your life conform to Jesus' Gospel,
- By the care you expended to reproduce Jesus' way of living,
- By your determination to never, not even in the little things, to never make any compromises with the Truth,
- By your ever renewed effort to make obvious Jesus' tender love to whomever you met in the course of your days, or your ways,
- By your steadfastness, by standing-your-ground, solid in your faithfulness in spite of the turbulence and storms that broke around you, and upon you.

Well, God took all of that in hand, and used it as the prayer that obtained our salvation! So, come on now, hurry up ... "take possession of the Kingdom that God has prepared for you from the beginning!"

October 12, 1991

10

As in a Mirror...

Around the year 50-55 A.D., in Jerusalem, the Apostle James headed-up the local Christian community. Some foreigners passing through the Holy City had been met by James. It might well have happened that one night, a certain Nicholas had stopped by to visit with James. He was a well-to-do Prefect, who had come from the Greek Province. Following in the footsteps of his ancestors, Nicholas practiced the cult of spirits. He knew little about this "New Way," as the beliefs and life-style of the Christians was termed. But, he was an inquirer, open-minded. Here is something that we might imagine of their conversation that night.

Briefly, James introduces himself. Very quickly, in the "style" of someone trying to make an impression, of someone who's "been around," Nicholas begins:

NICHOLAS: You know, I'm the Prefect up in the Greek Province. And, maybe you heard about the great numbers of people there! And, as you might imagine, my responsibilities are enormous. But, thanks be to the gods, we've been pretty successful in getting the people to be submissive. In fact, as I see things, we've quickly instilled the discipline and the obedience of a military unit! If I tell this one "Go!," he goes! And when I summon another, he comes, immediately! And when I utter an order to one of my slaves, "Do this, or that...," it's done, and immediately! It'd better be!

None dares to question my authority ... I've pretty well managed to instill this in them! After all, they know quite as well as I do that I also make the final decisions in the courts, so they'd better!

Really, it's a bit like captaining a ship. I am there to determine the course we will take. There's no doubt: I am certainly more knowledgeable, and truthfully, more competent than anyone else; and I know our ultimate destination! As a matter of fact, I control those who would "come aboard" ... so right there, any competition is eliminated. I am — and only, you understand, **I AM THE ONLY MATER ON BOARD.**

JAMES: So, there are no clouds on your horizons ... your life today is as your future will be, hopefully! Everything stands out black-on-white ... everything's under control...

NICHOLAS: Yes, I'd say everything! Well ... on second thought, I guess I'd have to say almost everything!"

JAMES: ... Uh ... come again? I didn't quite catch what you said. Your ship — and I think you're talking about your destiny here on this earth! — you've said that you're the Captain, that you are — in the fullest possible sense of the term — the ship's Master. So, really, there's nothing to raise any concern, is there?

NICHOLAS: Well ... in a way ... Since my "ship" — and, yes, I am really talking about my life! — well, I'm just not all that sure with regard to the final destination, to the final port of call...

JAMES: Oh! You're really talking about a journey without a destination, about going maybe, in circles? I guess that isn't all that sure a course, is it? I don't know that I'd care to be on your ship...!

NICHOLAS: Well, do you have any suggestions? Do you know where I might get some maps, or a dependable compass?

JAMES: Really, Nick, what I'd suggest is not something that can be "bought" ... and I'd quickly add, that is nothing that would enhance your standing, or your reputation. And, neither is it something that you will find by sailing vast seas...!

NICHOLAS: Yet, it'd be something that would give my life some direction, some consistency? something that'd help me to make sense out of it all? Have you heard of something that might have come — say from the East — or some place that we Romans haven't yet conquered?

JAMES: I guess that what I'm proposing would hardly be thought of as a "philosophy," not a established ideology ... it comes closer — I guess! — to being just Wisdom ... the Wisdom which can lead us to discover the One "in whom we live, and move, and have our being" as the great Greek philosopher used to say ... well, "said" some four hundred hears ago! It's simply knowing ... and coming to love the One Who is at the center, the core of everything that is, the creator of all that we can see and even what is unseen, the One to Whom we owe absolutely everything that we have, or want, the One Who constituted us as we are ... and ultimately, the One toward Whom our lives tend until finally...

NICHOLAS: Some "Supreme Wisdom?" Someone to whom we owe everything we have, everything we hope to have ... all that I am? Some sort of "super god," some god who would eclipse all the other gods in our Pantheon of gods?

JAMES: Your "super god," Nick ... he seems to me to be like the sun. You see it at dawn! And as it appears, the stars, and the moon are visible no longer. For us, they simply disappeared. They were "eclipsed" by the brightness of the light of the sun. And thus, neither the stars nor the moon serve any longer as a means of seeing our way clearly. Once the sun rises, the night is over, darkness vanishes!

You see, Nick, the moon and the stars, these represent the "spirits from above," all the countless gods and goddesses that human-kind has devised, that are the prayer-objects of different people. For us, the believers, OUR LIGHT, OUR SUN is God, "the Father of all light, the giver of all that is perfect; and with

Him there is no such thing as change, nor even a shadow caused by alteration." (Jas 1:16)

The light that comes and enlightens the life of our people, the believers, is the very Word of God. Through His Word, God comes to teach us that it is He Who is at the beginnings of life, Who accompanies us day by day through life. And it is He Whom we shall all meet, face to face, and at long last; and He will welcome us to live with Him forever, IF we have shown ourselves worthy of Him!

NICHOLAS: Now, you're saying "Through His Word, He teaches us..." But, what do we mortals have to do to hear that Word? Is it in heaven that He speaks? And if so, who will go up to heaven to bring it down to us so that we can hear it and learn from it? Is that word being spoken in some distant land across the seas? If that be the case, we all need to ask: "Who will cross those seas for us and bring it back to us so that we too may hear it and keep it?" (cfr. Dt 30:12-13)

JAMES: Now, you're making it considerably more complicated that it really is! For indeed, the Spirit of God speaks to each one of us in the depths of our hearts. "His Word is very near you, it is in your mouth and in your heart, so that you might observe it!" (Dt 30:13-14)

As you might expect, in the long history of our people, we have been hearing that Word for some time now, and we have carefully preserved that Word, writing down that which God has spoken and taught us. You have, perhaps, seen our Scrolls, upon which we have written His Word. We continually read, and re-read them when we gather.

If you will, I'd like to show you some of those "Words" that we have from God. Then, you might see, and understand what it is that makes our lives different. As we see these Scrolls and their contents, they enlighten us, they help us see, perhaps better and more clearly than others.

But let me first ask you something. What are the rituals and the customs that your people, your ancestors handed on to you? As I've heard, they are all "religious people." What did you get from them?

NICHOLAS: Yes, I certainly feel that they are! ... they are very religious! For generations now, we've turned to the gods who govern the universe. They reign above us; they rule the entire universe. They are greater, more powerful than any, or all of us! Our first duty to them is to honor their power, and to gain — if you will, to "win over" — their favor. For this reason, at different times during the year, — as we have received it from those who have gone on ahead of us — we carry out certain rituals, some of them quite elaborate, and meaningful. At some of these festivals, we kill a year-old calf, the most choice specimen in the flock. To express our respect, our submission to these heavenly "powers," *we offer the best that we have,* what is most valued, what we think "counts" most!

And we offer them to our gods. We burn them on the altar dedicated to that god ... and part of the ritual is to see that the animal is completely consumed in the fire. In this way we symbolize that *absolutely EVERYTHING is offered.* By this we signify that we do indeed "belong" to our gods, and we make these sacrifices so as to ensure the protection we all need. We use the term "Holocaust" when we enact these rituals ... and I'm sure you know, the very word "holo"-"caust" means to "burn everything"!

In some way, we are joined with those heavenly spirits by the rising smoke from our sacrifices which are burned to honor them. As we observe the rising smoke, in our hearts we renew the bonds that unite us to these heavenly beings. We sense that we are renewed in our attachment to our gods; and thus, they will preserve us from misfortunes and undue hardships and disasters. As we see these things, by our sacrifices, we "gain" the favors of the gods.

You see, by enacting these rituals, we are purified. It is this that counts most! For this we have instituted these rituals for our people. And now, they have become a part of our Roman culture ... something of that which we seek to propagate among the people among whom we live, when they are able to rise to this!

But, I've been talking about our religious rituals. Tell me, if you will, about yours! For you, what did you "inherit" from your ancestors, what are the customs of your people? Are they in some ways different from ours? What are they?

JAMES: Nicholas, I will try to answer your inquiry. But first, let me say something that I think is supremely important, and that is that you, and your people have really come to "ritualize" something that is very, very important for all human persons... for every human person! As you've just said, these sacrifices of animals are offered to the gods, the smoke rises up to the heavens where these divinities dwell, and somehow, by the rising smoke, you are bound, "bonded" to beings greater than yourselves. Let me say quite directly: this is something really great in your culture.

NICHOLAS: Well, thank you ... thanks a lot for your insights, for your appreciation of our ways... What you've said really says all that I was trying to say ... and says it beautifully! But, you ... do your people do anything similar?

JAMES: Among the Jewish people, we too — for generations now — we've offered calves in sacrifice to God, the Almighty. We make these offerings *as a sign of our submission, our homage, and our gratitude for all that He provides for us.* Here, in Jerusalem, at the Temple, we offer hundreds of magnificent animals in sacrifice. You know, the Temple is open; you might be interested in going up to see it for yourself

NICHOLAS: So, you'd say that there is little ... really, no difference at all?

JAMES: Well, yes, there IS a difference! You see, in generations past, God has given us the knowledge that **we must SEE further** than the smoke which rises to the heights. The "essential" is not there!

But, before speaking about this, let me ask you something else. Do those people you govern offer you gifts every now and then, on particular occasions?

NICHOLAS: Of course! This is one way they have to acknowledge that I am the Prefect, the "man-in-charge," the one man who has dominion over their land, their possessions really, over every one of them!

You see, there are those occasions — like the anniversary of my arrival, or even on my birthday, or the Emperor's day — anyone who "is" anyone comes to my palace ... one brings me fine cloth, another some precious stone. And, in this way they gain my attention ... an attention that "pays-off" handsomely for them in other circumstances ... if you know what mean!

JAMES: And, I assume, you are pleased with these "gifts" that they bring you?

NICHOLAS: Well, not always! I remember one particular fellow ... who wanted but one thing: to be appointed Prefect in my place! He was jealous of me, of my power, of my title ... of me, period! Recently, on one or the other occasion when they are accustomed to come, he came and offered this splendid ring which you see here on my finger...

JAMES: ...and, you accepted it?

NICHOLAS: Of course! But, let me tell you, I was considerably wiser than he thought! ... Of course, he had to come, to make his offering just like the others in the region. But, his gift was somehow ... well, it was hardly that! Yes, he gave the ring, but his heart was not in it ... **His heart was far from me.** He figured — I guess — that I would be so impressed by his gift that I'd never suspect his real intentions ... or at least, his hopes. Well, let me say that as far as I'm concerned ... he's just "out' one fine ring! You see, I'm sharper than that!

I might add: from that point on, I began to neglect him more and more, to ignore his interests ... really, to pass him by ... until, ever so gradually, I'd come to hate him more than anyone or anything else. I simply came to the point of ignoring him and his interests.

JAMES: Yes, you did repay him for his hypocrisy, his falsity ... really, it'd seem that he got just what he deserved in the bargain!

You see, Nick, something very similar has happened — for centuries now! — among the people of my birth. Down through the ages, the Prophets have risen continually reminding us that our holocausts were worth absolutely nothing unless our hearts were truly offered along with the sacrificed animals. So long as our hearts remained "far removed from God" (Mt 15:8), our sacrifices were hollow, empty! We should know that *we cannot approach God "with two minds."* (cfr. Jas 1:8)

NICHOLAS: You mention prophets ... who were they? How did they get into the picture? And, you seem to be saying that they had a great deal of influence among your people? How?

JAMES: Well, just for a couple of instances, we remember these teachings:

"Does the Lord like the holocausts and sacrifices as much as He likes the obedience to His Word? No! Obedience is better than sacrifice, submissiveness better than the fat of rams!" (1 Sm 15:22) What the Prophet has said is this: *What the Lord requires of us* is a complete **acceptance of His Word,** a heart that reveres Him, a dedicated love founded on a radical trust..."

"This love of yours is as momentary as a morning cloud, or the dew that quickly disappears!" (Hos 6:4) What I understand the Prophet here as saying is that *God expects* that we return to His Way with repentant hearts, with a new-found determination to love Him, and submit to Him irrevocably. Something superficial, anything passing would just not do it! It is certainly not this that the Lord God looks for from us! The acceptable "sacrifice to our God is a broken spirit, a broken, contrite heart He will not scorn" (Ps 51:17)

"The Lord our God is the one God. To love Him with all your heart, with all your understanding and strength, and to love your neighbor as yourself, this is far more important than any holocaust or sacrifice." (Mk 12:29-33) *What God seeks from us* it not some portion of what we possess, neither our money or our possessions, not our children or our slaves, not our animals. *What He looks for* is our love, our gratitude ... our hearts overflowing with appreciation for all He does for us. And, I believe that He is entitled to ask this from us: day after day, and day-by-day He watches over us, takes care of us faithfully and generously, with no strings attached.

He loves us passionately and cherishes each one of us to distraction! "He is in need of nothing, that He should be served by human hands; contrariwise, He is the One who provides everything — including life and breath! — to everyone" (Acts 17:25) "He is not far from any one of us, since it is in Him that we live, and move, and exist!" (Acts 17:28) All of these sayings are direct, and simple enough, but they outline an entire program for us. Well, what do you think?

NICHOLAS: Well, to even think about "a whole program" is pretty new for me, as you might guess! But, such words, such perspectives ... well, they assuredly do say more and go farther than what we Romans have from our traditions and customs.

When we sacrificed the finest of our animals to our gods, we considered this as "good." As we watched the smoke rise from our sacrifices, we thought of it as money ascending to the gods ... we sort of thought that it was "cash and carry," we paid, and we awaited the payoff! We "bought" favors from the diverse gods ... pretending that we could thus gain their protection and their assistance (Bar 3:29f). We'd thus avoid undue hardships and any sickness or disease ... IF we made our sacrifices at the right times and in the right way, everything would fall in place.

But now, with just this minimal "sampling" from your Prophets, it raises all sorts of questions in my mind. Maybe we were manipulating, calculating... It was ourselves "running" our gods rather than allowing our divinities to guard and guide us! We were subjecting them to our wills, our plans, our projections rather than seeking to know and submit ourselves to theirs! After all, what did we take ourselves for?

And we always were most cautious to carefully and correctly observe the rituals for the sacrifices. These were of supreme importance ... and value! But, even then, somehow we had the feeling that this was not the way it should have been ... that it was superficial, "as passing as a morning cloud, or the dew that quickly disappears," as you've said yourself!

Do you remember what I was saying earlier, when we'd just begun to talk? ... when I spoke of myself as the captain of a large ship. How I allowed no one aboard except those who would hear, and follow my orders? About how I thought of myself as the ship's "Master?" But now, after I've heard even just this "sampling" of your Prophets, I'd have to tell myself that "on board my ship, first and above all, ***there is but one Pilot, God!*** He will go with me through his loving, watchful presence, whatever course I follow through all my days. In my every thought, in all that I undertake to accomplish, in every word that I speak, whether I enjoy enviable health or am subjected to unforeseen sickness, really, it "all comes from God!" (1 Chrn 29:14) And all the rest ... well, it is simply His gift to me.

If I truly "knew God," the Master of heaven and earth, then I'd have but one thought in my head: to affirm, to tell Him humbly and excitedly of my gratitude ... that I have come to realize that ***I am the only master on board AFTER GOOD.***

JAMES: Yes, Nick, there is but one sacrifice that God finds pleasing, and that is:

- to rid yourself — as I continually try to do in myself! — of any futile pretension of autonomy,
- to let the Lord, the Master of our lives, ***"be at the wheel"***
- to eradicate any illusion of all of that "cash and carry" mentality that you mentioned, that attitude that IF/WHEN the rituals of sacrifice are carried out exactly, then we have a "right" to expect results.

As we come to acknowledge — and act accordingly! — Him as Master over, and in our lives, then we can more serenely know that the course is "best." And we have to persistently make the effort to keep "the eyes of our heart" on Him, so that what we undertake will truly be according to His Way. For this, we need to be open to the breath of His Spirit ... simply, to let Him "run the show!"

There can be — no longer! — those segments of our life that are "protected" by *No Trespassing*, or *Keep Out* signs! And, in this, we're just never done! we continually slip back into that thought-pattern of thinking of ourselves as being in control. We have to learn to let the Holy Spirit of God come to us, to strip away all of that foolishness... And nothing short of a constant effort will be

enough! After all, what we all hold most dearly and most tenaciously is our Ego, our heart, our own hopes and ambitions. And
the longer I live, and the more disciples that I talk to and discuss
these things with, the more convinced I become that we are all
called to offer this "as a living sacrifice, a holy sacrifice pleasing to
God!" (Rom 12:1)

One of the Prophets, Hosea, said it so clearly ... so clearly and
so concisely that it was taken up almost as a refrain right down to
our own day: "What God most wants *from us is our love!*" (cfr.
Mt 9:13)

NICHOLAS: James, you have served God and His people for so
many years now. May I ask you: has following the Way, truly believing been easy?

JAMES: Not really! Everyday I live I have to discover, and redis-
cover, with amazement, who God is! Everyday, as I read and re-
read what has been written, I find new perspectives opening to me,
new challenges, new opportunities... Everyday ... barring none! ...
I am astonished, astounded really! and elated, renewed in my utter
joy in pursuing the Way!

NICHOLAS: Just a minute now, James! What would I have to do
... how long would it take for me to get to know God's Word as you
do? It just seems that it'd be too much for me!

JAMES: Nick, I too have that same feeling deep in my heart! I
think that it is just too much really, impossible! to possess all the
Wisdom sayings that God wants us to live by. But God does not
demand that we be so completely acquainted with His Word ...
rather, what He demands of each of us is that we love Him in an
uncompromising way, day after day after day! Each day we CAN
improve the quality of that, couldn't we?

I can think of an old acquaintance ... an old, old man who
knows the Writings from top to bottom, from beginning to end.
He knows every dot of every "i" and every crossed "t" to the Nth-
degree. He is never without a "quote" from one or the other of our
Books, either the historical narratives, or the Songs of Praise, or

the Prophets. But when I think about it, I am tempted to have pity on him! In spite of all of his learning, in spite of his precise and exact knowledge about God ... well, let me put it this way: he knows how to talk about God but I have the feeling that he *doesn't know how to talk to God,* or *to let God speak to him.* He has never developed the ability to allow that Word to make demands upon him, to lead him, to guide him through the ways of life. Yes, his knowledge has made him to be quite renowned ... but is that what life is about? In my heart, I think of him as a "booming gong, a clashing cymbal!" (1 Cor 13:1)

What matters, really, is not what you, or anyone, knows ABOUT God, but rather how we *make that Word real* (cfr. Jas 1:23) in the activities and directions of our lives, hour by hour, how we allow it to center, to re-focus the direction of our life, patterning it on God's Way!

NICHOLAS: To make God's Word "more real," more applicable in your life, what do you have to do? Just offhand, it seems to be pretty complicated...

JAMES: Maybe it isn't as difficult, or as complicated as you think! Just take a minute or so to think about this: in your own family, is there perhaps someone who went abroad, and began a completely new life?

NICHOLAS: Well, yes! There was my cousin Alexander; he was just a couple years younger than me, and we got along really well. Two or three years ago, he went back to Rome...

JAMES: Do you hear from him from time to time? ... Does he write?

NICHOLAS: Well, yes, but not that often! But when he does, his letters seem to me to be almost poems! I know of no one who writes as beautifully as he does. When I hear from him, his is always the first letter I read ... and I can never read it but once. And when I've read his letters, my happiness, my joy in living as a human being is expanded ... tenfold! In a way, he lifts me up beyond myself. And, the "special" part of this is that he writes this, and this way just for me! And even so, I always want to pass his letters around ... not just because I'm so proud of my cousin, but because of the beautiful way he writes, and the splendid things he writes about! I guess from all of this you've probably concluded already that when I hear from him, nothing — neither business nor appointments! — keeps me from reading his letter. And when I get home in the evening, I read it again, and yet again!

JAMES: OK, Nick ... now, let's get back to the Word of God! It should be the same! We should have that same eagerness, that same interest and excitement in "hearing from God" as you've said you have when you hear from Alexander...

NICHOLAS: But, you see, he doesn't write every day. As I think about it, he writes from time to time, simply to affirm and to sustain the friendship, the closeness we'd enjoyed over the years. But when he does, I thoroughly enjoy ... relish reading them, treasuring them, reflecting about them...

JAMES: And, you know what, Nick? You've just answered your own question! You asked "How do you make God's Word real in your life?" I myself, **I try to "absorb" it** in much the same way as you do with your cousin Alexander's letters!
For three or four days at a time, just as you savor one or the other phrases, in Alexander's letters, well! ...this is also how I simply try to understand and penetrate every possible "angle" of one or a couple of verses, that I've found striking, something that has "spoken" to me in some special way. Every now and then, I strive to MEMORIZE an entire verse or two. You see! That Message of tenderness that God "mails" to me, I "clasp it to my heart," as if I was His one and only addressee.
For three or four days, I keep returning to that Word. I really concentrate my attention and my imagination on those words, on that short passage; and I seek to nourish my faith from those Words. And, slowly, but with equal certitude, those Words gradually unwrap themselves for me, they become more precious for me, certainly, than any of those jewels that you have in the rings on your

fingers! It is in, and through those Words that "I find my real happiness!" (Jas 1:25)

For three or four days, or more even, *that Word is — for me — like a hidden garden* in which I meet my God. Through those Words, it is God Himself Who comes to enhance and expand the dialog of faith and love that binds me even closer to my God.

And finally, that Word evokes, calls forth from me my own word, a word of prayer, a word of trust, which is itself fertilized by God's Word. It is as an echo of the Word God first spoke. And it is a very quiet word ... *a word spoken just between God and myself."*

NICHOLAS: I understand, James, what you're saying. And, if it wouldn't be prying, could I ask what Word you've been "chewing over" during these past days ... what struck you? and how did you reply?

JAMES: Oh no! It isn't anything! In fact, among us who seek to follow The Way, we generally try to share with one another the Word that God has spoken, and our responses. It is almost like a candle ... when one candle is lit from another, the first candle isn't lessened, or diminished, but the light is greatly increased!

Here is one Word. "Each day brings with it its own trouble. So do not worry about tomorrow; tomorrow will take care of itself." (Mt 6:34) Before I fall asleep at night, I think about those few Words, I repeat them quietly to myself. And when I do this, I entrust my night and my day tomorrow into God's hands. He will still be there tomorrow; He will walk alongside, helping me to carry whatever burdens the day might bring. As He has stood with me and walked with me today, so tomorrow!

And another Word: "Man, this is what Yahweh, the Lord-God, asks of you, only this: to act justly, to love mercy, and to walk humbly with your God!" (Mi 6:8)

These counsels are so simple ... but a whole life would be too short to really "live" them, hour by hour, in each circumstance that life presents. Up until now, I haven't succeeded! But, I'm still trying. And each morning, I begin by reminding myself anew of the task: to act justly in everything and with everyone, to seek to be patient and understanding ... and forgiving, to be merciful and kind and thoughtful to those who most need it, and who least expect it!, and to recognize that I'm doing this not through my own determination and power, perhaps even my own stubbornness, but through the power, the strength that God gives me to accomplish this. I listen to God's Word, you see ... and I really try to hear it! But, each day I must set about listening attentively to God's Word.

And, one final Word ... it is Jesus Who invites us to walk with Him, alongside Him even to the point of making His "fate" our own. He says: "Be courageous! I have already conquered the world ... The Ruler of this world has no power over me." (Jn 16:33; 14:30) To walk with Jesus, to "abide in Him" is to be beyond the reach, the attacks of the enemy, the prince of darkness and of this world.

His arms — as strong as a high dike, as resistant as a mighty dam — prevent the torrents of death (which is to say, **the onslaughts of our own selfishness and lack of faith!**) from ravaging and destroying everything we've built-up.

His divine Strength — the Holy Spirit! - will come to us and, little by little, will master whatever there is in us that does not yet belong fully to God.

And, He continues to hold out His hand, always lifting us up, bringing us to stand-tall, to raise us beyond ourselves ... to bring us to ascend to His Father and ours!

NICHOLAS: To put it another way, *God's Word is like a mirror!* I mean... how would we know whether our hair is combed without a mirror? How could we even smile to ourselves without a mirror?

JAMES: Precisely! Through His Word, God helps us to see ourselves, to see what we really are, to know our true identity. He reminds us time and time again that we are from Him, and for Him! And, He continually reminds us, too, that He is on our side, that His love for us is without end, without limit ... that He is always with us, even more present to us than we are to ourselves, and more real than the sun that warms us and makes our crops grow. Thanks to His Word, we can really come to see our life *through the glasses of God Himself!*

NICHOLAS: Unfortunately, the trouble is that we DO see ourselves, but we readily and quickly forget what we've seen! "We forget what we look like" (cfr. Jas 1:24-f), we are like amnesiacs! We just don't get "off the ground," to soar at the altitude God calls us to!

JAMES: Yes, you know ... if only we would let His Word and His loving Presence enlighten us, then nothing — not even death itself! — would ever cloud our joy of living...

NICHOLAS: "Nothing ... not even death itself!" But isn't this just a bit exaggerated? We're both getting along in years. Every time I even begin to think about my dying, all kinds of fears and apprehensions rise up in me. I know well enough that it is ultimately impossible to avoid it, that one day I'll have to let go of all that I have attained and all that I've come to own, that it'll all amount to nothing. I'll just fall into that fathomless pit, into that darkness ... almost like someone who is forced to go out of a well-lit house, into the pitch black darkness outside. When I look ahead to my own death, I'm fearful ... really, filled with fear! I am almost "scared to death!" ... and try as I may, I've never succeeded at ridding myself of the anxiety and the anguish. Really, when you think about it ... isn't life a whole lot of nonsense?

JAMES: Somehow, Nick, I can sense how deeply you are haunted by the thought of death. Suppose that the outcome of this is avoidance, to live day-by-day as if you were going to live forever, to banish from your consciousness any real thought about your death... And, I'd have to say: to think and act like this isn't at all uncommon!

NICHOLAS: No, I can't say that I'd be one of those... I don't ... I can't leave all my anxiety aside! ...refuse to *act as if death would never come* calling on me! It's just not my way. To live an "aimless life," that's just not my style. It's in this that I become bewildered...

JAMES: Well, God does speak words of comfort and consolation to me, to you, to everyone of us, words that can build or restore hope in us...

NICHOLAS: But, if God existed, there would be no death!

JAMES: Now, slow down, Nick! I wouldn't be quite willing to go that far! Contrary to what you're saying, it is precisely because God DOES exist, because He DOES love us that we can live out our life peacefully, tranquilly...

NICHOLAS: How's that?

JAMES: Well, God does not ask that we *"act as if"* there is no lessening of our stamina, of our strength with the passing of years; He doesn't demand that we act as if there weren't all sort of pain and suffering as the years progress, as if our pilgrimage on this earth were to go on and on...

He doesn't ask us to "lie" to ourselves! He merely wants us to accept whatever it might be that life gives us, and to live with it... even to the point of dying from it!

He doesn't ask us to submit passively to every bad situation, including death, that time and fortune put into our life...

But He does ask us to live eagerly looking forward to that "final Passover," through death to life. He does ask that we surrender consciously into His hands ... this He does expect from us! And so, we should walk steadily, and securely, toward that "final step" which we will inevitably one day take ... and that we make that step peacefully, not with some feeling of *"anything but this!"*

And, when these feelings of anxiety begin to take hold of you, maybe then it'd be time to repeat the words of Job: "I have spoken once, twice. I'd best put my finger to my lips, not to speak again. The time is over when I pretended to make some reproach to Providence!" (Jb 40:4f; 42:5)

NICHOLAS: When everything in your life is going smoothly, and when your health is no problem, it is easy enough then to believe in this God, in His Providence ... but the day will certainly come when my life slips out of my own control. Then...?

JAMES: Then, Nicholas ... then you'll simply seek to wait for that joyous moment when the Father opens the door of His dwelling to you ... when He holds out His hand to welcome you to His dwelling-place, forever!

You know, it is possible — even at that moment of dying — to thank God and praise His holy Name ... perhaps — again — as Job put it: "Naked I came forth from my mother's womb! Naked I shall return! ... The Lord gives, the Lord takes away; Praised be His holy Name! (Jb 1:21)

Every single time that we admit to ourselves that there is no such thing as "perfect happiness" on this earth, then maybe it's time to remember that it is God who inserted into our hearts *that hunger and that hope* for perfect happiness, that thirst for fullness. And that hope is also a promise: the day will come when that promise will be fulfilled! When its full reality will be ours. And, you now, Nicholas, those last moments of our life could well be *the most crucial;* it could be that precisely at that moment God comes to verify the depth, the tenacity of our faith ... almost as if He were asking: "You say you believe? or is it all just a sham? Do you cling tightly to Me in death as you always thought you did in life?

NICHOLAS: You know, James ... what you've said really fits together, it really makes sense! Now, if only I can remember ... and practice all of this! "I have been angry with God, but now that folly is finished!" (Jb 1.22) "We accept the good things that come to us from God, shouldn't we also accept the setbacks, the misfortunes, as well? (Jb 2:10)

February 13,1992

11

Not Without Us!

For many years after Jesus' Resurrection and Ascension, Mary lived at Ephesus. She took care of John, her adoptive son, the beloved disciple. There, among the other members of the small Christian community, she was particularly valued by John in his work. Slowly, her faith had deepened and expanded; and for this reason, Mary had shown herself quite willing, even eager to share with others all that she has come to perceive in faith.

One day, she had occasion to talk with Rachel, a recently baptized forty year old woman, who owned and operated one of the shops in the marketplace. She was quite successful, and thus has accumulated a certain status due to her wealth. And, she was well known by nearly everyone in Ephesus.

Can we imagine their conversation as Mary and Rachel met in Mary's house one afternoon? Would Mary find the "right words" and the "right way" to touch Rachel's heart and deepen her faith?

MARY: Yesterday morning, I was in your shop, Rachel. You have so many nice things! If I could afford it, there is much that I would have bought; but, being as how things are as they are, I bought myself this woolen shawl. It should be enough to keep me warm this winter...

RACHEL: I didn't see you, Mary; I must have been out for a moment or two! But, when you come in, please look me up! I'd be more than willing to offer you a discount ... not only to you, but to any of the brothers and sisters of our community. I know most of them, but I'm not sure that I'd recognize all of them! Just last Sunday, at the end of our Sunday celebration, I had to hurry right back to the store; that doesn't give me that much opportunity to get to know the others. And with business as it is, I can't be away from the shop for too long. When you're the owner, you really don't get days off; and you've got to be open, day in and day out, even Sundays!

MARY: Yes, like they say: "Business is business!" But ... (after a short time for reflection...) there's a question I'd like to ask you...

RACHEL: Oh, Mary, never hesitate a moment! After all, just like John, all of us in the community look to you as our "Mom." There's so much that we owe you; without you, how would we have ever received the Lord Jesus, our Savior? No, Mary, never hesitate a moment to ask as many questions as you like...!

MARY: Oh, Rachel, I don't have a dozen questions ... just one simple little one! You know, we all recognize that for you, business is your whole life; your whole life is taken up in just taking care of the store. So, there's something I've wondered about: do you think you could manage to spare some time each week — besides our Sunday celebration of Jesus' Resurrection — could you manage to take some time just to "sit down," to read and reflect on God's holy Word, and to pray? Do you think (and here, Mary smiles so pleasantly, undoubtedly to hide her shyness in the face of this boldness!), do you think that you do enough for our God, our Creator and our Father?

RACHEL: Mary, you see me at our Sunday celebrations, without fail! Unless some "catastrophe" comes up at the shop, you can depend on my being there. But, really, I feel that nothing should keep me from joining the community!

MARY: Yes, I have noticed, Rachel! For you ... well, really, for each one of us, that is essential ... when we renew the offering of ourselves to God and are again enriched by His presence among us ... in us. But, — again, excuse my brashness — don't you feel, sometimes, that the Lord might be expecting something more? Can any of us feel that we've done enough?

RACHEL: Well, Mary, really ... I feel that I'm doing enough right now; with the demands of the shop, at home, and all... After all, I feel that I'm doing what I have to, I'm doing what they told me is required! I just don't see anything more that I could, or should be offering to God. If you think about it, maybe this would make things clearer: after I've paid my taxes, everything is in order, and the tax-collector, he can just wait another year before he sees me again ... You see, I'm just finished with him!

MARY: Let me put it this way: everything we do, the very way we conduct our business, is that not God's concern? Isn't it "His business"?

RACHEL: I've never really thought about it that way! We have to face things as they are, simply and clearly! Sunday is the Lord's! That's our primary and indispensable responsibility, that is essential. But the rest of the week ... that belongs to us, that's our business! You see, Mary, there are some lines that you just don't cross...

To speak my mind, Mary, from time to time I hear one or the other talking too piously .. it just boggles my mind! And, to speak openly, I am sometimes ... well, overwhelmed... not to say, disgusted! When it rains, when storms hit, they say that it is God; when their businesses prosper, they claim that that too is God. And when they're sick, they say that this is a punishment from God!

How often have I heard one or the other say: "It is God's will! Blessed be His holy Name!" I just feel, deep down, that this is too pious ... somehow, that it's exaggerated! And, to say what I really feel: I just have to wonder if they aren't a bit fanatic!

I know full well that what matters is our eternal soul; but somehow, I sense that they forget that we also have bodies! And, when they insist so strongly on the spiritual, well, are they denying something of the human in themselves ... in all of us? I have to wonder: is this some sort of "denial" when they refuse to allow some modicum of joy and pleasure into their lives? As I see it, our soul is 50% of who we are, it's the soul that makes us human. When they somehow come to perceive that we can live in the here and now, and live as if in God's presence 24 hours a day ... well, I just feel that they can find only 50% of the joy and happiness that we — as human beings — are entitled to! Somehow, I feel that their lives are stunted, contorted. They try to have it "both ways," on God's side and still on this earth and in the process, put themselves at an impasse ... it's just a dead-end situation! Really, I pity them, Mary...

Don't you recall that word in the Book of Sirach: "There is no greater treasure than a healthy body?" (Sir 30:16)

After all, we have only one life to live, and God hasn't placed Himself against all satisfaction, all pleasure in this life! Deep-down I feel that He has to find great satisfaction in seeing His children happy, enjoying life! He enjoys our enjoyments! Life is short: play hard as they say! Enjoy life!

Like I said: those "fanatics" turn me off! Maybe, one of these Sundays you could just talk to them, help them understand that **GOD IS NOT ALL THAT DEMANDING OF US!**

MARY: Of course, Rachel, God never asks the impossible! He'd never expect us to remain in prayer 24 hours a day...

RACHEL: It just seems to me that this is what Jesus repeats on page after page of the Gospel. It is simply that our God is not a tyrant. He doesn't deal with us as a Master toward his slaves; His way just isn't that of Caesar, or of Alexander the Great!

As I have come to know Him, He is our Father ... our Mother! We are His children. He's in no rush after all, He does trust us!

MARY: And that, ... that's a thought that lies deeply within my own heart, You know, Rachel, whenever I remember the story of the Prodigal Son, I'm overcome with joy and gratitude. Day after day, that father stands waiting, scanning the horizon, hoping... "Will he come back today? What's taking him so long..."

What really frightens me is to see so many "who so value earthly things, who make their bellies their god!" (Phil 3:19). They find all their satisfaction, their pleasure in what they have. What they are — their success, their reputation, their riches — this dominates their hearts ... it overpowers them. They can't see anything else, or think of anything else. They are blindfolded ... in their hearts! There is space for nothing ... and for no one but themselves and their immediate satisfactions.

I somehow feel that for such as these, "God" is just a word, emptied of all meaning. Maybe, deep down, they're thinking: "After all, what could God give me that I don't already have?" And, unlike the Prodigal, they just don't go back to their Father's house ... in a way, they'd be like a sick person who'd refuse to go to the Doctor ... and finally, would just die!

RACHEL: You mention "sick people" ... which reminds me of a friend of mine, Andrew, who always really lived life; his life — so it seemed to me and to many another — was lived for the enjoyment he could find! He was well-off, and he certainly lived well enough! ... as they say, "high off the hog!" With that, there weren't many who'd try to resist his charms ... you know what I mean? There was nothing, absolutely nothing that held any fear for him. I remember, one day we were talking, and he said to me: "When I get sick, I just take whatever will take care of it! I hate those doctors ... they always seem to think that they have to know everything..." Well, for years he'd always found "the cure" for whatever it was that caught up with him. But then, just a couple of months ago, he got so sick that no one, not even the doctors, was able to help him ... and he died.

MARY: And, it is just that which we have to avoid. Any one of us could get sick ... to that point of being beyond anyone's help. And, in the very same way, everyone of us ... you, me ... our hearts can become so sick that God Himself will be unable to do anything to help us ... nothing at all!

RACHEL: Just a minute, Mary! I've lost your train of thought. As I see it, we all have that "heart sickness," but come what may, we can't lose hope. God is the great Healer of our hearts. "For Him, nothing is impossible." (Lk 1:37) Whatever comes our way, *God will always be there, ready, eager to heal us, to forgive us.* And if ever we forget that, what is there to hang onto? You agree, don't you?

MARY: Yes ... well, yes and no! God's mercy is limitless, that's sure! But there are other things that we have to remember too. God, our Father, is like the Father of the Prodigal Son. And each one of us, we're his children, lost, far away from Him, in a strange land. He waits, eagerly, hopefully, for our return. So the question: are we going to get up and begin to make our way back to His house? or are we going to turn a deaf ear, a hardened heart to His call? Do we pay attention to nothing and no one except our self and our selfish desires ... following our own pursuits, our own willful ways?

So long as we stay away, we'll never see the welcoming smile of our Father, nor will we feel the tenderness of His embrace. We'll never know the sparkle of the ring He puts onto our finger, nor the sandals He finds for our blistered feet, the clean tunic and the fatted calf ... and the finest bottle from His cellars ... well, we can't let ourselves forget any of that!

So long as we stay away, the Father, consumed with grief and sadness, will return home, alone still! Sadly, He'll let us make our burdensome way ... He simply has to let us go our weary and troubled way, separated from Him, forever ... to His great sorrow. There is nothing He can do to "raise us up and "restore life"!

Surely, Rachel, you haven't forgotten the manner in which the rich young man responded to my Son, to His call, do you?

RACHEL: He just refused to change. What Jesus asked ... for him, it was just more than he wanted to give. "Wow! What does He take me for? ... a complete idiot?" And Jesus ... He just had to let him go his own way...

MARY: And, as I recall so clearly, he was a good young man ... a generous young man. For years, he'd carefully lived according to the Law and the Prophets. When he spoke with my Son, that young man — proud of himself — added: "I've carefully kept all of these!

What more do I need to do?" Really struck by this questioning, Jesus invited him to an even higher way: "Get rid of all you possess ... of all that possesses you! ... Give it to the poor, the needy. Don't be enslaved by ... anything you have!" Don't collect "things" for yourself here on earth, where moths and woodworms can destroy and thieves can plunder... (cfr. Mt 6:19) And then, listen: Come, follow Me, walk in My way ... walk with Me. By walking in this way, by hearing My Word, you'll be opening yourself to be loved by God Himself, just as I do. Your love for God will be your true and imperishable treasure! Let God Himself become your treasure!

Rachel ... after he'd heard that invitation ... you remember as well as I do what he did ... what he couldn't bring himself to do...!

RACHEL: "When the young man heard these words, he went away sad, for he was a man of great wealth." (Mt 19:16-22)

MARY: They were both sad... (Mary remains silent, reflective for just a few moments).. .both of them, the young man, and...

RACHEL: ... and Jesus too! He was deeply saddened, sad unto death! The man had come to Jesus, hoping ... hungering for more. Yet, when Jesus proposed the liberation of his heart... He just proposed, he didn't impose! Jesus offered the fresh air of the Kingdom, but He wouldn't make him live on it... Jesus pointed out the "House of God," where God awaits our coming, but He wouldn't make him to go in... Respecting our human freedom, He took a chance...

MARY: Yes ... He took a chance ... of being excluded from our picture, from our horizons ... He left him free ... free to refuse the gift of himself to his God! ... He comes, knocking at the door of our heart (Rv 3:20), but He knows that we can refuse to answer the door, that we can slam the door in his face ... He offers us Salvation ... which means, He offers us Himself, but even *He is unable to save us without us* ... That's what makes every moment of our every day so dramatic!

To God's great sorrow, there are some who are boxed-in, locked-up inside themselves. What they have, what they are ... it seems that that is what matters to them. They are untouched by *the fear of the Lord, our God.* They could care less, so wrapped up are they in themselves. They "tough it out! ... and still, the very first words of our faith, "the ABCs" are so clear :

- "The Fear of God is the beginning of Wisdom!" (Ps 110:10)
- "The eyes of the Lord are on those who fear Him, on those who rely on His love, to save them from death and to sustain them in hard times." (Ps 33:18-19).
- "No one makes a fool of God!" (Gal 6:7)

So, little by little, they are estranged from God ... just a little bit at a time ... but so persistently that the final outcome is guaranteed! Then, what does their life amount to? Limited, twisted and tattered ... atrophied, as you said just a minute ago!

RACHEL: But, Mary, don't forget that Jesus brought the message of joy and of freedom to the world... Remember Zechariah's canticle: "Blessed be the Lord, the God of Israel! He has visited His people! He has come to save! ... He swore to our father, Abraham, that He would grant us — free from all fear! — to be His servants, in holiness and virtue all our days!" (Lk 1:67-75)

And, in that awesome page of Paul's Letter to the Church in Rome, a thought that inspires such joy in me every time I re-read it: "The spirit you have received is not a spirit of enslavement, bringing fear into your life! It is rather a spirit of adoption, of sonship which makes us cry-out "Abba!" "Father!" (Rom 8:15).

And, just recently, right here in Ephesus, John wrote those lines which sort of crystallize all the newness of the New Testament: "In love, there can be no fear, for fear is driven out by perfect love! To fear is to expect punishment, and anyone who is afraid is still imperfect in love." (Jn 4:18). As I consider it, "fear" is just not something I think about anymore! Before I began to walk in His Way, it was only too present in my thoughts, in my outlook ... but not anymore! I don't "fear" God! How could you still see things that way, Mary?

MARY: No, Rachel, I'm not unmindful of those splendid pages. I know them all by heart. But we can't let ourselves forget: we are being called to an entirely new "fear" of God ... because of Jesus' words. Walking in His Way, we have to live in His Love ... as best we can, and we can't let ourselves be satisfied with what we are now. As I see it, *what we have to fear is not doing enough for our God!* And, that's brand new, isn't it?

RACHEL: Wait a minute, Mary! I'm not sure I'm following you...!

MARY: Well, you do remember the word of Paul: "Work out your salvation in fear and trembling!" (Phil. 2:12)

RACHEL: I find those words puzzling! I know that when we are baptized, we become God's dearly loved children. We no longer have to fear our God! We are not like slaves, fearful of physical harm, of the yoke and the lash if we don't do what we're expected to do... As if our God were a terrible ... really, terrifying God, just waiting to see us step out of line ... that's what we grew up with, and it is this that was set aside by Jesus' Way. That was a long time ago...

So, those words of Paul, "Work out your salvation with fear and trembling..." what do they really mean?

MARY: To answer you, let me first ask you a question, Rachel. You have children, don't you?

RACHEL: Well, yes! You know ... there are the five boys and three girls. We were married twenty-two years ago ... and that whole adventure of bringing them up was no picnic, believe me! Yes, there were those tremendous joys, but there were the very difficult days, too!

MARY: Eight youngsters! Yes, I can believe that you had your hands full! But, during those years, did you ever find that you were afraid ... afraid — for example — of getting sick, or of dying ... and then, they'd have been orphans...!

RACHEL: Did I ever? Yes, and more than "just occasionally" ... the thought was there in the back of my mind, and frequently enough, believe me! Had I become sick, I couldn't have taken care of them as I should; I was afraid that I wouldn't be able to provide for them if I were unable to take care of the shop; I lived in fear that my husband might leave us ... just disappear...!

But, you raised your child, Mary; and I'd guess that you didn't count the times, the hours you devoted to him any more than I measured out my efforts and time that mine demanded. Really, I never thought of the demands this imposed... I waited on them hand and foot, and with all the love that I have in my heart ... for each one, and whenever... There were no "small details" ... everything was important. If one cried, I was right there; when they were hurt, I was right there, "right now"! When I had to leave the house — even briefly — I was constantly thinking about them... and I'd hurry back home as quickly as could...

I guess that I wasn't any different than you, Mary. My "kids," they were always on my mind ... and often enough, that left little time for myself. They were just first ... they came before anything ... everything else! When I'd be tired or hungry, at the "end of my rope," they'd still be first and foremost in my thoughts and efforts. And, I always worried about loving them enough ... loving them as they deserved ... and needed to be loved! I was continually concerned that I would get too busy with other things, and neglect them... And, I guess any mother harbors deep down the concern of being too concerned about herself and allowing her "being mother" to take second place in her thoughts, her life! Never ... ever did it enter my mind that I could do "too much" for them. Really, as every mother in this world, I simply "knew" that *you can never do enough for those you love.* They were just the reason for my being ... and, well, ... I'd have given my life for them, should that have been asked! There'd have been no question at all!

MARY: I can certainly understand what you're saying, Rachel. The fact of the matter is that I've never heard anyone speak with such heartfelt devotedness. "You can't do too much ..." "There was never anything ..." "Everything was always important ..." "I was always afraid of thinking too much of myself..." But, when I think about it, what you've just said describes perfectly the basic characteristic of our "fear of God"!

To "wait on our Lord and God hand and foot...," to listen carefully to His Word in precise detail, to belong to Him and to be haunted by the desire of not passing up any opportunity to show our gratitude to Him ... in a way, Paul said all of this: "Work for your salvation with fear and trembling!" We just have to recognize that the "slave-like fear" has vanished completely, and the fear of a child ... or a mother in regard to her children ... has taken over our heart, fully!

RACHEL: "Belonging" to my kids ... I just didn't belong to myself anymore ... just to them, to each one! I guess that you could say that I was being "consumed" by them, eaten up! And, as they grew, so too did my love for them grow. And, the more that I gave them, the freer I became! I'd never have imagined that I'd have the capacity to love each one of them as I do ... my heart just keeps expanding and expanding...

When I sit down to think about it, I think that no one other than a mother could even sense that kind of growth: as we loved them more ... and in more ways, so we became more and more free!

MARY: Yes, there is One ... Jesus, whose heart overflowed with that new "fear of God," our Father. Everything He had ... He put into the hands of His ... our ... Father. He wanted only to do His will... And, when there seemed to be nothing further that He could give, when those who flocked to Him simply devoured Him, when He was completely caught up in the Father's loving plan... it was there, on the Cross that Jesus showed the greatest love that could ever be imagined.

And, it was then that He was free ... freer than anyone can imagine! Nailed to the Cross, He was and IS the Model we're all called to imitate, the model of our perfection, of true freedom.

RACHEL: Mary, there's something I'd like to ask you ... I'm really embarrassed even to ask ... But, what will happen if I take Him for my Model? What will I get? What will become of me? How will I gain?

MARY: Well, He will gradually give you the light, and the strength to live up to that "fear of God," which drove Him every single moment of His life. He will gradually enrich you with that total "poverty of spirit" by which He belonged to God until the very end of His life.

What I think might be best... well, maybe, you could simply ask Him to give that, day by day...

RACHEL: Oh! I remember His word: "Ask, you will receive! Search and you will find...!"

MARY: And, you might wonder: just what would we ask Him for? I always think back to the Cross ... It is there that I find the answer...

- Ask that you might live of Him, with the very same love that He lived, with that devouring love that burns so ardently every single moment...
- Ask the Father that you might come to be caught up, possessed by the hope in that unchanging and unchangeable love of God...
- Ask the Father to engrave the Cross deeply in your heart...
- Ask that Jesus' freedom might become yours, too; and that day by day, you might find yourself more identified with Him
- Get rid of any smallness in your prayer. Ask Him for everything and you'll find yourself receiving more ... so very much more ... than you'd ever imagined!

In a word: it is Jesus reminding us: *Ask the Father for Me, and quickly enough, you'll receive what you asked for...!*

RACHEL: Mother Mary, I don't know when I've been as moved as I have been by what you've said this afternoon. Now, I see that the Lord, our God, must certainly be disappointed with me ... I really haven't been acting toward Him as toward a Father... I'd thought that participation in our Sunday celebrations was all it took, that that was enough. As a matter of fact, somehow, now, that seems to me to be the barest minimum... How could I have been so stingy with the Lord...? How could I have been so ungenerous with Him?

MARY: Rachel, it is useless to be worrying about the past! Simply focus on what lies ahead! It takes a long time ... a whole life time to begin to grasp the "ABC" of discipleship, of being a Christian. Even now, when I've grown so old, I still wonder sometimes whether I've grasped the "essential" myself...

We humans come only gradually to give ourselves to the Lord ... I mean, really, without always counting the hardship that that entails. To wait on Him "hand and foot" just like we did for our children ... we've always got new horizons to discover and to pursue...

Yes, God is exacting ... but He is also supremely patient with us.

He comes to us to take us to Himself ... but He knows well enough that our way home is long and tedious ... that sometimes, the nights of our pilgrim's-way are dark...

But, He gives us all the time we need ... and at the same time, eagerly looks for us to hurry along on our way to Him. It's almost as if He'd be saying to us, in His kindly and gentle tones, "Don't rest so much along the way! ... What you can do today, just do it ... don't put it off!"

Today is the day ... today is the day that it can all begin ... again ... and this, over and over again. And, somehow, we'll never get tired of hearing that. Every "today" is new and fresh. Yesterday? Why would you ever waste time worrying about that...?

And, his tone is so very patient, so very encouraging, and at the same time, so urgent! It never seems to be blaming us for our slowness, our lack of persistence. It's as if He recognizes that without us, without our willing and conscious effort, He is helpless in leading us home to Him.

How gentle, yet insistent is His love for us! He knocks at the door of our heart ... and it is for us to open it wide. He simply trusts us. Were we to turn Him down — by refusing to respond to Him in love as He has always responded to us and to our efforts — if we were to turn Him down, I think that we would greatly sadden our God. I don't know what a "small" failure to love might be ... each failure is so enormous ... It always hurts so deeply, Rachel!

Let's just sing together, Rachel: "My spirit proclaims the greatness of the Lord ... the hungry He has filled with good things ..."

July 15, 1992

Walking in Their Footsteps

12

Tomorrow, Just Like Yesterday...

One evening, Peter had a visitor; as a matter of fact, he was a very well-known person in Rome. One of the leading Senators, Gaius was himself a recent convert to "The Way." But there were still some questions in his mind that remained unanswered. On this particular evening, he had come to speak of them with Peter. Perhaps, we could "sit in" on their conversation as Peter tries to explain to him the newness of the Gospel.

GAIUS: There are some questions I've got for you, Peter. But before I forget, let me mention that a couple of days ago, I met one of your compatriots from Capernaum, James, the son of Bartholomew.

PETER: Oh, yeah! I remember him ... an outstanding young man!

GAIUS: He spoke very highly of you, too, Peter! He just couldn't finish talking about you from the time you were a fisherman on the Sea of Galilee. A fisherman...! You really knew WHAT you were doing! Whatever the season, you always managed to bring in a fairly good catch ... always just a bit better than any of the others out on the lake. From his stories, I'd have to guess that you must have been among the better fishermen on the lake — unless they were all telling me "fish stories!"

PETER: (smiling, and a bit embarrassed) Oh, maybe there is some truth to what you say. My crew, really they were "the better part" of my success. After all, they were the ones who did the work ... knowing where to go, how deep to fish, how to find 'em ... that's the fisherman's trade. And, that was my whole life, until that day when...

GAIUS: ...until that day when the Master called, you and the other fishermen... That day when He called you to come and follow Him, without looking back. (After a short time of reflection) From time to time, don't you look back to that life which you left?

PETER: Eh? For sure!

GAIUS: It's right there that I, at times, sort of get lost. You think back to your career as a fisherman, to when you lived at Capernaum. And still, for these past twenty-five years, you've been supremely happy being a "Fisher of Men," as the Lord called you to be. Peter, do you — sometimes — regret that day?

PETER: Oh, yeah, I suppose so! Often times I think back. You see: *if I'd listen to my heart, I'd be back at Capernaum in the blink of an eye.* I'd have fewer cares and worries; all the criticisms that I have to endure, they just wouldn't be! I'd have to answer to no one but myself ... it'd make so much more "good sense." In a way, I'd be content to repeat that time-worn saying: "Everyone for himself, and God for all!"

GAIUS: Well, what keeps you from going back?

PETER: To put it as clearly as I can: it's because I love Him, because the Lord Jesus captured my heart and my life, and because I feel this immense hunger to draw everyone — all my brothers and sisters — into this same love.
   "It is the Lord Jesus that we love, without seeing Him!"

"And it is in Him that we believe, without seeing Him now." (1 Pt 1:8)

GAIUS: But you had the chance to live with Him, to be with Him, to walk and talk with Him wherever He went. And that, Peter raises *my first question:* During those months, those years that you were with Him, what was it about Him that struck you? Is there something that's engraved on your heart even now?

PETER: Yes, when I think about it, I guess there are so very many things that are there. It seems like just yesterday. There are a couple of things I think about right now. First, there was that transparent way that Jesus was before God and among us, his brothers and sisters. And there is the way that all of us, gradually, grew and developed, ... patterning ourselves on Him, "walking in His Way." (1 Pt 2:21)

GAIUS: Yeah, that's it! What was it about Him, something He said that was new, unexpected, something extraordinary in what He said or did...?

PETER: There is so much, so many incidents that I recall. To mention just one or the other: **First,** day after day, we walked together with Him ... just as He walked continually in the presence of His Father. His inner freedom radiated outwards to everyone and everything He met. Looking into His eyes, it was as if we were gazing into the depth of an ocean of purity and calm, of peace and serenity.

Day by day, He showed us [and we, little by little, caught on!] just what it was that He wanted us to be and to become, that "better self" that was really the deep-down hunger of our hearts. Through Him, that "dream" of boldness, that self-control ... we were seeing and hearing that "dream" enfleshed, in Him!

Secondly, Jesus never wrote anyone off! Men and women, the young and the old, the little children ... and with such tact, such tenderness. He was so very gentle, so understanding and so patient with all of them, with each one! And what warmth! It is just unimaginable, something so completely new ... and different! Just take the little ones: Jesus knew how to be so simple, so small, with them. For Him, the sparkling joy of those children, their indescribable openness, their smiles ... it is God Himself Who was alive to them, and in them ... and Who is speaking His love through them! It is really so beautiful, so touching, that words fail me! When the little children came to Him, Jesus found no difficulty in echoing their bursts of laughter. He was so simple with them.

Every time I recall His gentle, overwhelming smile, His directness, His refreshing and satisfying joy, as pure and purifying as water from a spring, then I feel that I myself become a little child in whom He always finds such deep and enduring joy and peace. In those moments, I am not the old man that you're talking with now, believe me! Day by day, through Him, God comes and restores a youthfulness to us all

Thirdly, He was like a fire: He spread warmth, and restored the vigor of each one that God placed along His way. He seemed the "grandpa" with the elderly, "widower" with the widowed [and "the tears of the widow fell on his cheeks..." (Sir 35:18)] He was like someone who'd endured some lengthy sickness with those who'd spent years in bed, unable to get up, unable to see the brilliance of the sun. Those who were hurting, and even those who'd hurt us deeply, Jesus became friend to them, too.

Day by day, and day after day, Jesus embraced the miseries of the people and carried them in His heart, to His God and Father...

Fourthly, month after month, there was something that was really striking: He, the Master, the One Who came from God, God-with-us, alongside of us. Here, more than in anything else, He was so vulnerable to our moods as well as to anything we might've said, to our questions, our disbelief, our sarcastic laughter. We could always speak simply and openly with him, "without any embroidery ... it was just so natural and easy!"

It was always like those two followers of the Emmaus road told it. Their discouragement was immeasurable, their disillusionment complete; God had abandoned Him who "was to have delivered Israel." And Jesus, so calm, so gentle in bringing them to recognize the whole picture, brought them back to the Way of Faith. Often enough, He just had to point out how we were falling short, how we were failing to grasp what He was saying and doing, but it was always that same gentleness ... no one could ever have claimed to be ashamed, to have "lost face"!

Even now — in fact, this very day — the Lord is the One to whom we can go without pretense, in complete honesty and candor; He is not someone who would cause any kind of fear or reticence. His heart is unquestionably big enough to handle all of our "whys," all of our complaints, all of our unfaithfulness and all of our sins. Whatever might happen to us, all those things which bring us real joy and pleasure, and all that brings us disappointment and discouragement, our fatigue and our successes, it is just that day after day, Jesus takes all to heart. Nothing, absolutely nothing is foreign or strange to Him!

And finally, nothing ... no one was ever His "favorite." He could recognize and accept whatever it was, and whoever it might have been ... whatever was good and beautiful. Whether we were Jews or Greeks or Romans, we were all the same in His eyes. He certainly was not someone who considered the "pedigree" of anyone. (cfr. Sir 35:15; 1 Pt 1:17). Looking back, I'd have to say that there wasn't a single day that I wasn't impressed by the sureness, the directness of His judgment.

GAIUS: And so, living and walking with Him, what did you do? how did you act? Were you the same ... natural ... or were you, perhaps...

PETER: How could we have stayed the same?

He chose us! He wanted us as His own! And so, each succeeding day, He drew us out of ourselves, and enriched us with the freedom that was His as the Son of God. He, so close to the Father, drew us closer to the Father; as He was "in the Father" and we were "in Him." He brought us ever closer to the Father. He transfused His own Spirit into us, engraved It upon our minds and hearts, as day followed day. (cfr: Ez 36:26) Living with Him, we gradually became like Him.

Day after day, Jesus' joy at being tenderly loved by God, our Father, was like a well, that provided us with crystal-clear water. Then, we, His disciples, by living close to Him, were able to quench our thirst and be refreshed by His own joy.

He chose us! ... even when there was nothing in us, nothing about us that deserved it. Chosen, and enriched with the supreme honor of being a part of what He was. All our doubt and questions about being like Him just evaporated, gradually, one after the other. He became the Master of our hearts (Jer 31:31-34), and we became in a way, like Him.

He chose us! Just think of it! He, the Son of God chose to "need" the likes of people like us! And, even here in Rome, He is the Great Shepherd (1 Pt 5:4) exercising His task through the likes of me!

You see, Gaius, I have never quite succeeded at finding the right words to talk about this "supreme joy" (1 Pt 1:8) which He has given to me. In Latin, Greek, or Hebrew (or in any other language you'd like to use!) no human words will ever be able to express, to speak the height and the depth, the fullness of this joy. (ib.)

GAIUS: If I'm following you, Peter, you're thinking back to what you just said "If I listened to my heart, I'd be back in Capernaum, but..."

PETER: But, it is His word that won out! He unendingly manifests His love for me. His words re-echo in my heart more clearly now than ever, and overwhelm any feelings and desires I might have...

GAIUS: Then, are you saying that you just can't imagine exchanging your role as a "disciple" of the Lord, as a "messenger," for your old life as a fisherman...?

PETER: Exactly, Gaius! To leave God behind, to forget His immense love, to abandon His Spirit for anything...? Could you imagine someone abandoning a tremendously productive field of grain, when the heads are already heavy, bowing down toward the earth, ready for the harvest ... could you imagine him leaving this for a bright yellow daisy which burst into bloom alongside the roadway? Anyone who would, would have to be crazy!

GAIUS: Peter, I enjoy ... thanks for your honesty. Now, I'm beginning to see: it's far better to "hear the voice of the Lord" and to be transformed ever so gradually by His love than to listen to "our own voices" (Acts 5:29), and to act, or react according to simple human thoughts. And, I must say, you are — yourself — an outstanding example of this! And everyone of us here who seek to walk in "His Way" recognize you as a living example that we can follow!

PETER: Don't thank me! Thank the Christ, "in Whom we live and move, in Whom we are! (1 Pt 5:14) It is He who desires to occupy, and preoccupy our hearts, continually more! As we read in the Holy Writings: "Become holy in every facet of your lives. Become mature in the way that leads to salvation!" (1 Pt 1:15; 2:2)

GAIUS: From you, Peter, those words take on a very special meaning. You — who denied the Lord three times — you who yet dared to take the Lord's hand when He reached out to you. It was He who raised you up, so to speak.

But, *I have another question,* if you don't mind. During these past twenty-five years, you have never abandoned the Christ, our Lord. How did you do it? What was it that ... that made you so steadfast, so steady?

PETER: By myself, I could do nothing! I can do nothing by myself. I'm really far from being a dependable, or as you say, a "steadfast" disciple. You remember as well as I do how things went...

There was that time when I was in the fishing boat... I jumped out, and was as stunned as anyone when I found myself walking on the water as I went to Jesus. I had scarcely taken a few steps when — suddenly — I could think of just one thing, and the wind was so very strong. Right then, Jesus didn't matter. Oh yeah, *He was right there, but my heart, my thoughts were a thousand miles from Him* at that moment. The result? I began to sink... (cfr. Mt 14:22-23)

I survived ... not because I'm such a good swimmer, but because Jesus ... because His love reached out to me ... and saved me!

And that other time: I was outside there, in the courtyard, trying to keep warm at the brazier. Three times — as you've just reminded me! — I denied Him. I was just occupied, and preoccupied with saving my own hide. Undependable! I just "chickened-out!" ... A coward! That's what I was! That's when my own true colors

showed! (Mt 26:69-75) As it turned out, my faith in His power —
revived, came to life. It's because Christ, in His untiring love, sent
me His Spirit. Without that, I'd have simply been a "loser," believe
me! — It is He, *the Lord, always faithful,* always dependable; it is
He alone who empowered me to stand tall, who "saved" me from
my own weaknesses and who showed me just how shallow my
faith in Him is. By myself, a great big "Zero," that's what I'd have
turned out to be!

GAIUS: As you reminded us when you wrote in that Letter...
"Entrust yourselves to the faithful Creator, and do good all the
while..." (I Pt 4:19) "The God of all grace, Who called you to His
eternal glory in Christ, after you have suffered a little while, will
Himself restore you and make you strong, firm, and steadfast. To
Him be the power for ever and ever." (1 Pt 5:10)

So, your cry of anguish there on the water, your desperate
prayer, your cry of confidence "Lord, save me!" It must come back
to you from time to time over these past twenty-five years ... no...?

PETER: From time to time? Believe me! It's every day, and how
many times each day! It's my refrain: "Lord, in Your love, save
me! Do not abandon me!" (Ps 30)

GAIUS: Would you say, then, that all of us Christians, if we want
to be "strong in faith" (cfr. 1 Pt 5:9), we too should reach out our
hands and, without doubt or delay, ask for help?

PETER: Exactly! That's the only way to hold firm, to remain faithful come what may!

There was that day when we were on the lake, I was sinking fast;
I was up to my neck. In another moment or two I'd have been under.
Can you picture me? It was all of me that spoke in that desperate cry
for help to the Son of God, the Lord. Nothing else mattered except
one hand reaching out and grasping the other, His and mine!

Endlessly, we have to say, and say it yet again: Cost what it
may, I have to reach out for the Lord's hand, I have to "have faith in
the Lord God," and I will be upheld by His invincible power (cfr. 2
Chrn 20:20)

Endlessly, over and over again, ceaselessly, we have to make more urgent the bond of love which binds us to the Lord.

Endlessly, over and over again, we have to choose Him as our Master, our Leader, the Guardian of our spirit, the very center of our lives. We need to constantly renew our efforts to be totally present to God in love. And it is there that we — poor mortals that we are — there that we can begin to do some beautiful, some tremendous things with our lives. And that choice has to become ever more personal, and must arise from the very depth of us as human persons.

And none of this is something that we can "take or leave." This is the very core, the foundation of our being. It is this that connects us to the divine power which will bring us to that faithfulness which will hold firm, come what may!

GAIUS: You remind me of that phrase of Isaiah: "I will drive him, like a peg, into solid ground." (Is 22:23)

PETER: That is just what I think, Gaius. It used to be when we were landing the fishing-boat, I looked for something solid, an iron post firmly driven into the ground that I could use to tie up the boat, to keep it from drifting. Then I could sleep soundly. Let the wind come up; let the storm winds come up. I was sure that my little boat would still be there in the morning, that it wouldn't have been blown away.

GAIUS: In other words, in our Sunday gatherings, and in our own private prayers at home, we should be tying our lives onto the solid "peg" that will forever remain solid and firm. And, it isn't in the quantity of our words ... of our prayers ... that we count but in the sincerity, the quality...!

PETER: Of course, Gaius, we should all look at the sincerity, the "quality" of our prayers: the firm conviction, the unshakable faith that the Lord is hearing and heeding us. Then, we can really put ourselves, unreservedly, into those few, simple words. "You can save me and I need it now! Come help me, now!"

We have to come to believe what we're saying when we pray. We have to involve the very best of ourselves. Nothing else matters except those few words of gratitude, or those prayers of supplication, of petition that we utter, almost spontaneously, which — really — the Spirit puts into our mouths, our hearts. A little bit as if this were the only time, or the first time, that we were making these prayers to the Lord with our cry for help.

In the Book of Psalms, there are, here and there, a verse or two which can so precisely utter just what I'm saying, which contain that firm confidence which we need to have. "Lord, it is to You that I lift up my spirit. Those who hope in You will never be deceived." (Ps 25). [And, as Peter was repeating the Psalm verse, it seemed almost like a chant!] Or again, "I place all my hope in You, Lord! I have complete confidence in Your Word!" (Ps 130)

GAIUS: Let me check this out: You've remained faithful in your following of the Gospel, solely and completely because of the Lord, the Faithful One, as you've just said. The awesome love which He has shown in the past (all those times when He saved you ... mainly from yourself!) You've been mindful of Him, of what He has done, of what He can do. This is the basis of your undoubting confidence: Tomorrow, ten years from now, He will still be there, just as He has always been there over these past years. "The Lord's power has shielded me" (1 Pt 1:5), and thus, for tomorrow...

PETER: Tomorrow, ten years from tomorrow, He will be there! To put it simply,- I'd say: ***The past guarantees the future!***

GAIUS: Tell me more about that! What I'm especially interested in is just how Jesus was able, as our Master, to live His life — especially His Passion and Death — with the confidence that nothing could disturb...

PETER: And, we all — at one time or the other — have wondered about that! All of us, we need to take yet another look at what it was in Jesus that empowered Him to keep going, always. How could He have kept so resolutely to His resolve to go to Jerusalem? In saying "yesterday," Jesus was thinking particularly about the final three years of His life, during which He had traversed most of the Holy Land, when He had pretty much covered the whole land of Israel. And, in speaking the word "tomorrow," He was undoubtedly thinking ahead to His Passion which was soon enough to come, and of His glorious Resurrection.

a. "Yesterday," I was with the Father, fulfilling and accomplishing so many wondrous things in His Name. "Tomorrow," the Father will keep Me close, by that faithfulness which cannot be matched, equaled by any other

b. "Yesterday," the Prince of this world never took hold of Me, I was always delivered from his hands. "Tomorrow," most assuredly, he will be thrown aside, and one day, his power will come to an end.

c. "Yesterday," My followers shared fully in My joy. "Tomorrow," their happiness, their blessedness will increase even more.

d. "Yesterday," I was sown so generously and none fell by the wayside. "Tomorrow," those seeds will bear fruit, abundantly, a harvest, of 30, or 60, and even 100 to one.

e. "Yesterday," those whom the Father entrusted to Me, I gathered them together and I kept them safe. "Tomorrow still, they will all be safe, under the staff of the Good Shepherd.

f. "Yesterday," I cleansed and healed them, by the hundreds, by the thousands. "Tomorrow" they will come from every race, from every nation. It will be impossible to number them.

g. "Yesterday," I was faithful to those that the Father had entrusted to Me, those whom He had called. "Tomorrow," in return, they will remain strong, and faithful."

h. Even unto now, nothing has been able to erase from My heart that love which has kept Me "in the Father," "Tomorrow," assuredly, it will be they — in their turn — who will rest in the loving arms of the Father.

i. "Today," I go to the Father, clasping to My heart all those that the Father has given Me. "Tomorrow," they will be secure, and nothing more shall be wanting to them.

GAIUS: What you're saying now, Peter, I understand well. Jesus recalls all of His "yesterdays" which the Father entrusted to Him. Tomorrow, the Spirit will be there sustaining and accomplishing His will in the midst of great trials which are yet to come.

PETER: Together, we must learn *to live-up to the unconquerable confidence of Christ, the Lord:* (Gal 2:20 & Col 1:27)

(Singing: "Assured of your love and strengthened in our faith, We come to You, O Lord...")

GAIUS: There's yet *another question,* a bit more personal. Certainly, you are not unaware of the heavy responsibilities that have been mine over the years, Peter. For more than thirty-five years, I've been one of the most powerful men in the Roman Senate. Every time that something came up, every time some decision had to be made, I was among the first consulted. As I look back, my thoughts on most of the grave matters that came up were sought, and seriously considered. I was right at the center of power in our Roman society. And my reputation went considerably beyond just the City itself! ... even in those areas quite remote from the Senate chambers, they'd heard, and knew about the "great Gaius!" And then...

PETER: And then...

GAIUS: Recently ... well, it's about two or three years ago now, the Lord, Jesus called me, even me! ... He called me by name, just as He'd called you, there on the shores of the Sea of Galilee. Needless to say, Peter, a number of things have changed since the day I said "Yes!" Since I was baptized, I really began to involve myself in this "pledge of a good conscience before God" (1 Pt 3:21) Since those unforgettable days, proudly, I "carry the name 'Christian!'" (1 Pt 4:16).

PETER: (wondering whether Gaius has really yet said all that he wants to say.) Listening, Gaius, it seems to me that there might be some things that aren't quite settled in your mind just yet, things that are still a bit hazy. Is there anything in the Gospel which you find difficult, some things that seem to be just "too much" for you? (cfr. Jn 6:60)

GAIUS: No, not really! On the contrary ... What most disturbs me is the way that Christians are treated by the Roman authorities, and even the Roman people in general... It seems that they look down on us, they think so little of us... Things are just so different now.

PETER: Is there anything ... anything that you might have heard lately?

GAIUS: Yes, there have been what seem to me to be an increasing number of happenings... Some of them, I'll just never forget! There was one Senator who was talking with me really, standing right in front of me, and insulting me. I'd always considered him as one of my closest friends, a Senator like myself. We've known one another for well onto twenty-five years now. I'm talking about Rufus...

PETER: Tell me: what did he say?

GAIUS: First of all, he was extolling the past "Glories of Rome," of the Empire. "Gaius," he said, "we all have the very highest regard for you. And we're all so very grateful, so appreciative of all that you've accomplished, contributing to that 'Glory' and the glory and renown of the Emperor. And, just like us, you must be proud of the glory and splendor of the Eternal City. With the rest of us, you know that the Pax Romana, that unity that reigns within our frontiers, from Gibraltar to the Danube, from the Tiber to the Thames. Our Roman Legions maintain order and peace in so many regions and nations which have submitted to Roman rule and to our respected and beloved Ruler. The Roman Laws prevail everywhere. No other nation contests the power and the glory of Rome. And thus it shall remain for a thousand years! It goes without saying, for us that Pax Romana is a very significant source of pride.

"You know, too, like all the most distinguished persons of Rome, that the unchanging and unshakable foundation of this universal order, it's the respect and total submission to our universally respected, and all powerful Emperor. The orders He gives come from the gods themselves. In submitting to Him, we assure ourselves and our nation prosperity and riches. Not only that, but if we hold true to this, we shall stand firm for generations to come. We can attribute this and so much more to our sacred rituals, the honor we manifest toward our **Protective Spirits.** Without them we are nothing!"

Then, after a moment of silence, my friend Rufus spoke in an entirely different tone. He went on, saying: "Unfortunately, you're no longer one of us! You have embraced some strange religion that comes from who-knows-where! from some hidden, little country in the East. And, you question the absolute supremacy of Caesar. You refuse to afford Him the worship that is His due! You think of Him as just another human person. You are no longer there to make offerings to the 'spirits' who watch over the City. You're nothing but a backslider, a heretic! You, you've served with us all — and served well — in the Roman Senate. There's not a Senator who doesn't admire and appreciate all that you've done; and yet, now, you're rejecting the one thing that is our proudest boast. You now look down on that which has given us the glory and the power over the nations of the earth!

And, worst of all, you've become a follower of that man whom we Romans crucified twenty-five years ago, in Jerusalem... I think they called him Jesus, if I remember correctly. I faintly recall that they also called him 'the Christ,' and the members of that heretical sect call themselves 'Christians' ... Now you, the celebrated Gaius, you've become one of them. You, a Christian! I have to laugh!"

PETER: That really hurt, didn't it? I'd guess that Rufus would have been someone from whom you'd hardly have expected that kind of outburst!

GAIUS: That's for sure! And that wasn't all! He went on, and said: "If we don't do something to curb these weird beliefs and practices, and without delay, we can only expect the worst! The unity of the Empire, the Pax Romana itself will soon be ravaged!"

And, he wound down — finally! — saying: "I'm really sorry to have to talk to you like this, Gaius, but it is imperative that you understand once and for all: these strange 'believers' (Christians, they call themselves!) have no rights here in the Eternal City, nor anywhere else in the Roman Empire. They do nothing but disseminate their divisiveness, that uncontrollable weed, everywhere. They're nothing but a bunch of 'out-laws!' Not a one of them deserves the title of 'Roman Citizen.' I can only wish the worst for every single one of them. It would have been better had you never been born, than this! You're nothing but followers of someone who was crucified as a common criminal, an insurgent. And, if you'd ask me, you deserve the same! To preserve the honor and the splendor of Rome and of the Empire, nothing less will suffice for all of you, and — really — the sooner, the better!"

You see, Peter, since that day, all that I've accomplished, my very reputation has been reduced to nothing. Everything I've done is forgotten. It's just not that easy to lose out like this and to be the subject of ridicule on the part of those I've considered as friends. Ever since that day, I live with fear. All those insults, those threats ... I can't forget them! I'm living under a heavy cloud! There are very few hours of my days that I don't live with fear. I can think of nothing but this. Who knows what lurks just over the horizon! Really, it's crazy ... it makes no sense!

And this brings me to *my third question,* Peter: When you live a good and upright life, as all of us Christians are trying to do, how does it happen that we're treated so unjustly?

PETER: Gaius, that is the very same question that I — one day — asked Jesus Himself. He'd just told us that He was going to be arrested, that He'd be judged and condemned, He, the Just One as no other, He the Holy One, "so close to God," He so filled with love. When I'd heard this I sort of exploded in anger, it just boiled over. I took Jesus aside and I started to correct Him and His judgment in no uncertain terms. And I said: "God forbid! No! This will never happen!"

GAIUS: Had I been there, I think that I'd have said the same!

PETER: His answer struck me like a whip. Needless to say, I really didn't understand right then. Without hesitation, Jesus said: "Behind me, you Satan! You create an obstacle in my way. Your thoughts are not 'of God' but merely human reactions." (Mt 16:22-23)

GAIUS: And — knowing you — you didn't buy into that either! How long did it take you before you began to comprehend the full import, the full weight of what He had said to you? Today, are you completely ready to accept whatever it might be that God asks, as

Jesus taught us? Do you, somehow, understand all the suffering ... the insults ... differently?

PETER: You better believe it! Understand me well, Gaius. From time to time I reflect anew on what you've said earlier: 'This suffering, these disappointments, this rejection ... it's not normal! They're unjust! They're crazy!" And I was thinking to myself, all of these are empty words, totally meaningless.

GAIUS: ...They make no sense! But, you're stretching it a bit, aren't you? For me, I'd have to admit it openly, they disturb me, they upset me. I just can't make any sense at all out of this!

Called by God, we Christians we walk in the way of the Christ (1 Pt 4:19; 3:17; 2:15). We are faithful disciples — at least we try to be! — and we're beloved of God. He walks with us, drawing us forever beyond ourselves, just as He did with you during those three years. He makes us go well beyond anything we'd ever imagined, as we've all come to know. Gradually, His love overwhelms everything about us and within us which is not "of God"!

To put it another way, we put into practice that which you are forever repeating: "It is much better to submit to God than to men!" And, it's true!

"We do not allow the pattern of our former selves to continue!" (cfr. 1 Pt 1:14). "We avoid what is of this world, and which continually wage an insidious war against the spirit!" (cfr. 1 Pt 2:11) "We turn away from all that is evil, and do good — we seek to be at peace. This is our way! (2:18)

In other words, we seek in our lives to allow nothing that would be cause, or even occasion for blame or fault-finding.

"We submit to all human authorities, for the sake of the Lord. We respect every man!" (1 Pt 2:13, 17)

"We submit to our masters, and not alone to those who are gentle and understanding, but also to those who are harsh!" (cfr. 1 Pt 2:18)

We seek to be of one mind and heart, compassionate, enlivened by our love for one another, merciful, humble. We refuse to return evil for evil, or insults for insults; but, contrariwise, we offer the blessing of God!" (cfr. 1 Pt 3:8-9)

In other words, we live in such a way that no authority can find any fault with anything we do, or in any attitude we manifest. We carefully avoid anything in which they might find reason to blame, or accuse us of disrespect, or disloyalty.

And still, they calumniate us, finding and seeking every possible opportunity to find fault with us, and our faithful conduct in Christ (cfr. 1 Pt 3:16) They ridicule us for one sole reason: because we venerate Christ, and because we honor and love His Name above all others! (cfr. 1 Pt 4:4)

You'd have to admit: "All these insults in return for all of our efforts are unjust (cfr. 1 Pt 2:19). When you think about it, we're a bit like Daniel and the three young men who were cast into the flaming furnace. A very strange testing (1 Pt 4:12) It's really very hard to understand ... or endure!

And besides, God leads us in ways that are hardly the way we'd ever have chosen ourselves ... and that's definitely understating it! "His ways are unsearchable!" (Rom 11:33), impenetrable. Think of all our friends, our acquaintances, my fellow Senators ... all those people here in Rome who think that we've simply gone berserk, as if we were completely "off our rocker"!

It's a fact that they're mistaken, but I see no way of responding to them! What can you say...? What can you do to get them to change their views, to get them to put aside their threats, their insulting words and actions?

PETER: Really, **not a whole lot ... not a whole lot more than just to continue** living just as you've said: "We are compassionate, merciful. We refuse, absolutely, to return evil for evil..." And also, to put into practice that guideline: "Have no fear of those people! Be not troubled!" (1 Pt 3:14) Continue to stand firmly, irrevocably adhering to the Christ, who is Lord. Be at peace before Him, "there where He is, where He lives." (Jn 17:24)

"He was put to death in the body, but enlivened in the Spirit. He went to preach to the imprisoned spirits who had disobeyed long ago. They were few who were delivered through water, that same water that now offers you, too, salvation. It saves you by the resurrection of Jesus, the Christ Who has gone into heaven and is at God's right hand — with angels, authorities, and powers in submis-

sion to Him. (cfr. 1 Pt 3:19ff, passim) If we hold firm to Christ, He
— in return — will keep us close to God, His, — and our — Father.

If we remain faithful, He will share with us the glory that is
His as Lord.

GAIUS: What you've just said is most encouraging, Peter! You
have that gift! "Have no fear of those people! Be not troubled!" (1
Pt 3:14). "Stand steadfast in the faith!" (1 Pt 5:9)

What you've just said calls to mind those words of the Prophet,
Isaiah. At that time, the king of Syria and the army of the Samaritans were marching on Jerusalem, and the Holy City was about to
be put under siege. At that moment, "the heart of the king and of
the people were moved, like the trees of the forest are moved by
the winds." (Is 7:2) So, the king sent legates to the King of Assyria,
thinking to himself that the king of Assyria would surely have the
authority and the power to check the advance of his troops and
those of the Samaritans. And in that historic and threatening moment in the history of Israel, how did Isaiah react? What did he
say to the Jews of his time, themselves troubled by such fears,
such complete devastation? Isaiah knew well that those living in
Jerusalem were close to panic. If they had recourse to the king of
Assyria, that would be the same as acknowledging that it was not
solely nor supremely the Lord God of Israel in whom they placed
their confidence.

So, Isaiah raised his voice and spoke, clearly and unequivo-
cally: "All these nations that are conspiring against you, who ally
themselves one to the other to bring about your downfall, have no
fear of them! Fear but one! That you would alienate yourselves for
the All-powerful Lord. The one thing to fear above all else would
be to think that the Lord, our God, is deaf to your cries and your
prayers!" "The Lord, the Almighty is the one you are to regard as
holy. He is the one you are to fear, He the One you are to dread,
and He will be a sanctuary." (Is 8:13)

PETER: And we know well the outcome! The people refused to
listen to the Prophet; they alienated themselves from their God,
ignoring His limitless Power. For them, God would be unable to
aid them in their hour of grave danger, so it would be senseless to

turn to Him. And so, in the end, the Assyrian troops entered Jerusalem and conquered the whole beautiful land of Judah.

The king and all the people might have acknowledged the sovereign power of God, but they had placed their confidence elsewhere. The result? They were severely punished.

GAIUS: Now, I understand just what these words, what this story is saying to us in our present circumstances:

What God is asking from us today is that we not repeat the dastardly error of the king of Jerusalem and of his people. They feared those who were approaching, preparing for the attack ... and, instead of placing their trust, their confidence in the Power of God, they turned to the king of Assyria.

What God is asking from us today is that we see Caesar as God sees him, as a human being like the rest of us, as every single one of us. All those "Protector Spirits" of Rome, what are they? Less than nothing when you really look long and hard.

What God is asking from us today is that we embrace Jesus, the Lord, and love Him as the sole Master of our hearts, our lives!

PETER: Precisely!

If we cling to Him (as I had to, that day on the Sea of Galilee!) He will lead us through the dangers, and deliver us from our own fears and any threats coming to us from outside. His overpowering Love will sweep away from our hearts every question, every doubt, all of our frailties and faults. And, gradually, it will be the Peace of Our Lord Jesus, the Christ Himself that will surround us, that will overcome us completely.

No comparison at all with the PAX ROMANA which the Roman Legions imposed on the whole world by the sheer power of their military might!

If we cling to the Lord, Jesus, we all have a share "in what He is": by being so very close to us, Christ allows us to share in the very **Peace of God!**

For a while, all our fears and anxieties are still with us; they are part of the cross we bear. But the Lord calls us **to follow the way He has taken,** ahead of us: with Him and in Him, let us "unload all of our worries on God, our Father; then, God will take care of us" (1 Pt 5:7), the same way as He took care of His first-born, the Eternal Son! Apparently...

GAIUS: Apparently! When He was nailed to the wood of the cross, Jesus manifested nothing that would catch our attention. He cannot call up divisions of Legionaries nor thousands of slaves. In Jesus' life, there is nothing at all, compared to the glory and splendor of Rome, of the whole Empire.

Nailed to the Cross, on Golgotha, Jesus just hung there, between heaven and earth, made the laughing stock of those Roman mercenaries and the crowds of Jews who'd gathered. Together, they spewed out their insults and derision on Christ. Whether it was Latin or Hebrew that they spoke, there was but one thought: their triumph over Jesus! They were dead set against the one who — from their point of view, at least — planned to plant disorder and revolution, everywhere. Both the Romans and the Jews — who despised one another deeply — were united in their ridicule of Jesus. Together! That beats it all!

As you wrote in your letter, Peter, all those people looked like "roaring lions, prowling about, seeking someone they might devour..." (1 Pt 5:8). *But, really...*

PETER: *Really,* it is at that very moment that Jesus *is strongest, most exalted, at His very holiest* ... more than we could ever imagine!

GAIUS: What is it that makes His sufferings so crucial, so very important for us? Why or how does this give Him such power and glory? Why ... how did this contribute to His victory?

PETER: For many years, beginning at the time of His Baptism, Jesus was empowered by the Spirit of Glory (1 Pt 4:14). The Holy Spirit of God dwells within Him. And thus, there was no moment of His entire life that He really doubted the **Faithfulness of the Father** — The **Eternal Word of God** echoes from the depths of His heart. It was this echo that deafened Him to those shouts and blasphemies that swept across that lonely hill...

GAIUS: The **Word of God** ... I remember what you wrote in your letter: "All flesh is grass and its glory like that of the wild flower. The grass withers, the flower falls, but the Word of God remains forever." (1 Pt 1:24f)

Is there any particular word that Jesus might have had in mind? that would have sustained Him?

PETER: Who could ever know for sure? But, the thought that comes to my mind now is that the words He was hearing were the same as those He'd heard over the Jordan, and on the Mount of the Transfiguration: **"You are my beloved Son! You are my chosen one! It is in You that I place all my love!"**

That Word is forever engraved on His heart. It's there, unfailingly. It etched itself deeply. Jesus could never be unmindful of that "infinite love, with which the Father loves Him." (Jn 17:26)

That is why He — nailed to the Cross — gathered all peoples to Himself as His very brothers and sisters,. Then, Jesus had enough courage to "bow down under the powerful hand of God." (1 Pt 5:6)

His extreme love, and His great confidence enabled Him to "surrender His spirit to the Faithful creator." (1 Pt 4:19)

GAIUS: He is there, nailed to the Cross ... eight or ten feet above the ground, but ... really...

PETER: *Really* ... Jesus then found Himself closer to His all-powerful Father. He no longer was His own; He is completely in the hands of His Father. In the ardor of His prayer, a prayer filled to the brim with confidence, and fierce with love, He remains completely and peacefully convinced that "the eyes of the Lord are upon the just, and His ears listen attentively to their prayers." (1 Pt 3:12)

GAIUS: Let me put it this way: on the cross (and also through His victory on Easter Morning), Jesus reaffirms the perceptive words of the man born blind, after Jesus had opened his eyes: "When someone is devout and does God's will, then God listens to his prayers." (Jn 9:11)

When Jesus is nailed to the Cross, He lets Himself be overtaken, possessed completely by His Father. The infinite tenderness of God fills His heart. The Holy Spirit is His consolation. *The peace of God* overflows in His heart, transforming and transfiguring His misery into "a spiritual sacrifice, acceptable and pleasing to God." (1 Pt 2:5)

PETER: Because of His inexhaustible love, that's exactly what the Lord invites and challenges us to do:

- Strengthened by the Spirit of glory and power, we can allow Jesus to bind us to His cross, along with Him ... and in fact, close to the Father.
- We must be drawn out of ourselves, carried away into God, invaded by the indefectible love of Christ and by His unconditional obedience.
- Our struggle to remain faithful to God, our sufferings and our miseries ... let Jesus take them and make them His own. Our worries and anxieties will become, ever so gradually, *His Victorious Cross,* irremovably planted on our hearts.
- We have the privilege of being the continuation of His prayer of love which was the very essence of His life: continually, God invites us to make Jesus' commitment to the Father visible, tangible, and actual: "Christ suffered for us, leaving us an example so that we might walk in His way." (1 Pt 2:21)

GAIUS: From the depths of my heart, *I'd like to share in that great confidence and that all-powerful love* that filled Jesus' heart.
   I'd like to grasp something of that inward peace which makes His life so different from ours.

PETER: As a matter of fact, you can!, as I can!, as every Christian can!
- "We have been redeemed by the Precious Blood of Christ";
- "Purified by the Holy Spirit, we have been begotten (and each day, we are being reborn!) to the new life of God's children. We are sustained, encouraged, and enlivened by the same Spirit of glory and power, Who guarded Jesus, right up to the end of His life." (1 Pt 1:19; 1:22-23; 4:14)

- And it is thus that — one day — just as Jesus emerged victorious from death through His Resurrection and Ascension, so too we: *"Having shared in the sufferings of Christ"* (1 Pt 4:13), we shall also share in His glory.

GAIUS: One day! ... one day! But, how long must we wait?

PETER: "After you have suffered a little while, the God of all grace, Who calls you to His eternal glory in Christ, will Himself restore, support and strengthen you! He will make you unshakable!" (1 Pt 5:10)

GAIUS: You know, Peter, after this conversation, ... from what you've said, I feel that I'm more prepared to "defend to anyone, to be accountable for the hope that is in me!" (1 Pt 3:15) Like you, I "know the sufferings which the brethren are undergoing in this world." (1 Pt 5:9) And like you, I am even eager to come to share in "the inheritance which is imperishable, undefiled, and unfading!" (1 Pt 1:4)

PETER: Gaius ... my dear brother, ... within the community of believers, and equally in the eyes of those who misunderstand us, let us "continue to bear witness that it is truly the love of God which has been given to us. Let us stand firm in this!"

Gaius, "to you, and to all the brethren who are in Christ-Jesus, **PEACE!"** (1 Pt 5:12-14)

St. Paul MN
October 16, 1992

Walking in Their Footsteps

13

Make Yourself at Home

One evening, — it was the Day of the Lion! —, in the town of Ephesus, Demetrius, an Elder of that Christian community, visited John, the beloved disciple of Jesus. That same morning, John — in his Sunday homily — had reflected on a subject that was so dear to him: in Christ, God has made all things new; and in the Son of His Love, God has reunited all of us to Himself. He has already made a place for us in His heavenly Kingdom. Day by day, the Light of God comes to spread Itself more widely and enlighten more brightly.

Demetrius is one who is having some difficulty sharing John's deep, calm faith. Let's listen in on their conversation...

DEMETRIUS: John, I genuinely appreciated your reflections this morning at the Eucharist. My whole life long, I'll be so very grateful that you came here to Ephesus and that you have stayed with us all these years. And, having Mary here has really been a very special blessing for all of us. Had you never come here to settle, we'd still be in the darkness of our former ways. Yet, I'd have to admit, I'm a long way from having come to that enlightened faith, that transparent faith which you were talking about. Child of God, yes! and I'm abounding in the joy because of this, but...

JOHN: ...but you recognize that the pilgrimage is far from over!

- The light of God is still overcome by darkness in many compartments of your life;
- You are still struggling to become that "just man" you're called to be, and which you'd like to be;
- And lastly, there are innumerable things in your own life which haven't yet been radically affected, enlightened, ... brought to life and the Light by the love of God and the love of the brethren. Isn't it so?

DEMETRIUS: That's my trouble! You see, already so many years have passed by since I first became a child of God, by Baptism, since that day when I was "born of God," as you so often say. (1 Jn 3:9fff; 5:1-5). I wouldn't abandon my faith for anything, nothing could make me change! I'm "hooked" on that splendid word of Faith which you so often reflect with us.

- But, at the same time, I have to tell myself: The Lord has already brought me a long way on His way, ever closer to God, our Father. He has asked a great deal of me, and He can't ask anything more. Nothing! It's enough!
- You see, John, I'm so slow, even hesitant, to change things in my life. I am — I guess — really and radically afraid to entrust my life to the Holy Spirit, to guide me "there where I'd rather not go" (Jn 3:8; 21:18). Maybe it's just the fear of the unknown...
- Tell it to me again, John, after you brought the fishing boats to the shore, and after having abandoned your trade as a fisherman, and your own father, Zebedee, did you really understand what was ahead of you? You'd have to admit, you were launching into quite an adventure!

JOHN: Ah, yeah! I really didn't have that clear an idea of just what was going to happen in the lives of my brother James — he's older than me! — and of Peter, Andrew, and myself. I knew just one thing: "Jesus is the Master who comes forth from God!" (Jn 3:2). I'm going to listen to Him, to my heart's content. I'm going to be his confident ... and eventually I'll let Him become the center of my whole life.

- You, Demetrius, you see I really did entrust myself to Him. I just said to myself: in the past, God took care of those who turned to Him; in His time, Jesus, the Good Shepherd sent by the Father Himself, will guard and protect me.
- And as you just said, it was the beginning of a tremendous adventure... But ... really, I've never been sorry!

DEMETRIUS: And all of this goes back some fifty, or sixty years. Here in Ephesus, things just have to be different, somehow. It must be so much easier for you to hear the Word of God, of Jesus, and to have Him reign as Master over your whole life, over each facet of your life. That goes without saying, doesn't it?

JOHN: Not really! It doesn't "just happen," all by itself. Quite the contrary. I've still not finished being "converted" to the Lord, I'm still learning how to follow Him more fruitfully and more faithfully. And every single day, I have to re-affirm my intent to follow, more consciously, and more conscientiously. It's a constant struggle ... for the most part, just struggling against myself!

- To help you grasp something of all of this, I'd like to share three simple thoughts with you, comparisons which will — I hope — help you recognize just why it was that I left my father's fishing-boats and nets, and walked in His way...

FIRST REFLECTION

DEMETRIUS: First of all, give me an example from the Old Testament. Among our ancestors in the faith, were there any Israelites, believers, were there some who had to really fight for their beliefs?

JOHN: Of course, there are so many examples! But one that I frequently go back to is that of Jeremiah...

DEMETRIUS: Yes, I remember! On page after page of the Book of Jeremiah, he complains to God about the difficulties he was encountering in his mission.

- As one speaking for God, Jeremiah had been charged with re-calling God's people to their vocation, to fidelity!

"Your gods have become as numerous as your cities, Judah, and the altars on which you offer your burnt sacrifices to the Baals are as numerous as the streets and passageways of Jerusalem itself!" (Jer 11:13)

- As one called to speak for God, Jeremiah's heart was literally broken. He was stupefied and horrified to find that the people had abandoned what was — for them — their most precious possession, their faith in the Lord God, the Living and True God. Israel had walked away from the All Powerful, its Source of Life. And, what had they gotten in exchange?

I recall his very words: "My people have committed a double outrage, says the Lord; they have abandoned Me, the Source of Living Water, and they have dug cisterns for themselves, cracked and broken, which are unable to hold water." (Jer 2:13)

JOHN: And how eloquently Jeremiah cried out, exhorting Israel: those cisterns incapable of holding any water, those are the hearts which turn to alien gods. All those alien gods are without power, are absolutely unable to come to their aid. He cries out: Israel, come to recognize that you have been sadly deceived, that you have allowed yourselves to be deceived.

DEMETRIUS: And Jeremiah couldn't help but speak further: "They say to wood: 'You are my father!' and to the rock, 'It is you who brought me forth!' They show me the back of their heads, not their faces, but in their stubbornness they say to me: 'Arise! Come to rescue us!' But where are those gods that you'd made for yourselves? Let them arise if they are able to save you in your tribulation, because these gods have become as numerous as your cities, O Judah! You, all of you, are in rebellion against ME, Yahweh declares." (Jer 2:27ff)

JOHN: And lastly, Jeremiah, with all his determination, reminds Israel to be on guard: God will not allow those transgressions and infidelities to go unpunished:

- "Your own wickedness will punish you and your apostasies will convict you. Know and see that it is an evil and bitter thing for you to forsake the Lord, your God!" (cfr. Jer 2:19)

- "Assuredly, I am going to bring disaster upon you, such that you cannot escape; although you will cry out to me, I will not listen!" (Jer 11:11)
Jeremiah could not have spoken more clearly!

DEMETRIUS: And still, no one listened. The only response that he got to his warnings shouts of alarm was disgust. He was ignored, brushed aside. Jeremiah himself complained to God: "Whenever I speak, I must cry out, I must shout, 'Violence and destruction!' For the Word of the Lord has become for me a source for mockery and sarcasm, of ridicule and reproaches constantly." (Jer 20:8)

- Jeremiah had plenty of reason to complain to God, don't you think?

JOHN: Yes, he certainly did! Discouraged, Jeremiah went on to say: "I will no longer mention Him, or speak another word in His Name!" (Jer 20:9)

DEMETRIUS: And, still, he went on...

JOHN: He had to! And how searing the word he spoke! Yahweh! You have made me feel Your power, and You have overpowered me! You accomplished your purpose: The Word has become like a burning fire within me. I have worn myself out seeking to restrain it, but was unable!' (Jer 20:9)

DEMETRIUS: That picture of a "burning fire," reminds me of the forest fire some months back, right here close to Ephesus. So quickly, a strong wind came up; there was no way to control it. The best efforts were of no avail at controlling that raging inferno. And, the whole forest was totally consumed by that fire ... you remember, don't you?

JOHN: Of course! For some time we were afraid that the very city of Ephesus would be engulfed.

DEMETRIUS: As a matter of fact, what is it that Jeremiah was saying: "The Word has become like a consuming fire within me, deep in my heart..."

JOHN: I think that what he was saying was: by myself, I could be at peace, could take care of my own affairs, and I would warn the people of Israel no more. But, in fact, that was impossible! **God has chosen me.** From the day of my birth, His hand was upon me. (cfr. Jer 1:9) The All Powerful chose me to speak in His Name. He sent me to rekindle a flame that would re-ignite the faith in His people. That was the empowering "mission" that He entrusted to me. Most assuredly, a very broad mission...

God chose me to beget — among the brethren — **new life**, the true life for which they'd been created. To lead them to set aside their idolatries and turn back to their Maker, to their Father, their hearts burning with confidence and with love. Then they "will know their Lord. All of them — the great and the small — they will know that God will pardon their infidelities and their sins. They will become — in His sight — a people, and the Lord, the God of Israel will again be their God! He will unceasingly shower His blessings upon them. His joy will be to fill them with all good things." (cfr. Jer 31:33f; Jer 32:38ff) What a splendid undertaking, an awesome mission ... to help them to come to live the fullness of life!

DEMETRIUS: In other words, *what's at stake here,* is the return of Israel to the true God, the living and life-giving God!

What's in the balance, is to guide this people to live — again — their faith in its purest form. It was to renew the bond of love by which God was united to His people ... not just the few people of Israel, but all the peoples who — at some future time — would pursue the ways of this people. Isn't it this that he was doing?

JOHN: Precisely! And Jeremiah undoubtedly continued his reflections, saying to himself: How can I ever refuse so sublime a mission? But, how can I get myself ready for it? Mightn't I be frightened and intimidated by the task, by their insults which will rain down on me?

Their mockery and persecutions are — beyond all doubt — the "price" that I will have to pay in order to win them over to the Faith that lies deep within their hearts.

And, it is God Who permits these "trials." It is God Himself who will employ my tears to water the fields, to bring to harvest all those who return to Him.

His Word had become like a devastating flame in me, in the center of my heart; I've exhausted myself in trying to control that fire, but to no avail. The more that I dreamed about, and sought a simple life — without trials and difficulties — the more that mission as "God's spokesman" imposed itself on me.

It is impossible to stand up to God, to fight against His Word which had been entrusted to me. Nothing else matters except to faithfully carry that Word to the people of Israel, cost what it may. It was impossible to turn back!

Just as a forest is consumed by a wild-fire, this is what happened to me and my own plans for my life: they were consumed, reduced to mere ashes.

It became impossible to dwell on anything else but the renewal of the Faith of the people of Israel. I was simply incapable of shedding that fixation.

And, it was God who put this burden on my shoulders. He had the upper hand; He was simply stronger than me. It's just that I can't help but speak His word, in His Name. And, then, nothing else mattered but to allow myself to be "used" by God Himself... It serves me right!"

DEMETRIUS: I am struck by Jeremiah's openness, his simplicity in speaking to God. What he said was: "God, my God, You have finally won out, overcome me. You've got me! Isn't this a fine mess now!"

JOHN: You can understand better now just why it is that I choose to reflect on our friend, the great Prophet, Jeremiah. His example really reaches and touches the depths of my heart. He accepts — in spite of himself — to seek to accomplish the mighty mission from God; he gave himself over completely to the service of His Word. And, it is this that sustains me, especially when our little community here in Ephesus faces the reality imposed by those who insult and calumniate us.

SECOND REFLECTION

JOHN: I'd like to think about another image that comes to mind. You see, Demetrius, at the very bottom of our hearts, there where we really "meet God," it seems that it all happens like it does in the arena, where the combatants meet...

DEMETRIUS: I like that image you've just suggested, that of a couple of athletes competing in the arena. After a while, it becomes apparent that one of them isn't as well conditioned as the other, he comes less well-trained. He's faced with an opponent who is more vigorous; and ends up begging for mercy. He is completely dominated and, finally, reduced to defeat. The one who is better prepared simply overpowers him; he is forced to give in, to give up ... to put himself into the hands ... and the heart of the other. But, are you suggesting that God Himself would come as an adversary, to engage us in such a competition?

JOHN: Well, as I see it, every single day, God comes before us through the proclamation of the Gospel of Jesus: "He unveils whatever it is that lies hidden," and by the power of His Holy Spirit, He wants us for Himself. He wants us to live for Him alone; He wants us to be constantly "reborn" (cfr. Heb 4:12f; 1 Pt 1:23f)

DEMETRIUS: We ... we who are so deeply centered on ourselves! We consciously or unconsciously seek that day when we'll depend on absolutely no one; we don't like to envision even the possibility of someone else giving orders, forbidding or commanding us to do this or that. We'd go so far as to say: "I alone am the one to judge what I can, and cannot do! I render accounts to no one!" We'd like to see the day come when we'd be completely "on our own." We'd like to have every facet of our life in our own hands. But, God, in His immense and unconquerable love...

JOHN: ... You know? ... God — simply because He loves us so — confronts us. His divine Spirit speaks to your hearts. And, He speaks, too, through His Word when we hear that Word in our Community.

That "dream" of being totally autonomous, that futile hope of being completely dependent on no one... it's precisely this that God seeks to overpower in us.

Through the power of the Gospel, God desires to be all-powerful ... to have the first place in every aspect, and at every moment of our lives. And, it is just this that we ask, when we pray: "Our Father in heaven ... may Your Kingdom come!"

DEMETRIUS: And, we are after this constantly! But, I have to ask myself: If I ever really took this prayer seriously, what would eventually be required of me? If God really reigned as Master over every aspect, every moment of my life, what would happen? what would I become? This is not at all clear in my own mind. I need something concrete (and after a brief moment for thought...) John, if it isn't too personal, what ultimately happened to you during those three years when you were walking and talking with Him? How was it that Jesus, little by little, really became your "Master?" How did He win out?

JOHN: Let me try to explain! And ... as you've noticed! ... this is what I'm continually talking about in our little community here at Ephesus. First of all, *the Word of God is Light.* Following Jesus, we walk in the Light, and we live the Truth (cfr. 1 Jn 1:7) And then, Jesus' presence in our lives, we come to know the over-powering Love that God has for each of us. And then — again, walking the path Jesus walked, and in His footsteps — we walk the true Way of Love.

DEMETRIUS: You say, John, that *God is Light.* Through His Gospel, all that is darkness, that is shadow within us, all of our just "going through the motions," of our half-heartedness, this is all exposed in broad daylight. Is this what you're saying?

JOHN: Precisely! By His Word, Jesus leads and helps us live in the Light of God. Thanks to the Gospel, we somehow turn our eyes away from that which is only appearances and which blinds us to the Truth.

You undoubtedly remember the words ... "The Scribes and the Pharisees speak well, but they don't practice what they preach! All of their actions, their rituals ... they're all done so that others will notice ... Cursed are you, Pharisees and Scribes, hypocrites! You like to be seen as 'good men,' but within, you are filled with hypocrisy and deceit!" (cfr. Mt 23:3, 5, 13, 28)

DEMETRIUS: Wait a minute, John! Tell me, all these complaints, these criticisms, *there was nothing particularly new* in any of this, was there? In times past, all of the prophets condemned these same things. How often they repeated that incisive word that the Lord had spoken to Samuel: "Men see appearances, but God looks deep within the heart!" (1 Sam 16:7)

JOHN: For sure! All of us — me as well as any other! — we remembered what was written but we, too, were a long way from putting it all into practice! Gradually, we'd all come to say to ourselves: "The Scribes and the Pharisees, who don't recognize themselves as sinners..." but (and here, John smiled gently at Demetrius...) that means us too! Us too, we were so taken-up with noticing their ways, their behaviors that we were forgetting...

DEMETRIUS: You forgot? But, you weren't alone: all of us, at times forget what you never get tired repeating to us in the Assembly: "If we say that we have no sin, we separate ourselves from our deeper self, and the Truth does not dwell in us!" (1 Jn 1:8)

JOHN: Every day we have to let God's Word penetrate into our deeper selves, there where darkness and shadows, all our hypocrisies and delusions hide themselves ... it is each day that the Lord wants to be Light for us, enlightening our way. Only then can we begin to get the upper hand, finally beginning to master those darknesses and shadows, that we'll be able to begin to "walk in the Light and to live in Truth." (1 Jn 1:6-7)

And we have to remind ourselves of that other word, too! Jesus returned to this time and time again! And it is this that sustains me in my mortal combat with the Evil One. Certainly, you must have heard me speak about this ... and more than once!

DEMETRIUS: I see what's coming! I know it all by heart! "This is how God's love was manifested to us: God sent His only begotten Son into the world so that we could live of Him. This is what love is: not that we have loved God, but that He has loved us, and sent His Son as an atoning sacrifice for our sins... *God is love!* And, anyone who lives in love, lives in God, and God is alive within him!" (1 Jn 4:9f, 16)

But, tell me, John, *all of that wasn't really that new,* was it? so many of the prophets had already proclaimed that. Generation after generation of prophets, they'd all come back to that, one after the other...

JOHN: What was new... radically new about it is to grasp something of how Jesus understood it, and invited us to live "in His love..." And, not just "understand" it, but to make it — somehow — a part of our own lives, our very being: "Jesus gave his life for us; we therefore have to give our lives for our own brothers and sisters."

"My little children: we need only love! And, this... not just with words, in what we say repeatedly, but in what we do, how we live our lives."

"If anyone were to say 'I love God!' all the while harboring some bitterness, some unforgiveness toward a brother, he is a liar! The fact is: anyone who fails to love his brother whom he can see, simply cannot love God whom he has never seen!" (1 Jn 3:16,18; 4:20)

DEMETRIUS: In other words, Jesus dying on the cross on Calvary was "love in action," love pure and undiluted ... and that's the way we are to walk. (cfr. 1 Jn 4:17)

I remember those beautiful phrases in your letter, but sadly, I'm a long way from "measuring up" to what I believe. I'm like an athlete on the floor of the arena: I don't want to be defeated by the example of love given by our Savior. I struggle against it, I'm not about to be "outdone," even by Him...

JOHN: *What could be more valuable* to us in life than to accept, willingly, that the infinite Love of the Lord would come to us, and really "sink in," to the very depths of our hearts, to give the Lord all the room that He needs?

What would be more splendid than to let His blood — His love! — flow through our veins?

Here, for sure, is the supreme dignity, the royal Way that God proposes to us. Here is the secret of an entirely different way of life, a life expanded in height and depth!

DEMETRIUS: If I'm understanding you, John, we have to do just the opposite of those competing in the arena! Full of ambition, and perhaps even spite, they are forced to "surrender" to the more powerful adversary (Phil 3:12).

We, for our part, with complete willingness and in all the faith that we can muster, we ought to let Him defeat us, overcome in us all that bespeaks pride or egoism. We have to let the Lord "capture us" (Phil 3:12). And, little by little, "we will walk the same Way that Jesus walked" (1 Jn 2:6). Is that what you meant?

JOHN: Precisely! And then, little by little, the Lord Jesus will share with us His purifying love, an unshakable firmness and stability, a deep peace of soul, and a courage that surpasses every challenge, an unconquerable optimism, the invincible Power of the very Spirit of God, the tranquil joy of finding ourselves, finally, on the "right side," "the side of salvation" (cfr. Heb 6.9), in the serene conviction of the unending and merciful faithfulness of our God.

Just remember, Demetrius, it will never be possible to make a list of the spiritual gifts which the Lord grants to any one of us. And, besides, these gifts will vary from one person to another...

DEMETRIUS: No need for details, John! For you, for me, for every one of us, it will always be an impossible task to list the gifts that the Lord gives us: "The whole world would not be large enough to contain the books that could be written on this!" (cfr. Jn 21:25), as you yourself wrote in your Gospel, so insightfully and so eloquently!

THIRD REFLECTION

JOHN: I come now to my third example : often we read and pray the 131st Psalm: "Lord, my heart is not proud, nor are my eyes haughty. I do not chase after lofty matters, after things that are beyond me. No! I have stilled and quieted my soul. Within me, my soul is **LIKE A CHILD, LIKE A LITTLE CHILD CLOSE BY HIS MOTHER"**

DEMETRIUS: Strange! I too admire and pray that Psalm. You know, whenever I see a little baby — completely satisfied — at rest on the back of his mother, two things come to my mind:

First of all, through that strip of fabric, the baby is being tied to his mother's back. Or sometimes, it's an older sister. That baby has a hard time fidgeting, even moving; he is much too weak to loosen the bonds that bind him. There's no escaping! He just can't get out! Isn't it strange! Then, I think to myself: what a pitiful sight!

But, at the same time, I reflect and say to myself: when all is said and done, that baby has got it made! His mother's back *is the best spot in the world* he could ever be. That's an ideal situation. His mother is right there, close to him. She is his sustenance, she's his whole life. In just a few moments, when he wakes up, his mother will be there, to feed him. She will care for him — He need have no worries about what is to come: nothing will be lacking. HE IS TIED AND BOUND TO THE VERY SOURCE OF LIFE TO HIM! What else could he need? What more could he possibly want? Yes, I like your comparison!

JOHN: Tell me! that little baby, asleep on his mother's back, and bound to her, what does that remind you of? Or, perhaps, what does that bring to mind?

DEMETRIUS: I'm thinking of every man ... of any man ... but more especially of all believers, of those "born of God." Just as the tiny baby is bound close to his mother by that strip of fabric which surrounds him ... well it's the same with the believer, who, through his faith in God's Love, is closely bound to his Lord and Savior, the Source of life.

Each believer feels secure, close to his God, the Giver of life, who provides him with nourishment and nurture, his God who sustains and comforts him in all his struggles with the Evil One.

Every single one of us, we're "just sure:" God will never fail us... He is our Mother.

JOHN: God! our Mommy! It's so true! he is the Father and Mother to each of us.

And, as you've just said, we are "born of God:" we're all part of his house and family. Undoubtedly, you remember those words: "How very great is the love the Father has lavished on us, that we should be called 'children of God.' And that is what we are." (1 Jn 3:1)

DEMETRIUS: And, every day — as you are forever reminding us! — we are re-born of God, by the merciful Power of His Holy Spirit. We are in good hands! What should we be afraid of? All fear is swept away by Jesus Himself! (1 Jn 4:17)

"I know my sheep! My Father — who gave them to me — is greater than all. And there is no one who can snatch them out of my Father's hand." (cfr Jn 10:14 & 28-29)

JOHN: Maybe ... maybe we should think of ourselves more often as that tiny, helpless baby ...*who can't think of an other place* he'd rather be than on the back of his mother, right there where he is... and maybe we need to repeat to ourselves, too, ten times... or a hundred times... a day: "Anyone who is born of God, just look to Him who was the only-begotten of God, Jesus! He will protect and shelter him — The Evil One has no power to snatch him away." (cfr 1 Jn 5:18)

Perhaps, we should call to mind more often that we really are God's children, dearly loved by God! And then, we'll live in a deeper and more lasting PEACE. What do you think?

DEMETRIUS: It's only too true. (And, after a moment's reflective silence...) John, *I too have an analogy, a comparison.* It's hardly as rich as yours, and those which you've just suggested, but...

JOHN: Perhaps it's even better! What do you have in mind?

DEMETRIUS: Well ... sometimes, I think of myself as a swimmer, caught in the current in the middle of a river. And, when the swimmer is buffeted by that current, he has to swim with all his might. The current is stronger than he, and gradually, the swimmer is swept along, downstream ... farther and farther... there where he hasn't chosen to go!

JOHN: I like that! The force of that irresistible current ... it's Jesus' all-powerful Love which carries us far, so very, very far along ... to God, Himself!

DEMETRIUS: Ought we simply surrender ourselves to be carried along by Him?

JOHN: Hardly, surrender! Just the opposite! You see, the Lord beckons to us, just as one day he called us fishermen from our boats there at Lake Tiberias. And, every single day, He awaits a new acceptance, a new response...

And, that acceptance is the most important that we'll ever be able to make ... simply to say "Yes" to the Lord!

Not a "yes" and a "no;" after all, who are we to place conditions, or limits on our response to the Lord? In all the diverse pathways of our lives, all those changes that the Lord asks of us in the course of our days, what right have we to say yes to some, and no to others? When God calls, it is hardly a "take it or leave it" call!

Every single day, the Lord awaits our "yes," open and total, clear and vibrant ... not unlike the "yes" of Mary, His Mother when She received Her mission to become the Mother of Her Savior.

But, above all, just to follow the Lord Jesus: "In Him there was no YES and NO, there was only the YES, every day of His life." (cfr. 2 Cor 1:19)

DEMETRIUS: I like that ... yet different from that swimmer fighting against the current which is carrying him along, *we let ourselves be borne along by the Power of God to which we subject and submit ourselves.* Is that it?

JOHN: Yes! That Power... that's the Lord's Love! Day after day after day, we ask: Lead us... to God! *Make Yourself at home, in* *me, among us!* Accomplish in us that myriad of faith, hope, and love, which You've dreamed about for all eternity!"

DEMETRIUS: And then, all of us — Christians and everyone who inhabits this earth — we will become living pages of the Gospel. We will have become living "Words of the Lord." We will have become the proclamation of that joyous Easter message: "It is true! The Lord is alive!" We will proclaim to the whole world: Look and see! "He who is among us, within us, is so much greater than he who is in the world." (1 Jn 4:4) "God's Word has made Its home in us, and we have overcome the Evil One!" (1 Jn 2:14)

JOHN: Let's sing together: "The LORD is my light and my salvation! Whom should I fear?" (Ps 27)

October 6, 1993

14

But that... That's Just too Much!

It was a Sunday evening, in Rome The year was 62 AD. The Apostle Paul had just completed his second year of "house arrest," under continuous guard, night and day. Still — with all of this — Paul was "able to receive those who came to visit him." (Act 28:31) Perhaps, among those visitors, Clement had also come. He was about thirty years old. He was a member of a Christian family in that first Roman Christian community.

That morning, the Apostle Peter has presided at the morning gathering, the Celebration of the Lord's Supper. And — as could have been anticipated — Clement spoke with Paul about this first; Paul, for his part, rejoiced to learn that the peace of the Risen Christ was gradually rooting itself ever more deeply among the members of that community in the Imperial City.

Could we just imagine their conversation?

CLEMENT: Paul, for a while now I've been wanting to talk over a very personal problem with you...

PAUL: Why did you hesitate? I know your parents, your family, well. I trust that your family's business continues to prosper. I also know your sister, Aquila. Your family, especially your Mother and Dad are the very pillars of the community here: they display an outstanding example of faith... Are things not going well with them? ... well, as well as you'd like to see them working out?

CLEMENT: No! It's not that at all! You see, my folks, and particularly my Dad, seem to want me to do one thing with my life... and — as I feel about it myself — that way just doesn't fit...!

PAUL: I don't understand, Clement...

CLEMENT: What I'm continually hearing Dad say is this: "You are our only son, and you're already thirty years old. It's time for you to be thinking about getting married. Your Mother and I, we're not getting any younger you know, and it'll be you who'll have to take over the business. Without you, our business has no future. You just have to get married."

PAUL: Well, after all, you could hardly find fault with that, could you? But, what are your own feelings about all of this?

CLEMENT: To get married? Well, that would be easy enough for me. In fact, given the family's situation, there are quite a few young women who'd delight in the thought... I know one in particular: she's from one of the more outstanding families here in Rome, and — really! — she is something to see! Wherever I go, her gentle smile is with me. And every time we meet, it's like a new sunrise in my heart. Were I to marry her, I just know that we'd have a very happy and blessed home; we'd certainly get along wonderfully. I could be tremendously happy with her; she'd certainly lack for nothing... But... (here, Clement hesitates for just a moment...)

PAUL: Just a minute now, Clement — (and for the observer, you could add that there was slightly more than just a hint of a smile in Paul's eyes!) — just a minute now, Clement, have you ever considered the possibility that God is calling you to consecrate your life completely to Him, "as I have done?" (1 Cor 7:7) Would this be a suggestion that Jesus is showing you that He'd like you for Himself alone? Maybe, He's suggesting that you be "attached to Him," with undivided heart and hope! (1 Cor 7:15)

CLEMENT: That's unbelievable, Paul! What you've just said echoes perfectly what is in my own mind, and heart!

PAUL: On the one hand, your Dad seems bound and determined that you be married. On the other, you've thought of remaining celibate, so as to focus all your energies on the spread of the Kingdom...

CLEMENT: But, I wonder...! I'm continually pulled one way then the other by each of the options. What should I do?

PAUL: Tell me, Clement, just what does your Dad say? What does he think...?

CLEMENT: Often enough ... really, too often ... he keeps repeating the same old thing: "You're not different from any other man. You are made for marriage. You'll wreck your whole life if you choose to be a celibate. We'd be obliged to will our beautiful home, and the business to some stranger. All that we've worked so hard and so long to accomplish — your grandparents as well as your Mother and myself — it'd all be lost, it'd simply collapse; and all because of you! Our family, our family's reputation, and our whole place in society, it'd all be just so much dust. Or, are you unconcerned that with such a move, the family would "lose face," right in front of the whole City of Rome?"

PAUL: Clement, you know as well as I do that — for your Dad — his business has been, and is his whole life. And, you shouldn't be surprised, it is natural enough that he'd like to see you assume the family responsibilities there. I'd have to feel that — in his place — I'd not be saying anything terribly different...

CLEMENT: My Dad is just about as stubborn as he is tenacious (Here, Clement is silent for a moment...) Understand me, Paul, I'd never question his unshakable love of God. Nothing ... absolutely nothing could bring him to deny his faith... The problem is this: he's obstinate, and he gets so very, very angry with me. How many times have I heard him say: "You're my only son, Clement! God can't take you for Himself alone! **THAT'S TOO MUCH! JUST TOO MUCH!**

PAUL: Then ... what did you do? What'd you say to your Dad to — maybe — get him to see things differently, to bring him around, to deepen and broaden his faith? ... I'd have to guess that that is no easy task!

CLEMENT: For sure! I do whatever I can to reason things out with him, to help him understand that Jesus taught and that he lived this kind of life. More than once, I've told him: "As Christians, we have to be identifiable, we have to make known the life of Jesus. We have to focus our hearts on what is unseen, which is eternal, and not become too attached to that which is seen, but which will pass." And in this, I don't think I'm very different from you, Paul. You made this only too clear in your letter to the people at Corinth (2 Cor 4:11, 18)
But, I'd have to acknowledge it, Paul: I'm a long way from getting him to change his mind...!

PAUL: As a matter of fact, it is a tremendous task to understand the mystery of Jesus... that each one of us Christians — as a result of our baptism — is called to replicate, to make it visible in our individual lives...

CLEMENT: ...a radical change of heart; a new way of thinking, of seeing things! This — as I've come to understand it — is the new way which each of us Christians — my Dad and me too! — are called to follow...

PAUL: And, your thinking is "right on." This alone is the Way to Salvation! There is no other!

CLEMENT: But how'll I ever make him understand that he has to look farther, deeper? ... and that, to really live, there is more than lust money and success, and good-standing in the eyes of others?

PAUL: By yourself, I don't think that you're going to convince him. Clement, just pray! Pray steadfastly, and one day, if God so wills it, your calling will become — in the eyes of your Dad — a singular honor, a proof of God's love which Jesus, the Lord, is bestowing on your family.

CLEMENT: Right now, my Dad can recognize none of this: he's really fighting God, and he's holding to his outlook tooth and nail (cfr. Jb 9:4) He's just so opposed to this calling that he closes himself off to any consideration or perspective other than his own. (Clement stops to think for just a brief moment...)

You've just said, "...one day, if God so wills it.." One day, is God going to change my Dad's outlook, and his heart? Will it be changed by God's love, "renewed by God's love?" (Zep 3:17) You believe that God will have the last word? If God would accomplish this... I'd be awe-struck!

PAUL: Well, that's precisely what happened to me, you know. I've told, and you've heard my story more than once. I persecuted the followers of "The Way," those Christians, with wild determination. Finally, Christ radically and suddenly changed my heart. My fury, my tenacity, my tireless determination: He wanted all of this for Himself, for the service of His Gospel He turned the whole thing around — radically — from a tireless persecutor, He made me into the Apostle to the Nations, a missionary among the unbelievers. Just one more confirmation of His Word: "Nothing is impossible for God!" (cfr. Gn 18:14)

To draw us closer to Himself, and for the development of His Kingdom, God turns every branch into an arrow: the destruction of our own undertakings, that "loss of face," our disappointments, our illnesses, and too, all our half-heartedness, God — perhaps, only God! — can use any and all of these. And lastly *"for those who love God, God makes everything work together for their well-being"* (Rom 8:28)

CLEMENT: And, I can think of so very many examples of this in the Holy Bible, that confirm that!

I remember what happened to Joseph, the son of Jacob. He was detested, really hated by his brothers. They sold him as a slave to those Median camel drivers en route to Egypt.

PAUL: And, *in the end,* Joseph became a leader, a prince in Egypt; when his family came seeking rations there, Joseph saved them from starvation. The Israelite people survived, even prospered there in Egypt.

CLEMENT: And, I remember what happened much later to those Israelites who were exiled in Babylon. For quite some time, they remained convinced that God had abandoned them. Their name, their fame had been completely obliterated from the face of the earth.

PAUL: But, *look at the bottom-line,* it was precisely through that time of exile that their faith was purified, refined and affirmed. God had sent numerous Prophets to them, calling them back to Himself, whose "mercy is without end." Zion said: "The Lord has abandoned me, my God has forgotten me! Could a mother forget the child at her breast, would she forget to show the love, the tenderness to the fruit of her own womb? And, even if she could, I would not forget you. Look! I have you engraved on the palm of my hand!" (cfr. Is 49:1Sf.)

In other words, even during those lean years of exile, of enslavement: "God made all things work together for their good." (Rom 8:28)

CLEMENT: And, above all, we can't let ourselves forget what happened in the life of Jesus Himself. He, the perfect man, He — wholly innocent — endured a merciless death.

PAUL: And *in the end,* God used this horrible crime to give us access to His infinite Righteousness and Holiness, to His innocence and His heavenly purity." (1 Pt 2:21ff)

CLEMENT: And, He was handed over to His enemies by His own friends, His very own! They had put a price on His head, the ridiculous thirty pieces of silver! When you think about it thirty pieces of silver, hardly the price of a slave. For Judas, or for the Jews themselves, Jesus was not really that expensive!

PAUL: Yeah, "His precious blood, the lamb without stain or defect, bought us back from those empty ways we received from our forefathers." (1 Pt 1:18f) His sacrifice, that was the price paid to buy us back from our bondage and to deliver us from our captivity to sin and death.

CLEMENT: Nailed to a cross, Jesus was wiped off the list of the living. He, the Beloved Son of God, He was rejected by the very ones He'd come to serve. He was mocked, ridiculed. He was plunged into shame.

PAUL: But never forget, Clement! "Because of this, He received a Name that is above every other Name. He received the power with which He can subdue the whole universe." And, thus, He made us fellow-citizens with the Saints; we are "of the house and family of God!" (cfr. Eph 2:19)

CLEMENT: He was detested by the very ones He had enlightened, healed, and saved. He was dealt with as the lowest of criminals... It was Barabbas who was set free!

PAUL: Yes, but, it was through His death that Jesus showed us the final proof of His love for each of us, for every single one of us...
"My present life, in the body, I live it in the faith of the Son of God, who loved me, and handed Himself over for me!" (Gal 2:20)
And, after His resurrection, day after day, Jesus gives each of us a share of His very own Spirit, of that divine Love which unites us to Him, to His Father, Who has become, our Father!

CLEMENT: Handed over to death, Jesus had nothing more to give. In any merely human consideration, He is reduced to less than nothing. He is the One despoiled as no other!

PAUL: And, Jesus, "seated at the right hand of God's very throne, He calls us to fix our eyes on Him, triumphant over the Cross." (cfr. Heb 12:2)

Day after day, Jesus is the "source of life, of peace, of love." He is our healing, and our Healer; He enriches us through all that He is. His act of complete surrender to God because of His love becomes the whole of our life. In Him, endlessly, we are drawn to God, ever closer, as dearly loved children.

CLEMENT: I have to say it yet once more: *For those who love God, God makes all things work together for their well-being.*

I begin to understand something of what you're saying, Paul. You feel, you hope that one day my Dad will turn the full measure of his energies and attention to work as a co-worker with God, and will be able to recognize that which has — until now — been so much a part of his life, his insistence on his own way. Isn't this what you're saying?

PAUL: Precisely! We must remain at peace, certain of one thing: God will forever be able to bring about a change of heart in and for your Dad.

Rather than thinking first and all but always of his business, he will be able to begin to center his life's energies on the acceptance of God's will. His love will effervesce!

Rather than interfering, or even obstructing your response to God's call, he will embrace it as generously as you seem to be doing already. He will walk with you as you remain "attached to God alone."

Rather than remaining stubbornly obstinate, he will eagerly and knowingly accept, and be deeply grateful for this grace with which He has blessed your family.

CLEMENT: If Dad would come to work along with God in this — as you've explained it so well — he'd have everything to gain.

Through him, here and now, the Lord Jesus would once again hand Himself over to His Father, with inscrutable love.

Through him, here and now, the victory of the Christ on Easter morning would appear even more radiant, like a lighthouse guiding the pilgrim ships through the narrows, into port, the Kingdom...

Now tell me, Paul, what can I do now so that Dad might be induced to "come around?"

PAUL: Well, Clement, that's something beyond both of us! All the arguments which you could come up with, all the words contained in all the books of the Bible — all of this is of inestimable value, but nothing like this would ever "convince" him...

CLEMENT: Then ... there's nothing we ... or I can do?

PAUL: Don't say that. There is much that you can and must do! Pray for your Dad, more even than you've been doing! Pray that the Lord Jesus grant him a fullness of His Spirit, of that Spirit: which sustained Jesus Himself in His ministry of service, and unshakable acceptance of the Father's plan, His will.

That Spirit was given to me, and has been my Guide during these thirty-plus year that I've been serving the Gospel. It was given to me ... and yet, I have to ask this gift for myself every single day. That Spirit is my very life: He lives with me, within me. He makes me "come alive!" Every single day I have to remain open and receptive to whatever the Spirit calls forth from me, and through me.

CLEMENT: But, not only you, Paul! All of us, all Christians, simply because we've been baptized, and confirmed in our faith, we've all been filled with that same Spirit, our hearts overflow with that fullness. Each Sunday, when we come together to celebrate the Lord's Supper, we are again taken in hand by that Creator Spirit Who transforms us anew, deeply, reshaping us in the image of the Risen Christ.

PAUL: Just call to mind that phrase which I wrote some time ago, Clement: "It is God who makes us stand firm in Christ. He anointed us, set His seal of ownership upon us, and put His Spirit in our hearts as a deposit, a guarantee of what is yet to come." (20 Cor 1:21-22)

CLEMENT: Two words really strike me, there: "seal," and a "deposit."

The Spirit is the "seal" by which God has marked us, engraved something unique in our hearts.

And this, as a "deposit," and "advance" on the inheritance which God holds for us until we take full possession, on the day of our final deliverance, to the praise of His glory (cfr. Eph 1:13) Let me repeat... let me savor those words yet again, Paul: *"God has marked us with His seal: the Spirit who lives on in our hearts."*

That makes me think of the branding the soldiers receive on their foreheads, or sometimes, on the back of their right hand, when they pledge themselves to the service of Imperial Rome, as a member of such and such a Legion. That mark, that seal, often enough is the initial of their commander: JT for Julius Tiberius, HA for Herodius Antipas. It cannot be erased; it'll be there until their dying day.

That mark, that "seal" is an indelible reminder that they no longer belong to themselves alone. From that day forward, they must remain dedicated, body and soul, to the service of their commander. In life and death, they've pledged to obey his orders, without complaint and with no hesitations whatever. They've committed themselves to complete, unbending and unending obedience.

And, in return, the Roman Legionaries have the promise of compensation according to their needs from their commander. He is committed to watching over them, providing for their needs and wants in so far as he can... And, at the end of the month, on "payday," they need produce nothing more than their "seal." This is the only ID required. Thus, they'll receive their promised wage, each one according to his rank.

PAUL: Your understanding, and your explanation of the Roman soldiers' seal strikes me as very enlightening. They are pledged to serve their master in life and in death.

CLEMENT: How can we say: *"In our hearts, the Holy Spirit is like a seal imprinted by God in us...?*

PAUL: "...in us, in our hearts..." but — before all else — that Spirit has come to us in Jesus, in the waters of His Baptism, but most particularly, after His Resurrection. He, Jesus, is the Son of man upon Whom the Father has marked His seal (cfr. Jn 6:27). And then, "consecrated and sent into the world, Jesus was able to accomplish all that the Father anticipated in and from Him. (cfr. Jn 10:36)

The most awesome thing of all is that — day by day — each one of us Christians, we can be caught up in awe and wonder that that same Spirit, "the Spirit of glory and of power," rests upon us. (cfr. 1 Pt 4:14)

CLEMENT: I must admit, Paul, the Holy Spirit who imprints in us the very face of Christ in all His splendor and beauty, and Who ever so gradually fills us with His Goodness, His holiness and His courage... I'm a long way from allowing that Spirit to be the very center of my own life...!

I keep recalling in my mind the words which you yourself wrote: "Hope will not deceive us, because God's love has been poured out into our hearts by the Holy Spirit Who has been given to us." (Rom 5:5); "We have — all of us — been baptized in the one Spirit so that we might become one Body, Jews and Greeks, slaves and free-men, and we have all been given to drink of that one same Spirit." (1 Cor 12:13)

PAUL: Or, to put it another way, the Holy Spirit enlightens us to see to the bottom of things with — so to speak — the very "eyes of God." Thanks be to that Spirit, we are able to establish a set of values, completely new and other than what we might have learned before, or elsewhere. Through that Spirit — ever so gradually — what we are comes to prevail over what we have... what is eternal comes to displace what is only temporary.

CLEMENT: If I understand what you're saying, Paul, all those divisions, all the criteria by which we separate persons one from another ... that has all been turned topsy-turvy, overthrown! On the one hand, we would think in terms of the "rich" and "well-off," those who've had a good education, prolonged studies, and all of the aristocrats, and those in the higher echelons of the government; and on the other, we'd place the poor, the illiterate, those subject to masters of whatever kind. And now, all those barriers, all those "classes" are simply eliminated.

"All of us have drunk of one same Spirit;" "all of us are — through faith — children of God in Christ, Jesus." (Gal 3:26)

All of us are loved to the point of foolishness by God Himself. It is the Holy Spirit who affords us this unanticipatable status. And, thanks be to that Spirit, we've all become ... "Generals!" And who could ever begin to count the stars on our epaulettes?! The Holy Spirit accords us a dignity greater, a prestige more pervasive than the Prefect of the City of Rome! In fact, we've been placed higher even than Caesar himself!

PAUL: Sustain your faith, Clement, and nourish it day-by-day, untiringly! And, don't overlook, or forget that through the Holy Spirit God incessantly recreates us, so long as we allow Him to work in us. Keep recalling in your mind some important words that I wrote: "IF we live by the Spirit, we move forward unceasingly, driven by that same Spirit..." (Gal 5:25) —"You are no longer ruled by the things of the body, but by the very Spirit of God Who dwells within you!" (Rom 8:9)

Tell me, Clement, have you ever considered how you have "radiated" this faith, in your family, among those with whom you've been lately? Have you borne witness to this immense love of God? Have you yourself perceived how God is at work in a way that infinitely surpasses anything you might have been able to do on your own?

CLEMENT: In a way, yes! There's something almost every day! One incident that comes immediately to mind, something that happened just the other day. I'm talking about my sister, Aquila... you know her! She's been married now for nearly ten years. Her husband is also a member of our Community here in Rome...

PAUL: What's been happening? Have they healed the sick? Have they spoken in tongues?

CLEMENT: Oh, none of that, Paul. First of all, let me say that they've had five children, one healthier than the other, two boys and three girls. And, then, about two years ago, their sixth was born, a son; but, he was born with a handicap. He is unable to walk, or speak...

PAUL: How did your father take this? What did this do to him?

CLEMENT: You'd never believe the tremendous disappointment, which quickly enough turned into an unbelievable anger. For quite a while, actually, for months he carried on like a barbarian, with neither trust nor law. "It's a disgrace for the family" — he'd cry out — "how can we shelter or give life to anyone like this who'll bring embarrassment, even shame to the whole family?" He was actually thinking of poisoning the baby, feeling that the sooner they could be rid of him, the better it would be for all of them...

PAUL: And, this went on for months? How did he finally resolve his anger, or did he? Was he able finally to accept the little guy, did he finally come to love and cherish him, just like the other five?

CLEMENT: In fact, he did! My sister really brought this about, I think Aquila consistently showed an indefatigable love, the patience of an angel. Never once did I know of her having been angry with that poor little guy. Her mother's-love expanded, quite literally exploded. And, soon enough, — I guess — her husband caught the drift. Afterwards, it was my own Dad. His anger turned into an unbelievable attentiveness. He'd never miss the opportunity to stop by and play with the little guy. And I must say, my admiration grew as I saw this change in each one of them. My Dad was soon expending more time and energy on him than on his business! ... and that was really a switch!

PAUL: How did it happen? What brought about the change? How do they themselves see, or understand their change of heart?

CLEMENT: It's really quite simple! It was God's Spirit who "worked them over," who completely "turned them around." Day by day, I could see them coming to live more deeply "of the Spirit." They were overwhelmed by the Spirit. There's just no other explanation...!

PAUL: Well, with regard to your question, the one you were worrying about earlier ... your desire to turn your life over to the Christ and His Gospel, isn't it possible that one day your Dad, under the direction of that same Spirit, might turn the whole thing around?

CLEMENT: Will he? Will he accept? Will he quit "making deals," "striking bargains" with God? Will his anger let-up, will he be able to overcome his fear of "losing face?" Will he grow in his faith? If he's to accept what I feel as my own calling, he'd be not one cent ahead, that's for sure! But in God's eyes, his entire life would glow with a deeper splendor and beauty ... more than anything he could ever imagine ... or hope!

PAUL: Yeah... yeah! Then one day he might be able to swallow his "too much" with a very simple and humble *"Who am I — a simple man — to argue with God?"* (cfr Rom 9:20)

CLEMENT: Paul, thank you ... even those words seem so trite! We do have to live with a "shatter-proof" hope... "like those who see Him who is invisible, we hold firm..." "God who calls us is ever faithful," and He will not quit acting in us and for us as time, and our lives move along. (cfr. Heb 11:27; 1 Thes 5:24)

August 25, 1994

15

Assured of that
Which is not Yet

*A week or so after an earlier visit with Paul — who
was still under house arrest in Rome — Clement returned
to visit him again, and talk with him. After that earlier
visit, Clement had begun praying, daily, for his Dad: that
the Spirit from on high would overcome his stubbornness
and obstinacy; that the godly Spirit might obtain that his
Dad's refusal to even consider what Clement was beginning to perceive as his own call from God to a life of service to the Gospel and to the Gospel-people. Little by little,
ever so slowly, a deep peace was gradually coming to be
all-pervasive in Clement's heart and mind. Calmly, he was
finally able to place all of his tomorrows into the hands of
God, come what may. And, he'd see, and accept this as
God's will...*

*Additionally, there were some points that had come up
from their earlier conversation that Clement wanted to
clear up. And, for this, he'd decided to go and visit Paul
again.*

CLEMENT: When we were talking last week, Paul, there was one
thing that really helped me understand those words: "God has
marked with His own seal those He has called, those who — in

return — have come to love Him; that seal — indelibly engraved on their hearts — is the Holy Spirit, Who dwells in their hearts" (cfr. 2 Cor 1:21f) Paul, I can't tell you how much I've come to appreciate, to really treasure those words!

PAUL: That mark, this taking-over of our hearts by God's divine Spirit, that's the origin, the basis of all our confidence! It accomplishes that which — of ourselves — we'd never accomplish; but we must remain calmly and firmly convinced that God can do it, through His overpowering Spirit!

CLEMENT: ...and, Paul, there was another thing which we didn't have time to explore last week, that other phrase that you wrote: "The Holy Spirit, dwelling in our hearts, is the pledge, the "down-payment" that God gives us as a foretaste of our inheritance, which we can possess partially, even now, a "pledge" of what our ever-lasting inheritance will be like, to the praise of His glory." (cfr. Eph 1:13) "first-installment," a pledge ... just what do you mean by that?

PAUL: Well, remember when I bought that piece of property from you for 10,000 deniers. At that time, I couldn't come up with the full price. So I gave you 1,000 deniers; and you understood that this was but a pledge, a "down-payment" on what you would finally be getting. In giving you the thousand deniers, I provided some kind of assurance, a promise of the full price.

CLEMENT: OK! Which reminds me of one of my cousins. It's Rufus; he lives, oh, about 25 or 28 miles from here, out in the country. He farms; and he has a large family ... seven children. And just to feed them all, he raises and sells wheat. Unfortunately, he doesn't have any means of transportation, so as to do his own selling in the Imperial City of Rome. So, in August, when the grain has been harvested he gets in touch with a sort of middle-man (a man who does quite a business out there in their neighborhood.) He entrusts to him all his wheat. In the months that follow, the miller mills the grain, and takes the flour and sells it to different bakeries in Rome. Knowing his territory, that middle-man realizes that Rufus needs some money just to keep his household fed. And so, from August on, long before he's been able to have the wheat milled, and then sold, he gives Rufus and his family a pledge of what will eventually be theirs. It's an "advance," a "first-installment;" but Rufus has it as the pledge of what is yet to come. And, with this, he can live from day to day, until he gets paid for all his wheat, the full amount that is due.

PAUL: Exactly, Clement! It should help you to understand better those words which I wrote to our sisters and brothers in Ephesus: "God chose us, and little by little, we've come to love Him. The Holy Spirit, dwelling within us, is the pledge, the first-installment, the assurance of the inheritance God has prepared for us and which will be ours on the day of our final deliverance. May God be praised!" (cfr. Eph 1:13) (Paul remained thoughtfully silent for a brief moment. And then, he posed this question to Clement:) Tell me, Clement, since that day when you were baptized, has the Spirit been your deliverance?

CLEMENT: Yeah! Is there any other explanation of *the joy I find in simply being Christian?* Time and again, I've re-read, even learned by heart, what you wrote to the brothers and sisters right here in Rome: "All those who are led by God's Spirit are His children! For, the Spirit that God has given you does not make you slaves, nor is that Spirit a cause for you to be fearful; no, rather the Spirit makes you God's children, and empowered by that same Spirit, we cry-out "Father! my Father!" God's Spirit is attuned to our own spirits, declaring that we are children of God. And, since we are His, we will come to possess the blessing He has reserved for us, and — along with Christ — we will inherit what He has already prepared for Him; for, if we share in Christ's sufferings, we shall also, surely, share His glory." (Rom 8:14-17)

Paul, as long as I live, I'll remain deeply grateful to you for having written those lines. Thanks to you, God the Holy Spirit, made the faith take root in me, and flourish. And the confidence I have now ... it's just so very deeply rooted in my heart!

PAUL: No. Clement, don't thank me! It is the Lord, Jesus, that we should thank, Him, the "first-born from among the dead." (cfr. Col 1:18) It is He — in His inexhaustible goodness — who calls us to live in faith. It is He who by the gift of the Holy Spirit made our community of believers to come about, right here in Rome.

CLEMENT: Here, in Rome ... it's good to remember that! Rome, the Imperial Capitol, here where Caesar claims to be god! Rome, where thousands and thousands of people make their sacrifices, the blood of bulls and goats to the "protectors" of the City and of the Roman Empire. Rome, this city where so many of those from the "better families" have turned away from these idols and turned themselves to God, the living and true God, and who — in these times — *await the coming of the Son who rose from the dead, for Jesus,* who protects us from the approaching terror. (cfr. 1 Thes 1:9f)

PAUL: Clement, you're speaking some very basic, down-to-earth things now, and things that are supremely important! Blessed may you be! And you live in expectation. Who could ever enumerate the gifts of God's grace which give you the happiness that is now yours ... and at the same time, prepare you to look forward so eagerly to what is yet to come...

And, not only you, Clement, but all of us Christians, *we find a deep happiness in what already is:* day by day, in our hearts, "the gifts of God's grace are there, infinite, inestimable!" (2 Cor 2:12) God has made us His own beloved children. The very Spirit of Jesus transfuses His own life into us and it is this life that we now live: how could we ever imagine any greater happiness?

And, even now, along with all of this, we live in hope: this inestimable gift of God's Spirit is only the "down-payment" of that which God has set aside for us. The Holy Spirit indwelling in us that's a pledge of those unimaginable gifts which God has reserved for us: we await that day when "we'll take full possession of that glorious inheritance of the saints in light" (cfr. Col 1.12f)

All of us, we wait calmly, but *assured of that which is not yet* ... that "it will exceed, simply transcend anything which we can figure out, or even imagine!" (cfr. Eph)

CLEMENT: As you've written so well, Paul... "We await that which no eye has ever seen, which no ear has yet heard, that which no one could possibly imagine, that which God has prepared for those who love Him..." (cfr. 1 Cor 2:9)

PAUL: That's it, Clement! Day by day, we need but to look and *see, to rejoice in seeing those observable signs of the presence of the risen Lord among us ... and, at the same time,* believe fiercely that we haven't seen anything just yet, that God will fulfill all that He promised: *we have come to believe in the future!*

CLEMENT: Which reminds me of John ... I've heard that he's now living at Ephesus, with our Mother... I'm thinking of that early morning when Peter and he were racing to the tomb. They both saw — obviously! — the same thing: an emptied tomb and the large stone rolled away from the entrance, the head covering and the burial-shroud. The head covering was there, but separate from the rest. (cfr. Jn 20:1-10)

PAUL: Peter and John were both there when Jesus' body had been carried to that tomb. And what they were now seeing was the shroud in which the one from Arimathea had wrapped His body. There was certainly no doubt about that!

CLEMENT: *Peter SAW all of this* ... and he was awe-struck. He had to ask himself the question ... Who would have dared to steal the body ... to put it where? Peter was seeing no farther than that! He wasn't connecting what he was seeing: the empty tomb and these folded cloths, and all that had been foretold in the Scriptures, and which Jesus Himself had promised...

PAUL: And, just like Peter, John took in all of this. And then, almost instantaneously, *John believed!* "...the Lord lives!" — Somehow, "He took flight from the tomb!" He overpowered even the tomb, and He was caring enough to leave some trace of His passing ... and what had enshrouded and bound Him ... and now, that was it, there was nothing more...

CLEMENT: "He took flight from the tomb..." it reminds me of something beautiful that happened to me this very morning, out in the yard...

PAUL: In your yard? I don't know as how I'm following you right now...!

CLEMENT: Well, a couple of weeks ago, on one of the trees in our backyard, I noticed a cocoon, still unopened. Day by day, it grew. This morning, at sunrise, I saw the cocoon burst-open: a beautiful butterfly appeared. Slowly, so very slowly, it unfolded the splendor of its wings, and for a short time, it was bathed in the warm sunlight. It was really something to see. If they'd allow you to get out of your own present situation, I'd take you into the yard ... but you'd see nothing but the empty cocoon...

PAUL: Hey, Clement, I like that! What you were able to see in that simple, very natural process of a cocoon and the butterfly really strikes me! I'm just sorry that I couldn't have been with you to see for myself all that you saw.

And, every one of us — as Christians — and following the teaching of John, we believe deeply in the Resurrection, and the empty tomb. Just like that butterfly, being freed from the enclosure of the cocoon, He was freed!

And, right along with John, we believe that that which Jesus left — the empty tomb, the burial-shroud folded and left there — it is God's Word for us. God wants us to understand that Jesus DID overcome the powers of death. It's His way of teaching us, of helping us to realize that the words spoken by the Prophets have been accomplished. And, what Jesus had promised, was done...!

CLEMENT: Yes, I keep all of that in mind... "The Holy One, the Just one, God did not abandon Him to dwell among the dead. His body did not know corruption. God raised Him from among those who had died and placed Him — once again — onto the pathway of the living. Henceforward, God, our Father, enriched Him with the joy of His presence." (cfr. Ps 16:8-11)

"In my desperation, I cried out to the Lord, and He heard my cry. This is — indeed! — the Day of the Lord; and for us, a Day of joy!" (cfr. Ps 117:5, 24)

PAUL: And further, Jesus Himself announced His victory over death. And He spoke those words: "Anyone who gives himself to fulfilling God's will, will be heard by the Lord when he turns to Him in prayer..." [cfr. Jn 9:31]

God's fidelity lasts well beyond time. He "had" to save Jesus, His own beloved Son, from the pain and humiliation of death, because of His complete submission...

CLEMENT: *John believes* so much more deeply than any poor mortal's eyes could ever see. "Today" — he seems to say to himself — "today those words of the Scriptures are being fulfilled: "Death, you have been swallowed-up by this victory. Death, where is your overpowering triumph? [cfr. Is 25:8; Hos 13:14; also 1 Cor 15:54)

PAUL: John believed, and now leads us to believe too: Death would no longer overpower Jesus, the Son of God. From now on, "the fullness of life, and the glory of God show forth awesomely" in the figure of the Risen Jesus. (cfr. Col 2:9)

And we sincerely believe — again, as John teaches us! — the dark and dank tomb, the bonds of death have been conquered, even though they had seemingly won-out!

But even this was not the whole story. For John, as for me, and for you, Clement, and for every one of us who seeks to walk in "the Way," Jesus' victory over the darkness of death, it is a pledge, a "first-installment" as it were, that God will pay-in-full to those who put themselves and their destiny into His hands. This triumph of Jesus is like a *fore-telling, and subtle sign,* an affirming of what God will accomplish in some unknown future...

CLEMENT: As I hear you, Paul, you're saying that the empty tomb and the shroud and cloth, these are — in some mysterious way — God's promise to us...

PAUL: Don't say "in some mysterious way"! This is God's truth, His promise to us that we too will pass over from this world to the Father (cfr. Jn 13:1) And, when that pass over happens, we too will find ourselves there where Jesus is! (cfr. Jn 14:3)

Just as death was not the final word spoken of Jesus, so for us. We will become then what Jesus has already become, and which He is now and will remain forever. This is God's solemn promise: "One day, we will be with the Lord Jesus!" (cfr. 1 Thes 4:17)

Do you remember what I wrote in my Instruction to the Christians at Corinth? "Sown perishable, the body shall rise imperishable. Sown corruptible, the body shall rise bursting with glory. Sown negligible, it shall rise full of strength." (1 Cor 15:43)

CLEMENT: Just a minute now! You're moving a bit fast for me! You say: One day, we'll share that which Jesus came to be, and is, and will remain for all time? What He became through His Resurrection ... we'll have a share in? It sounds to me like the hymn we sing when we gather on the Lord's Day, after we've sung the Lord's prayer: "For yours is the Kingdom, and the Power, and the Glory, now and forever more!"

PAUL: Yes, *each Sunday,* it is the Lord, gloriously Risen who brings us together, and so together we sing out His victory! And thus, the promise of our own eventual victory deepens and roots itself in our hearts.

Each Lord's Day, the risen Lord brings us together in His Name; together we proclaim Him as our Lord, as our future! And thus, we more deeply enroot our own desire to share that which He is, in the very glory, light, and splendor of the Father.

Each Lord's Day, we recall His passing-over to the Father, and thus we renew our faith that it is "to Him, Jesus, the Lord, that all glory, praise and honor is due." *And that reality, already now we've begun to share;* His inheritance will be fully ours one day, on the day of our own passover, to the praise of His glory.

CLEMENT: Let me check this out, Paul! You're saying that that which Jesus now possesses, is ours, already now? ... Are you saying that the splendor of that life, which transcends any diminishment or corruption, fortified by the very strength of *God, is already in us,* among us, even though this be in a very subtle way? Yes ... I think I'm beginning to understand!

PAUL: Yes, already ... in a very subtle way! We must not let ourselves overlook that! We must look forward to the things in heaven, where Christ is, at God's right hand!) "The life we have is hidden with Christ, in God!" (cfr. Col 3:2f)

Day by day, the Lord Jesus, King in power, busies Himself in associating us in His passage to the Father.

Day by day, He remains Emmanuel, God-with-us: He transfuses into our hearts the love of the overpowering Spirit.

Day by day, His Spirit is at work within us, in so very subtle a manner, just as you've said, Clement!

CLEMENT: His Spirit is at work within us, changing our hearts. *It's like the yeast in the dough...* "The Kingdom of heaven can be likened to the yeast which a woman takes and mingles with the flour, until it rises..." (cfr. Mt 13:33)

PAUL: The yeast is not outside of, or alongside the dough. Outside, it would remain only yeast, accomplishing nothing. But mixed with the flour and the other ingredients, worked by the cook time and time again, it really becomes part of the whole. You don't see it, yet it is accomplishing its purpose! Only by becoming "hidden" can it do what it is there to do. And, the cook puts the dough outside, under the warm rays of the sun, covered by a towel so that it'll not collect any dust. Then, after sufficient time, perhaps just as the sun is setting, the cook takes the dough which has risen by now, and puts it into the oven.

CLEMENT: The yeast is hidden in the dough ... and then only can it begin to work. The whole mass of dough rises. And, what a marvel to see: the tiny, insignificant amount of yeast, makes the whole mass of dough rise! Yes, it works so invisibly, so subtly...!

PAUL: And we can draw our own conclusions... Think about it! The Lord Jesus — "who is our very life..." (cfr. Col 3:4) — at what point does He come to possess our hearts by the yeast of His Spirit...?

CLEMENT: Yes, that I recognize! It's when we come together to celebrate the Lord's Supper that we share in a special way in the very Body of Christ and in His Precious Blood, through our communion. But, His presence is "veiled." Still, if I understand what John has said, "It is the Lord!" Who "comes among us, and dwells within us." (cfr. Jn 21:7, 12)

PAUL: Yes! As we hold out our hand, all that we touch, all that our eyes perceive is the bread. But, when we swallow it, our heart speaks out, assuring us that "it isn't just bread!" That's what we hold to, dearly.

CLEMENT: We believe! ...and, I believe; however, I have to try to explain what our Savior, triumphantly risen, is accomplishing. I have to admit it: it is simply something beyond words ... at least, beyond any words that I can find!

PAUL: ...and don't worry about that, Clement; it's something that surpasses what any of us might try to say by way of explanation. (Paul then is silent for a moment or two, and then he continues...)

Just now, you made use of two comparisons. You spoke of the "down payment," the "pledge" that your cousin Rufus gets from that middle man, when he consigns his wheat harvest to him, when he has gathered the first of the harvest.

And, you used the image of the yeast, the leaven, which a housewife mixes in with the other ingredients in her recipe; soon enough, the whole begins to rise, and finally it's ready for the oven. These two ideas might serve us well in our coming to understand the Mystery of the Eucharist. Don't you think so?

CLEMENT: The Body of the Risen Lord, which we share in our Eucharistic Communion, would be as a "down payment," a promise of things yet to be ... Could you talk about that a bit more?

PAUL: Rufus appreciates the work of that man with whom he deals. The first installment that he receives gives him the where-with-all to hold him over for a few weeks, or even months. And, Clement, that "Rufus," that's you, that's each one of us...

CLEMENT: ...and the middle man, the go between ... that's Jesus... He is Goodness itself, and infinite Mercy. And, He keeps repeating to us, a hundred times — no, a thousand times — that one day we'll be "paid-in-full" that which is due us: "He will let us join the saints and with them inherit the light." (Col 1:12)

That very special sign of His infinite love ... or perhaps, that which sustains us as we journey along the road of life while we await our grand entry into the Kingdom of heaven, it's ... well, it's the gift of His very self in the Eucharist.

PAUL: That's exactly what I'm saying! Jesus continually repeats to us,to each one of us, individually "...His words of everlasting life..." (cfr. Jn 6:68)

"The bread which I give you, it is my flesh, given so that the world might come alive!" (Jn 6:51) You receive Me ... Risen from among the dead. You receive Me, and I come to you so that you might have some "taste of the power of the world to come" (cfr. Heb 6:5) In you — if you allow Me — I will be healing the "old man," healing all that in you which turns you away from the Father. Just "hang loose!" ... let me lead you to Him, to raise you to those heights. Little by little, ever so gradually that cleansing Light of My Spirit will "in-spirit" you, guide you, and become the power of your own life.

"He who eats my flesh and drinks my blood has everlasting life, and I, I will raise him on the final day." (Jn 6:54) I come to you so that step by step, stage by stage you might become love itself, in Me! Let Me increase within you: together — you and I — we will eagerly wait for that great day when you too will shine in splendor in the Kingdom. My power, My glory will find itself echoed in you!

CLEMENT: Week after week, when the Presbyter places the Holy Bread into my hand, I utter my "Amen!" Acknowledging that this really IS the Body of Christ ... that this is my Lord and my God ... as my gratitude for His closeness expresses itself ... (And, he stops; he chooses simply to think long and hard...)

PAUL: And, you spoke too of the image of the leaven, and of the butterfly which emerges so slowly from its cocoon. It takes some time for the yeast to do what it is there to do ... or for the butterfly to emerge fully, and take to its wings...

CLEMENT: Yes, it makes sense to me now! It is a lifetime task, a steady effort to become "strengthened in our inner being with power through His Spirit, that Christ may dwell in our hearts through faith." (cfr. Eph 3:16f) Each week, the Lord comes and dwells within us. He is the leaven of our own resurrection, the healing of our mortality, and the antidote to death itself.

Each week, each time we gather on the Lord's Day, He becomes "more" in us "until each of us comes to the unity of the faith and of the knowledge of the Son of God, to maturity, measured by nothing other than Christ Himself, come to full stature!" (cfr. Eph 4:13)

PAUL: The leaven is hidden and only thus can it do what it is meant to do! In our Eucharist, the presence of Christ is "veiled," hidden, but walking in the footsteps of John, *we "see and believe"* that Christ, "the living Bread comes down from heaven," comes to us to fill our hearts, our lives endlessly with the unsullied and holy love with which He — and we! — will love the Father for all of eternity!

CLEMENT: Paul, I can't find the right words to tell you how much I appreciate all that you've said. I just hope ... ask that you'd keep praying for me, even in your confinement here. How I'd want to see things like you do, to have the confidence you obviously have, to leave this "earthly dwelling-place of my body and to live with the Lord." (cfr. 2 Cor 5:8)

May 29, 1995

16

He Should Have

Along with Maria of Magdala and Mary, the mother of James and John, Salome had gone to the sepulcher. Early — at dawn — on the day after the Great Sabbath, she'd seen the Angel, had heard the Message, the Good News beyond any Good News: "He is risen!" (Mk 16:1-8)

Later, some few weeks after the Pentecost-event, Salome went to visit Mary, Jesus' mother. For all intents and purposes, she'd decided to go back to her own village, way up north, in Galilee. She'd felt an urge, a need to go and announce the "Good News" there, to her own family members and to the others in her village. And, she was already anticipating the questions and difficulties she'd be running into up there. And Mary answered in her very straightforward, simple way. This might have been their conversation.

SALOME: You know, at home, there were quite a few who had believed in Jesus, the holy Son of God! There were numerous sick people who had been cured; and still, there were a lot of things about Him that they found difficult, that they just couldn't get a handle on. Mary, could you help me find answers to some of the questions I'm going to be running into?

MARY: Are you thinking of all the torture and suffering that Jesus endured?

SALOME: Yes, especially that! That's one of the first things that I expect to be faced with: the all powerful Creator in-dwelt Jesus; it would have been the easiest thing in the world for Him to simply call upon His Father, Who could have dispatched twelve legions of Angels (cfr. Mt 26:53), and Jesus would have emerged from it all as a triumphant hero! His enemies would have been overcome, completely, quicker than you could bat an eye! And God's Kingdom would have come about.

Tell me: why did Jesus will to undergo all that His enemies inflicted on Him? even death on the Cross?

MARY: Well before the actual Crucifixion, Jesus had anticipated, and foretold: "Is it not necessary that everything that has been written in the law of Moses, in the Prophets and the Psalms should be accomplished? (cfr. Lk 24:44)

SALOME: I remember that, but I'm afraid that that alone will not convince those people up there...!

MARY: The beloved Son, Jesus, had to fulfill perfectly the will of His Father: "love my Father, and I conform Myself to all that He has prescribed..." (cfr. Jn 14:31)

SALOME: And, it is that, precisely, that the people at home will find difficult to accept! I can already hear them saying: "God could have, and should have acted otherwise in demonstrating the love He has for us..."

In their minds, it'd seem that all of this happened and made God some kind of terrible ogre, as "less-than-human," unbending, before Whom Jesus had simply to submit, yet without breaking. Jesus was called to be a puppet, a marionette in the hands of God!

He was to submit Himself, just like a slave, to the point that "...not a letter, not the smallest part of a letter of the Law would be trammeled, until everything would be fulfilled" (Mt 5:18) Face it: there's not a lot there that would be very understandable to them...!

MARY: Look at it another way, Salome: "God is Love, and He so loved the world that He gave His one and only Son: and so it is that anyone who believes in Him will not die, but will have eternal life. It is for this that God sent His Son into the world, not to condemn it but so that — through Him — it would be saved." (cfr. Jn 3:16f)

SALOME: Mary, those words, I remember them too! I can understand that God has undertaken a way that is quite contrary to the way we'd have anticipated. When He comes to be with us, "live and in person," He will quite likely come in some unpredictable way.

Think about it! A baby, clothed in whatever clothing was available, lying in a manger as the poorest of the poor; then, as an unassuming workingman, calloused hands, nothing singular much less flamboyant, ... indistinguishable from many another there in Nazareth, and at the end, one crucified, a "nothing" there with the cursed of this earth...

Yes, I can already feel their taunts, the hesitations and doubts. The refrain that I'll be hearing: God should have done ... otherwise...!

MARY: "He should have...!" Keep going along that route, and we'll have made ourselves the judges of God and of His ways, as we make our merry way...! "He should've...!" It's us imposing our ways on God! And, by what right...?

Tell me, Salome: what are we — in fact — saying, and thinking? What are we making ourselves out to be? Who are we to place God under our microscopes, submitting Him to our ways of seeing and judging things?

I simply recall: for your family and your relatives up there, for you, for me, and for any who would believe in Him, none of this is easy to accept. It takes an effort, and it takes something really deep to acknowledge that God is not like us!

SALOME: You know, Mary: what you've just said reminds me of something that Judith said so many years ago: *"God must not be threatened as a human being might be, nor is He, like a mere man, to submit to any arbiter"* (Judith 8:16)

MARY: I see that for you, Salome, Judith's story is very much alive in your mind and heart.

SALOME: Naturally! Judith — like Esther, and Ruth — I've always looked up to them as heroines and examples, God given...

Way back in those days, Holofernes, the general-in-chief of the Assyrian army, laid siege to the Palestinian town of Bethulia. In his army, he had 170,000 foot soldiers, and 12,000 cavalrymen, not counting those who were in his supply train. It was a markedly superior force, without a doubt! Not only that but the fortress, Bethulia — was strategically located, guarding that whole region, even Jerusalem itself. It was the last stronghold that the Jewish people still held. Defeated there, their entire country would lie open to pillage and rape. The very Temple in Jerusalem would likely be destroyed, not one stone left upon another!

Instead of launching a direct attack on the garrison at Bethulia, Holofernes planned a tactic which would give him a much easier victory: he would blockade the city, station soldiers on the nearby hills so that he could control, who could enter or leave the city. The Jewish fortress with its garrison would be completely surrounded. And most problematic: they would be unable to go out for water which flowed so abundantly at the base of the mountain. Every one of the springs was under the eye and the control of Holofernes. The siege had already endured for thirty-four days.

In the fortress-town itself, the situation had become desperate. The cisterns were all empty. There wasn't a drop of water anywhere. The children were dying of thirst, the elders and the women were exhausted and collapsing one after the other. The townspeople began to complain and murmur against their leader, Uzziah: "It'd be better to surrender than to die of thirst! So we will be enslaved! At least, we will be alive, and we won't have to stand by and watch our own wives and children dying right in front of us, before our very eyes!"

Uzziah understood; so — speaking to the assembled people — he went so far as to put God on trial. In that speech, he delivered an ultimatum to God! Uzziah said: "Hold out for five more days! At that time, if God fails to intervene, to assist us within the next five days, then I will accept the position you've proposed..."

At the time, in Bethulia, there was a dedicated and devoted widow, Judith. Quickly enough, she heard of Uzziah's proposition that if no aid came at the end of five more days, the fortress-town would be surrendered.

Judith summoned Uzziah and the leaders in the community and said to them: "Who are you to put God to the test? You understand nothing, and never will! You have no right to demand guarantees where the plan of the Lord God is concerned! You are forcing God to intervene on your own good time! Acknowledge and confess your infidelity to our God! *God must not be threatened as a human being might be, nor is He, like a mere man, to submit to any arbiter.* "Look here now, this is what the Lord God asks of us: together, let us beseech God's mercy, and He will hear our call, if such should be pleasing to Him." And, Judith betook herself to pray. She cried loudly to the Lord.

Some hours passed. Afterwards, Judith along with her servant, went forth from the gate of the town. She had clothed herself in her finest clothes, clothes which she'd last worn when her husband, Manasseh, was still alive. She'd prepared herself to seduce anyone who might cast an eye on her. And, she went all the way to the enemy's camp. Naturally, Holofernes was indeed seduced by Judith's splendor and beauty. In the course of a banquet, Holofernes drank very generously, considerably more than he had ever drunk before. After some time, Judith went with him to his tent. He was dead drunk, and soon enough, he passed out on his bed. Gathering up all her courage, and with both hands, Judith took hold of his sword and beheaded the great Holofernes. Then, Judith went back calmly to Bethulia, Holofernes' head lying hidden in the bag which she carried.

That very day, the Jews attacked their enemy, and their victory was complete...

MARY: You know, Salome, I too admire Judith as one of our heroines. Her faith renews my strength, and her example is as a light as I make my pilgrim way here on this earth. Oftentimes, I reflect on those beautiful prayers Judith uttered:

"Lord God, my God, hear me! I am a lowly widow. You have accomplished marvelous deeds in other ages, and will continue to do so, now and in the days to come... (Jdt 9:4-5)

"Your strength does not lie in numbers, nor Your power in strong armies, for You are the God of the humble, the Help of the helpless, the Defender of the weak, the Protector of the abandoned, the Savior of the desperate ... (Jdt 9:11)

"God, our God, is with us, to make manifest His mighty power in Israel!

"Lord God, You are great and glorious, awesome and supreme is Your power!

"Who can stand against Your Word? (Jdt 13:11; 16:13f)

SALOME: Lately, I've thought about that story of Judith quite often. I've told myself: These people who murmur against Uzziah, and he himself — who seeks to force the hand of God by his ulti-matum — well, in our own times, it seems to me that it is my own family and our neighbors who repeat in their own ways: "God should have..." should have done otherwise in bringing us to our salvation!" Jesus should have made use of His might and power to impose the Kingdom of God...!

MARY: And you, Salome, you who seem to be called by God to act as the "Judith" to your own, what will you say to them, to lead them to heighten and deepen their faith...?

SALOME: I'll simply do as Judith did! Yes, that's what I'll do! Certainly, I can't just stand there and tell them that they are think-ing wrongly!

MARY: For sure! You will find the right words, words which will inspire them to lift up their minds and hearts, so as to better under-stand Jesus and His way. Ever so gradually, little by little, you will let them be enthused by the meaning Jesus has put in His life...

SALOME: During the whole time that I was with Jesus — and served Him as best I knew how — there is one thing that I learned: that God DOES watch over us, over each one of us. It was what Jesus Himself lived right there, for us to see. And He did this, radically, completely! By the uprightness of His life Jesus ful-filled completely and radically all that God had foretold in the Scriptures...

MARY: I'm sure that you keep in your heart those snippets from the Law, the Prophets, and the Writings...

SALOME: Yes... There's that one, from one of the Psalms: "In the way of Your commandments, I find my joy, a joy beyond all treasures..." (Ps 119:14)

MARY: I love that verse too! In the depth of His soul, Jesus submitted to Him who is supreme, to His Father in heaven. And, therein He found His happiness. Living heart-to-heart with the Father, Jesus found His fulfillment as a human being. And, therein too He found a freedom, a freedom unknown by any of those who had gone before Him...

SALOME: It was the great prophet, Isaiah, who said: "The upright one, my servant, will justify many by taking their guilt upon Himself ... for having exposed Himself to death and for being numbered as one of those in rebellion, whereas He was bearing the sins of many and interceding for the rebellious." (Is 53:11f)

MARY: The Servant of God ... numbered as one of the rebellious... There, raised on the Cross, and raised to the heights of heaven, Jesus intercedes for us before the Father. "Father, forgive them for they do not understand what it is that they are doing..." It was for this that Jesus came; it is the very purpose, the focus of His entire life. It is "the Hour in which his whole existence was concentrated, found its meaning...

Then, Jesus cannot ask the Father to put twelve Legions of angels at His command. Had He done so, how would the Scriptures have been fulfilled which speak of the Servant who "had to suffer," to save all humankind from their sin?

SALOME: And there's another text in which I find great consolation: "The greater you are, the more humbly should you act. Then, you will find favor with God." (Sir 3:18-20)

MARY: It's brief ... and it says so much! Jesus could only have lived humbly, and with His singular sincerity. Submission to the Father, and the salvation of all humanity ... there because of His love. And, it is precisely in this that He is most Himself!

Because of this, in our hearts, Jesus is the way of the Truth, the Way we must all walk towards our heavenly Father! Through Jesus, we can find favor with God.

SALOME: And, so often the words of poor Job come to mind. "I know that my Redeemer lives, that He rises-up from the dust of the earth. After my own rising, He will set me close to Himself, and — in the flesh — I shall see my God. He whom I see will defend me: I shall behold One who is no stranger... (Jb 19:25ff)

MARY: What I understand Job as saying is this: realize that my Defender is alive! It is in faith, and through faith that Jesus lived His final hours. Simply call to mind those final moments when He — enflamed by His passion for God and for His brothers and sisters — He was so completely overwhelmed...

At that moment, that consuming flame spread and destroyed in Him all those "passions" which destroy so much in so many lives, in so many hearts...

SALOME: And, there is another word, recorded by our great Prophet, Isaiah. "The Lord God will come to assist me; insult and ridicule will not touch me..." (Is 50:7)

MARY: From the depths of His soul, Jesus — with a faith stronger than iron — believed that His Father is, and would continue to be with Him, close to Him, until the end ... and then, even beyond death itself...

Then, Jesus set Himself resolutely on the road to Jerusalem! Armed with the courage of God, He walked erect right to the end, with the Father always before His eyes... (Lk 9:51; Jdt 13:20)

His sufferings, His crucifixion ... this He underwent as an offering made with tremendous love, it is truly "the Hour" when — for us, and before us — Jesus remained focused on His Father, bound almost as by chains which no one and nothing could ever undo.

From that time on, deep within, Jesus on the Cross is one Who is bound to God, binding us too to our heavenly Father. Passover!

Yesterday, and through humanity's every tomorrow! Passover is unending!

Guided by God's Spirit, Jesus envisions "both ways at once!" looking at humanity's need, He is the Deliverer; and — at the same time — He is totally focused on, completely given to His Father, Whom He loves with every fiber of His being...

Mysterious, loving presence of the Christ, the Messiah Who delivers us by taking upon Himself our suffering and death ... the mystery that we need to worship on bended knee, our hearts overcome with gratitude.

SALOME: What you have just said, Mary, really, it is striking! Jesus puts Himself on both sides at the same time! He gives Himself to God for our human race, and for each one of us. His glance goes both ways at the same time. Which reminds me of something my cousin — the one living at Damascus — so often repeated...

MARY: At Damascus? Is the world so different there?

SALOME: Not really! One day, not too long ago, she was walking beside a creek; she was taken aback by a chameleon, feasting on the passing insects. The chameleon's two eyes were looking in two different directions, one looking to the left, the other surveying possibilities on the right. She'd never noticed anything like that, ever!

MARY: Well, neither have I! I never noticed! Yet, that simple recognition of nature at work can help to bring us to an understanding of what Jesus experienced: on the one hand, He "belonged" to humankind which He loved ardently, to every human being, no exceptions...

SALOME: You don't have to tell me ... I oftentimes witnessed that when I was traveling round with Jesus ... for almost three years. He belongs to us all, a "universal Brother," as if we all belonged to His own family

Lepers ... cursed lepers, shunned and outcasts in the minds of everyone ... Jesus went to them, touched them, and ... and, they went away healed...

The children ... so often neglected, seen as insignificant by so many, in so many families Jesus embraced them, held them to His heart, like a hen gathering her chicks under her wings. (cfr. Mt 23:37)

Pagans and aliens, the blind, the shepherds, widows and public sinners... Jesus received them all! Accepted them, and welcomed them ... embraced them!

The marginalized, the "nobodies," the desperately poor, Jesus was so very concerned about them. He was attentive to them, to the "little people," those closest to the bottom...

MARY: You know, as I sit and remember Jesus' way: each day He practiced that "golden rule," so simple and yet of such great consequence: "Whatever you would want from any other, do that for them!" (Cfr. Mt 7:12)

You know, for Him, to love authentically was to love limitlessly, never even considering the cost. No one ... not one single person was outside of, beyond the touch of His love!

SALOME: And, He took us, accepted each one of us just as we are. He never placed any pre-conditions, not even for those, like myself, who would never have merited a second glance! "Come without fear" — He would have said! — "Come, so that I can share something of My Spirit, My life-giving Spirit with you..."

He took us, accepted each of us then and there, however much we feared going to Him. "Come" — He would say — "Come, be not afraid! I will satisfy your heart's deepest hungers, will be all that you need, except a pitiless judge!"

And, we could go to Him! No need for masks; we could go just as we were. He was always there, always ready to take our hand and lift us up. And, afterwards, coming back to ourselves, there was that feeling of enrichment, of refreshment given by His Spirit of love.

MARY: Among all the children of man, Jesus unquestionably stands out, He is certainly one of a kind!" He was forever "for others," never, ever measuring the cost!

And He knew the meaning of forgiveness, there where we'd have seen or expected nothing but punishment, pitiless rejection...

He knew the meaning of compassion, and understanding ... especially where hatred, or any kind of alienation held sway, or self-centeredness in whatever form it might take...

SALOME: And another thing: the way He dealt with us women. He was so warmly welcoming toward each of us, so loving towards us with a tenderness so real and yet so pure, as if we were His own family ... His mother, His sisters, or His children!

Nowadays, in our whole society, what do we matter? where do we fit in? When it comes to making some sort of decision or other in our villages, who would ever think of asking us, "the women?" But Jesus allowed us to walk with Him, to be part of His company. And, He was always so attentive ... how often He expressly spoke His gratitude when — with our caring — we'd provided for Him and for His disciples?

In the course of these past three years, there are just so many things that impressed themselves on me: His deep and natural respect for us, His thoughtfulness, the authenticity that radiated out from everything He did. Day after day, we really mattered in His eyes we, unlettered, unimpressive women ... in His eyes, we "counted"!

And, most impressive of all, perhaps, was that final gift He gave us just before He returned to His Father. It was to us that He first appeared in those early morning hours, the morning of His Resurrection. I'd have expected something else! Had He asked me, I would have suggested that He should first appear to Peter, or to James, or to one or the other of the disciples; but, certainly, not to us! When I think back, all of this was just His way of reminding us again and again: Your God is not like you!

MARY: Like you've just said, Salome, Jesus is, and will forever be a brother to every single one of us! And still, He remains focused on His Father. Remember how often He spoke of this?

"My very sustenance is to do the will of Him Who sent me..." (cfr. Jn 4:34)

"It is by my submission to His commandments that I continue to live in the love of the Father..." (cfr. Jn 15:10)

Jesus' love, His unmitigated devotedness to the Father was such that never, ever, would He ask the Father to provide for, to guarantee His own happiness, as we might have expected or demanded! Never would He have thought of subjecting the Father to His own point-of-view. To think "ultimatum," ... it's just inconceivable!

Jesus leads us along the way of humility, inspired as He was by His complete and total love: walking ahead of us, and still walking with us, Jesus followed that "narrow way," the only way which would enable us to live in the true freedom of God's own children...

SALOME: In God's name, Jesus founded the New Family of the children of God: a divinely inspired mission. For Jesus, birth without bloodshed was unthinkable!

MARY: Because His heart was aflame with the love of God, Jesus lived on a "different" level ... well beyond any one of us...

Through Him, and thanks to Him, a fresh flame came among us, the flame of the very holiness of God! At each moment of His life, His life was marked, so to speak, was scarred by that fire of God's Presence within Him.

The silence of God in those terrible hours of His passion and death, the Father's seeming absence weighed heavily on Him ... and yet, despite everything, Jesus believed that the One Who had sent Him remained with Him; He had not abandoned Him because Jesus did always what was pleasing to Him. (cfr. Jn 8:29) And, we all know well enough: on the third day, the Father raised Him from among the dead.

Oftentimes, I recall two things that my Son often said: the first: "The Father and I are one. (cfr. Jn 10:30) Jesus' heart overflowed with the very splendor of God, possessed that unique, persistent goal centeredness that surpasses any comparison... And the second is: "The prince of this world is on his way. He has absolutely no power over Me... (cfr. Jn 14:30)

And now, Jesus stands at God's right-hand, forever placed in power! In His eyes, there is that resplendent joy, the serene contentedness of knowing that He is the Beloved Son of God. Nothing will ever be able to take that away... Nothing can ever take His divine Sonship from Him, or His presence with the Father at the throne of glory.

The prince of this world will seek, will try, but will never succeed. Jesus cannot be touched by his wiles; He is much too holy, too far removed. The lies, the hatred of His enemies, their insults and the abiding contempt ... all of this will forever be frustrated. Him, they cannot reach! From His place on high, He is well beyond their power to hurt or to harm!

SALOME: Those words, Mary, they resonate deeply within me! "The prince of this world is on his way. He has absolutely no power over me..." The image that comes to my mind is that of a prince, high-up on the turret of his fortress. The city-walls are solid, more than capable of resisting any assault. Outside those walls, the enemy can gather, in however great numbers. They can unsheathe their swords, mount their ladders, and only live to learn that their ladders are far too short. They can shoot their arrows, but they will never strike their targets. The prince is there, well beyond their reach...

MARY: At what time in His life do you compare Jesus to that prince?

SALOME: It's when He was "lifted up from the earth..." (Jn 12:32), raised on the Cross. It was then that His love of His Father, and of all humanity was most obvious and most intense.

MARY: Henceforth, all of us ... each one of us has taken our place with Jesus on that turret. With Him, we stand "on the right side, on the side of salvation..." (cfr. Heb 6:9) From now on, come what may, we stand with Jesus, and He with us. And, "when it is nearly evening," He will still be there with us. He is the never diminished newness of God, and our consolation.

There is no bruised or wounded soul that His hand cannot heal. There is no tear washed face upon which His peace cannot blossom. There is no failure, or litany of failures which a new tomorrow cannot overcome. "By allowing Christ to dwell in our hearts through faith" (cfr. Eph 3:17) a new Springtime, a new Youthfulness can spring forth.

SALOME: Tomorrow, Mary, I'll be going back home, back to my village. And going there, everything you've said will be very much in my heart and mind... I'll not easily forget our visit!

MARY: And when you're there, be like a spark. Reflect brightly the infinite love of our Savior. In everything you do, be as a transparency of Jesus. Day by day, you'll come to discover that there are those who will open their hearts to the Good News of our salvation in Christ, Jesus. After all: "Love is stronger than death!" (Song 8:6)

Allow Christ to "come alive" in you, over and over again. In His willingness to serve, in His humility, His intense passion for God and His incomparable simplicity... Know and be unshakably confident that little by little those who will walk in the Way of the Christ will come.

Salome, I'll be praying for you. May His peace be with you as you continue on your way!

Jerusalem
April 22, 1996

———————

17

The Happiest Day

Some months had come and gone since Salome had left the Holy City. She'd gone back to her native village in Galilee. Mary too had left Jerusalem; she'd gone back to her village, Nazareth. As you might have expected, en route, she'd made a "side-trip" to visit Salome. Ever since their earlier visit, she'd so often wondered: after Salome had gone back home to bring the Good News to her family and fellow-villagers, what had been her successes, and her difficulties as she went to proclaim that "He is alive! He reigns now as Lord and Savior!" How had they received her when she got home?

SALOME: You know, Mary, the first thing I did when I got back was to talk with them about how Jesus had been such an upright and kind man, who — at the same time — had been consumed with an inexhaustible passion for His Father. And how — at the end — He'd come forth from the tomb, alive, radiating a new-found glory through the power of the Spirit...

MARY: Yes, for so many months, all of them had seen or heard of all that Jesus had done, openly receiving and embracing each person whom He met along the course of His days. And, through it all, Jesus remained focused on fulfilling His Father's will. How often did He repeat — in one way or another — those words: "My nourishment, it is to do the will of Him who sent Me, and to accomplish His purposes..." (cfr. Jn 4:34)

Did they remember any of this up here?

SALOME: They could accept that He was an upright and gentle man — He stood head and shoulders above any other. They'd really recognized that He was someone very special, so much to be admired. He'd become one of their "heroes!" They all readily acknowledged that none of them had ever met anyone as kind and gentle, as receptive and ...well, just plain "good" as He had shown Himself to be. "Everywhere He went, He accomplished great things. He healed all who were subject to the powers of the evil-spirits. Because, God was with Him!" (cfr. Acts 10:38)

MARY: And then, did you remind them of one or the other of the passages from the Sacred Scriptures which they might have been having some difficulty accepting...?

SALOME: Precisely! I remember having spoken with them about that one verse from the Psalms:" The Lord tests the upright." (Ps 11) And, they, too remembered that, but...

MARY: But, it all seemed just "too strange" for them, didn't it? Some sort of contradiction, something sort of twisted and contorted ... How did you ever manage to bring them around to see that "God does confide in the upright whom He puts to the test..."?

SALOME: Well, I recalled with them that text from the great Rabbi Eleazar: "Think of the landowner who owned two oxen, one strong, the other pretty old and weakened. On which one does he place the yoke? Obviously, on the one that is young and strong. And, that's exactly how the Lord God — may His Name be praised! — puts the just man to the test...

MARY: That farmer, in going into his fields, is intent simply on getting his work done well, and as quickly as possible. That ox who was already thirteen or fourteen years old was having a hard enough time just standing up; it was no longer of any great use to the farmer. On the other hand, the two year ox was only now coming to full strength. And, the farmer could depend on it. She'd tolerate well the yoke, and drag the plow from morning until night ... Did that convince them?

SALOME: Yes, I think so ... at least some of them! Some were saying that when misfortune comes their way, they turn to God in anger, angered in some none too clear way. They wonder about God's providence, and His love for each one. And, in a very real, but quite hidden sense, they rebel. At times, they even say it: "Why this? why me? I am no greater sinner than many another! I deserve better than this! Why then this? It's just not right! Why should I have to put up with this?"

And, right away, someone else would speak up: "God, our Father, knows you better even than you know yourself! As He sees you — and please excuse this comparison! — He sees you as that two year old ox, full of strength and vigor."

And, right along with this, someone else would speak up: "God knows that you can endure this, because your faith and your dedication and love are such that you will bear up under this trial." He has manifested His confidence in you. He trusts you enough to "just know" that you will transform this misfortune, that you will, somehow, accept this demand out of your trust and your love ... Because of His great and powerful grace, all of God's people, - all of His people! - will come to be closer to Him. The very holiness of God will be more manifest, more diffuse ... God trusts you! why then this rebellion again Him? I'd think that you should be grateful, that your heart and your lips would overflow with thanksgiving...!

MARY: Yes, beyond all shadow of a doubt, "the Lord tests the upright!" It's so succinct a text, yet so full of light when we ponder it... After all, think of what happened to Jesus: He was a just and upright man, One Whom God loved more than any other! And in how many different ways, and different places, He manifested the presence, the action of the divine Spirit. When He was tempted, and during those three years when He travelled the length and breadth of our land preaching the Good News, what had He shown Himself to be? He showed us the eternal youthfulness of our God, and His unconquerable strength! By His love, He remained unshakably attached to God, His Father, bound inextricably to Him. And, just as obviously to anyone who'd look and see, nothing at all could distance Him from any human being. His sisters, His brothers...

God knew well enough that His beloved Son had the courage, and a faith sufficient to surpass any tests, every form of suffering. The love which filled His heart would be strong enough to keep Him solid, firmly anchored, come what may! And, simply because He loved so tenaciously, He could overcome, conquer all sin ... even death...!

SALOME: And that's just what we know from the Canticle of Solomon: "Love is stronger than death..." (cfr. Song 8:6)

MARY: The Father placed absolute and complete trust in His Son. And Jesus — for His part — went about fully involved, "wholeheartedly, with all His soul, with all His strength." And He endured His dreadful passion and death, for all of us, to save every human being whom He sought to bring-back to God...

SALOME: In the name of every human being ... to bring all of them back to God! I did talk to them about this, all of this. Jesus underwent all of His sufferings, His "emptying-out," His agony... It was not His own sins — He was 100% innocent! He was the "just One," beyond all others! — but for ours, for the sins of all humankind of all times and all places. He died for us, for each one of us ... for me...!

MARY: For us, and leading the way for each of us, Jesus undertook that way of obedient submission, the way of humility, the way of complete trust in the Father. He is the Way — the Way He invites us to walk after Him. It is by Him, by Him alone, that we can return to the Father. And, that "return to the Father," He — first of all — He accomplished just that. It is IN Him, and THROUGH Him that God comes to us, finds us... us who were lost. And, He takes us to Himself, not withstanding the fact that we had abandoned Him...

SALOME: "We were lost, far removed from God..." And see how God's mercy was shown to us: He sent His own Son to become one of us. He was in every way, just like us, except for our sinfulness. He came to meet us there where we were.. and He took to Himself our deep desire to return to the Father... It was about all of this that I tried to talk with them. I used what I consider to be the most beautiful parable that Jesus ever told...

MARY: You're talking — I presume — about the parable of the Son who was lost, and who was found...?

SALOME: That story has always struck me deeply, so deeply that I pretty well know it by heart. Of all of His parables, I'm convinced that that one will always be the one known best! My eyes fill with tears each time I think of that story, even just in my mind...

"A man had two sons. One day, the younger of them said to his father: 'Give me what I have coming as my inheritance.' The father, however reluctantly, divided all that he owned. And a few days later, that younger of the two sons got everything together, and left his father's house for a far distant place. There it took him little enough time to waste it all on a pretty wild life..."

MARY: Yes. When I think about that story, I recognize that he'd had all that anyone could have wanted there in his father's house. He had everything; he could ... he should have been happy. But he left his father ... that father who'd worked so hard to provide all of that for his family ... And as he got farther and farther from the "home-place," he saw this as a "liberation," as limitless freedom. From then on, he'd be answerable to no one; he'd be "in charge." He'd be his own boss. He'd be calling the shots!

SALOME: And Jesus went on: "When all had been recklessly spent, a famine came upon that land, and he found himself in great want, and need. He finally found a job with a hog-farmer in that country, who hired him to feed pigs. And, how that boy was longing to eat some of what was being fed to those hogs; but, no one would let him..."

MARY: Lost, and in a distant, a strange country. And there he was, poor as old Job! He had nothing to his name. And then, that job feeding hogs. For us Jews, a pig ... we all know how despicable, how unclean a pig is! So, that had to be the absolute pits, the final degradation...

SALOME: And Jesus continued: "One day, he came to his senses: so many of the ordinary laborers on my father's place have more than enough bread ... and here I am, dying of hunger! I will go home, back to my father and I'll say, simply: 'Father, I have sinned against heaven and against you. I know that I can no longer be considered as your son; would you take me on as just one of your workers?' And so, he got up, and began that long journey homeward..."

MARY: Alone, abandoned, there was no longer anyone who really cared about him, who really loved him. It was his own fault, he's the one who'd walked out, who'd wasted it all; with nothing, without even any really sound reasons for going on ... he was like a dead man walking! Burdened by all of this, he thought to himself: "dying of hunger, and my father's laborers have so much to eat there at home..." You wonder why he was so determined to go back home?

SALOME: And the scene in the whole story that touches me most is the very end: "When he was still far-distant, his father saw him coming ... and was moved to pity...!

MARY: "...his father saw him coming ..." Just think of all those weeks and months that he'd dreamt and hoped for this day! How often in all that time that father must have scanned the horizon, leaning — as he must have! — on his cane, for he'd grown old. He so wanted to believe that he would — one day — come back. And, he'd hoped ... and waited...

SALOME: And, that son! ragged, and so skinny ... little more than skin and bones! He seems more like the poorest of beggars with hand held out, hoping for a crust of bread. He has no sandals on his feet ... he's like any slave And those worn and torn clothes... Seeing this, the father's heart melts...!

MARY: "The father ran up and threw his arms around his ... his son!" For an older man like him, should he have run like that? With the temperature already pretty high, shouldn't he have taken it a bit easier, even just a little...?

SALOME: "...he embraced him, tenderly..." It had been so very long ... But now, there was neither time nor space for "doing it right!" The day ... dreamt of for so long, had finally come! Finally he'd found a chance to show his tenderness, his love, his generosity, his forgiveness... if indeed this was needed ... His son had come home!

MARY: "The father embraced and kissed him ..." That younger son hadn't even had the time or the chance to interject a single word of his well-rehearsed speech. He hadn't mouthed even one of those three sentence he'd put together and had repeated time and time again as he made his way back home. And ... here he was: already forgiven. That embrace, those kisses displaced any need for words. What would have said anything more?

SALOME: The son collapsed at the feet of his father. Finally, he spoke: "Father, I have sinned! ... against heaven, ... and against you! I don't really deserve to be considered as a son..."

MARY: The father didn't wait for that last phrase ... "hire me as one of your workers..." He'd seen his son's sadness for the bitter ingratitude he'd shown. The last thought in that father's mind would be blame ... any kind of "blame": "You left ... you went off on your own, you already have what was coming to you! I have nothing more that is yours, and that's just what you'll get! From now on, I refuse to think of you as a son; you'll be the last and least among all the workers. What more do you think I owe you? You got what you wanted ... now take it; it's your life, now live it!"

For that father, any such thoughts ... well, perhaps that might better suit someone with a heart of stone! Maybe that's the way of someone without trust, with no idea whatsoever of ultimate goodness...

SALOME: After he'd stuttered those two phrases, the father cut short his little "speech." "That's enough of that now!" And, turning to some of the workers who'd gathered around — probably some of his older and more trusted workers, who remembered! — he said to them: "Quick now, go and find some decent clothes for him, the best that we have! And, put a ring on his flnger and some sandals on his feet. And go out, get the fatted calf; slaughter it. We're going to have a real feast tonight... Think of it: my son was lost, and he's been found! He was ... well, he was like dead, and he has come back to life...!" And, the celebration began!

One or the other of the workers must have gone to the wine-steward, ordering him to bring up some of the finest of his master's wine, something he'd been saving for just the "right occasion!" And, as the evening wore-on, that father, along with his wife and those of the servants who shared in the joy and gratitude of the family ... a new, a deeper, a joyous sense of being together...!

MARY: And, the happiest of all? The father! His heart could scarcely contain his joy. His son had — at long last — come home. And he could now— again — love him as only a father ever could; this son would be the consolation and reassurance of his old age. For him — although he might not have had the words — this was the happiest of all his days!

SALOME: Just think, Mary! When I retold that parable here at home, it appeared to me that they were overwhelmed just in hearing again that story of the son who'd been lost and was found. They found no difficulty at all in understanding that the father in the parable was our heavenly Father...

MARY: We all recall the Psalm: "The Lord is merciful and tender, slow to anger and constant in His love. He does not treat us as we deserve, forgiving us all our faults and failings. As a father is loving towards his own children, so is the love of our God toward those who fear Him..." (Ps 102)

How often I silently pray these Psalms ... God is all love, complete generosity. His compassion and His faithfulness know no limit. Any who turn to Him are forgiven...

"As far as the East is from the West, that far does he remove our sins from us..." (cfr. Ps 102)

SALOME: ...and, that younger son ... that's you, that's me! How often we've acted in this same way, just like that prodigal son. We've turned our back on our Maker, on our Father. We chose — in one way or the other — to go it alone, by ourselves; we'd be our own master! And, we reap what we'd first sown! Far removed from our God, we lost our way. We were off the beaten path; we were lost wanderers. Left to ourselves, we found no way out of our miseries, of our loneliness, of our "lostness." Just like that son, we were as if dead...!

MARY: For hundreds of years, we humans — and especially, we Israelites — we were looking forward to the coming of the One who would lead us back to the House of the Father...

SALOME: We were looking for a new Moses, for someone who would show us the way to that land flowing with milk and honey ... the House of our Father!

MARY: And that new Moses, the Messiah-king, that leader ... what greater gift could God have given! It is His only-begotten, His beloved Son. It's Jesus, pure and simple...

SALOME: And, that's precisely what I told them! Jesus, brother to all, and to each ... as you called Him when we talked together before I came back home. He walks with us, He stands among us. And, He loves us, each one of us, without ever growing tired. He holds us to His heart ... the Good Shepherd Who takes care of His lambs and His sheep ... and in such a special and loving way, the one that had wandered astray. And for us, try as we might, we can never turn Him away. Having but one heartfelt hope for us, there was only one thing He sought: to redeem us, to restore us, to re-create us within, to turn us once again to the Father, as His loving children...

MARY: And right alongside this, His gaze remained unceasingly turned toward the Father. Just like the chameleon looking two ways at once, Jesus was face-to-face with His Father, and eye-to-eye with each of us...!

SALOME: He stood with both God and with us! In His prayer, He bore every single one of us; in His prayer, He sought nothing other than to find and bring back that lost son. It is for us, and with us, that Jesus returned to the Father.

MARY: And, what you've just said, Salome, we must never let ourselves forget... It is us — the wayward wanderers, all of us sinners who've wandered far (cfr. Act 2:39) — that Jesus carried in His heart when He took His place at the right hand of the Father, in glory...

Nailed to the wood of His cross, it was for each of us that Jesus, the beloved Son, "offered prayers and supplications, with loud cries and tears, to God the Father, so as to save us from final death..." (cfr. Heb 5:7)

He returned to the Father... but He didn't go alone! He took all of us with Him... It's this that we cannot allow ourselves to forget. It wasn't only "yesterday" in Jerusalem (...well, "yesterday," ... some months ago) on Calvary! It remains here and now that Jesus stands with us before the Father...

SALOME: Wasn't it this that Isaiah wrote so long ago: "Here I am, I and all those that You have entrusted to Me..." (cfr. Is 8:18)

MARY: And it is also in this "here and now" that Jesus continues to come forth triumphant from the sepulchre. With God, time is not the same as it is for us. We live time as a sequence of swinging pendulums counted, and numbered... but it isn't that with God!

SALOME: That's something that we all recognize, Mary! Here at home, they all believed that without any trouble!

Yes, "a thousand years in Your eyes are as yesterday; a day passes as quickly as any of the hours of the night..." For the Lord, a single day or a thousand years; are they so different? And, a thousand years, isn't it like a single day?

I remember what Isaiah wrote so long ago: "Our human words are like the flowers of the field that dry-up, the flowers that bloom and wilt; but the Word of our God continues forever..." (cfr. Is 40:6ff).

MARY: Which is just another way of saying: For God there is no "before" and no "after." What Jesus did "yesterday," He continues to do today, and every single day, forever more... His prayer of supplication yesterday, uttered from the Cross on Calvary, it resounds still today, and through every tomorrow. His offering then is being offered now too, and will continue until time is no more!

For God and His Christ, "yesterday" and "today," "now" or "then" ... it's all one same thing...

SALOME: As I recall, our elder sister, Judith, spoke in exactly that way: "God, my God, hear my prayer! I, a poor widow, pour out my heart to You Who made the past, what is happening now, and what is yet to be..." (cfr. Jdt 9:4f)

MARY: Maybe, it'd help to rephrase another word she spoke: "God is not like a human being to be confined within the narrow boundaries of one or the other country, nor is He, like a mere man, to be subjected to the constraints of time, in any way "

SALOME: we were there, at Calvary. There, side by side, we heard Jesus' heart-felt prayer, so filled with unquestioning confidence ... There and then, His unshakable confidence in God, His love sustained us... And there, too, we were caught-up by His calm submission and abandonment into the Father's hands...

MARY: First, there was that prayer: "Father, forgive them! They just don't understand what it is that they're doing..." (Lk 23:24) Speaking for us, on our behalf, Jesus made His own the prayer of that younger son.

On our behalf, here and now, Jesus prayerfully implores the Father ... imploring forgiveness for us...

SALOME: And, at the very end: "Father, I entrust myself into Your hands..." With what calm, with what peace ... to Him to Whom

He had entrusted Himself in ultimate faith ... His trust was limitless. Nothing ... not even all of that could lessen it...

MARY: It is in our name, on our behalf that Jesus entrusted Himself and His mission into the Father's hands.

Here and now, Jesus invites us to repeat His prayer ... to make it ours...

With Jesus, we're invited to pray ceaselessly "Father, forgive us, we just don't grasp what it is that we're doing..."

"Into Your hands we entrust our very selves ... our very existence here on this earth as well as our endless life in eternity..."

In our name ... here and now, Jesus calls us to life in His return to the Father. He allows us to live there "where He has already gone;" nailed to the Cross, yet clinging to His Father's ineffable love... and where He lives in heavenly splendor, in the glory of God our Father... Here and now ... we are there, with Jesus, taking our place at the right hand of the Father, in the glorious splendor of heaven ... forgiven, purified, passionately loved by the Father...

SALOME: Here and now, we're safe from the Prince of Darkness. We stand with the Prince of Light, on His citadel walls...

MARY: Satan, the Divider, no longer has any power over us. Sharing in the very power of Jesus, in His very holiness, we live with Him, already now, at the awesome throne of God the Father. And, what "Better News" than this could anyone announce?

SALOME: When I spoke of this here at home, when they'd heard this Good News, there were quite a few who replied by admitting their hesitancy, and what they now saw as their mistake in having felt that "God should have..." It is we who should have said: God couldn't have done more, or other ... in bringing about the salvation of the world!

And, no sooner had they really opened their eyes to this than a number began posing the same question that those who'd heard Peter on that Pentecost Day, in Jerusalem: "What do we need to do...?"

From many mouths I heard their prayerful question: How are we to "return to the Father" so as to live with Him, in His Kingdom?

MARY: And, what did you say?

SALOME: In the same way that the Apostle did that day: "Change your ways! Be baptized in the Name of Jesus, the Christ, so that your sins may be forgiven, and then you will receive the fullness of God's own Spirit...!" (cfr. Acts 2:37ff)

MARY: They must come to experience their own passing over to God through their descent into the waters of Baptism... then — with the Christ — "pass over" and attain salvation. (Here, Mary was silently thoughtful for just a moment, and then she continued.) In reflecting on this, they must certainly have thought back to the Exodus experience, to the Passover at the Sea of Reeds, didn't they...?

SALOME: Did they think back? How could they have failed to? That memorable miracle of God's love by which they were delivered from the hands of the Egyptians ... who among us Jews could ever fail to remember?

"The Lord, our God, allowed those waters to overwhelm the Egyptians; they were annihilated; of all the soldiers and charioteers of the great Pharaoh, there was not a single one who did not perish..."

MARY: Yes! Jesus, our Lord and Savior, the new and authentic Moses... He comes to us through those baptismal waters. This is the real Exodus! This is no longer just a "sign!" He delivers us... He saves us from the consequences of our sins..

What did you have to do, Salome ... how did you lead them to some understanding of the breadth and depth of this mystery?

SALOME: Well, first of all, I reminded them of those crowds who went out to John at the Jordan...

MARY: And, then...?

SALOME: They remembered how so many, even some Pharisees and Sadducees, had gone out to be baptized by John...

But I didn't stop with that! I spoke to them about how they'd gone out into the desert, and come to the banks of the Jordan and submitted to that baptism calling upon the Name of God, the most Holy. And, in so doing, they separated themselves — in a very real way — they separated themselves from their past! They committed themselves to renewed generosity toward the little people, the outcasts; the tax collectors among them committed themselves to collecting only what was due. Even the soldiers saw fit to renounce injustice, from any and all forms of extortion or bribery; they'd be content with their salaries...

MARY: Yes, Salome! But, what was the result of all of that? What came of all of that?

SALOME: Well, many ... perhaps most of those who were baptized by John returned to their old ways; their good intentions remained — for the most part — just that, intentions! Do I have to explain?

MARY: They pretty much forgot, or at least neglected what John had said: "I baptize you in water, to symbolize your change of heart; but One will come after me Who is more powerfull than I. He will baptize you in the Holy Spirit, in fire!" (cfr. Mt 3:11)

SALOME: My kinsfolk, the people up here in Galilee, they remembered well that Jesus was filled with the power and the invincible strength of the Most High God!

They remembered the blind who'd come to Jesus, whose sight had been restored; they recalled the cripples, the lame who'd gotten up and walked. God alone knows how many, and in what ways Jesus' power was their salvation...!

Jesus also forgave so very many ... Mary Magdalene, the man who'd come to Him paralyzed, Zachaeus, and even Peter himself.

He let the overwhelming power of God flow through Him, to give life to the dead ... the son of that widow at Naim, and his friend, Lazarus... the one He visited so often, with whom He used to stay there in Bethany...

"Everyone in the crowds tried to touch Him, because a certain "power" radiated out from Him, a power for healing..." (cfr. Lk 6:19)

Through Him, the powers of darkness, the reign of Satan was ended and the Kingdom of God came among us. "The finger of God ... the supreme Power of God empowered Jesus to be the conqueror of all the demons..." (Lk 11:19-22)

In fact, Jesus, Emmanuel, God-with-us, showed Himself as the all-powerful God, the mighty Savior. There was nothing beyond His power, His strength! (cfr. Jer 32:17f)

MARY: And — with all the unforgetable miracles that Jesus accomplished — you undoubtedly seized upon those words of Peter, when he'd said: "Let each one of you open yourself to be baptized into Christ, Jesus, for the forgiveness of your sins, and then you will receive the gift of the Holy Spirit..."

SALOME: And that's just what happened! ... Ever so gradually, they came to see that "in leaving this world and returning to the Father," Jesus gathered. and continues to bring together all those wayward, wandering "sons" into the House of His Father...

Just ever so gradually they came to understand that — through Baptism — Jesus yet again, the true Moses, comes to save them, to obtain for them the forgiveness of their sins...

MARY: You helped them to see that the Lord lives — most assuredly — among us, but more importantly, that He continues to live: that He is NOW the Savior of His people...

SALOME: The awesome story of the Exodus — which we never fail to recite over and over in all of our prayers, which every one of us Jews knows by heart — "He struck down the first-born of Egypt, for His fidelity and His love endure forever." (cfr. Ps 136:10)

MARY: Daily, we Jews remind ourselves and one another that the Lord God destroyed the army of the Egyptians, their horses and their chariots. Just as you've said: "God poured the waters upon the Egyptians at the Sea of Reeds, and He subdued them in allowing them to drown! Of all the armies of the Egyptians who had pursued Israel, not one survived! The depths of the sea overwhelmed them! They sank to the bottom of the sea like so many stones!" (cfr. Dt 11:4; 15:5; Ex 14:28)

SALOME: Mary, isn't that why we Israelites so love to tell and retell the story of the Exodus, of our deliverance from the land of Egypt where we were dealt with so miserably, as slaves? That's all in the past... it goes back more than a thousand years!

It goes back well over a thousand years ... and still — for us — among us — it's as yesterday: the passage of time means absolutely nothing to God. You've said it yourself just now: with God, there is no "before" and "after," no "yesterday" or "today," no "now" or "then" ... with God, that's all one same thing...!

MARY: A land as beautiful as this, and — for that matter! — all the lands of the earth ... God watches over them, He cares for each one of them, and for us, and equally for everyone on the face of this earth ... and everyone who'll come to life for the next thousand ... or ten thousand years... God knows ... cares for ... watches over each of them.

SALOME: Isn't this just what you were saying a minute ago, Mary? Remembering a word of Judith, you said: "God is not like a human being to be confined within the narrow boundaries of one or the other country, nor is He, like a mere man, to be subjected to the constraints of time, in any way."

MARY: All of us Jews, as well as all women and men who live on the face of this earth, before us and after us, we all hold dearly to one undeniable truth: We were not "there" when — long ago! — our God delivered us from the hands of the Egyptians, but we remember this as having happened to each of us, in our own time and place...

God's infinite love is far above and beyond times and places ... and He thinks and watches over each of us. We are all a part of that people which He chose to save, to deliver from bondage. Each one of us, such as we are, we're the ones He is saving, rescuing...

In that long past "yesterday," the Lord God in that awesome Exodus event manifested an extraordinary love for His chosen people, Israel; "today" that love is not diminished; it is as fierce and as strong as ever ... and such it will be for each succeeding generation...

Isn't this the reason why each of us Jews must come to see ourselves as if we are one of those being delivered from Egypt's slavery?

In our own time and place, each of us is loved, infinitely, by our God, today as yesterday. His love, strong and fierce as ever, is there to save us, to deliver us, to lead us to a new freedom, to a new land of promise...

There is always that one thing that we'd never question, or deny: every single one of us Israelites is as the whole people; and yet, each of us is loved uniquely by our Lord God. We can count on Him... His loving care, and His caring love will never fail us...

SALOME: And this, precisely, is what we sing out when we pray the Psalms:

"The Lord-God will do this for me. Lord, Your faithfulness is without limit in time or in space. Lord, do not abandon the work of Your hands..." (cfr. Ps 137)

"My soul is at peace before the Lord God. My salvation comes from His hand; He is my rock of refuge; my safety and my deliverance is in Him ..." (cfr. Ps 62)

MARY: For me, there's one little verse in one of the Psalms that recurs time and time again:

"The Lord is my Shepherd, I shall have my fill (cfr. Ps 23)

SALOME: You know, what you just said strikes a chord in me, Mary! All of us — and each one of us — we ought to see ourselves as if we are one of those being delivered from Egypt's slavery! When you think about it, what is "past" continues even now. That salvation granted us by the Lord God is even now being accomplished among, and in us...

MARY: And now, with Jesus gloriously Risen, gloriously returned to the right hand of the Father, we know Him to be the Savior, the new and authentic Moses. Egypt — from which we all come — it's not miles and miles from here, but it's within our own heart. And it is this that is completely "new" for us, for those seeking to remain faithful to Him, for His disciples...

SALOME: Daily, we have to seek to become more "real!" We who are the slaves of our hypocrisies pretending to be those who are in "good standing" while — in reality — we're living an illusion! We've simply blindfold ourselves!

Having our Law, the commands of God, which were given to channel us in our struggles and our efforts and energies toward becoming truly "holy," as God is Holy, yet, we are no more "saved" than the pagans...

We've been chosen from among all peoples to be God's own, in His righteousness and His love, under His ever watchful care; yet, the reality is simply that our hearts remain fixed on the here and now, on our meager possessions, on our actions, our own activities... It's only too true: that land that bespeaks "slavery," from which we so want to go forth ... it's really in our hearts that it roots itself!

MARY: And Jesus, He's the One who came to lead us out...

Coming among us, Jesus holds all of us, prodigals, and all the "prodigals" of the whole world, from the time of Adam until the last human being, at the end of time — He holds all of us in His heart...

On the Cross, Jesus endured that terrifying humiliation, yet His eyes and His heart remained irremovably fixed on His Father. And, it is His love which heals us!

On the Cross, and in His victory on the day of Passover, Jesus is the same "yesterday" and "today," and for all time to come. He did it all! He did it completely! Attached so intimately to His Father, and He allows us — His disciples — to share in His very identity as the One dearly beloved by the Father. Alive with His Spirit, Jesus transforms, recreates us in His own likeness...

On our behalf, before us and for us, Jesus underwent the real Exodus, deliverance from our encompassing enslavement. He, the first of many brethren, escaped the powers of that Enemy, the Prince of Darkness and Death...

On our behalf, before us and for us, Jesus returned to the Father. Here and now, and in each succeeding "here and now" for all ages to come, He is the Way to the Father!

SALOME: During those years of His ministry up here, my family, and the townspeople had seen how Jesus had healed the sick. I simply reminded them: "By your accepting the Baptism of Jesus, the Christ, you are simply doing what so many of those have done. You go to Him and simply ask ... you repeat — in your own way — the prayer that was theirs: "Lord, I want to see. Lord, I want to walk. Lord, son of David, grant that I might hear again!" Or perhaps, you simply cry out, a bit like Peter when he saw that he was about to be swallowed up in the sea: "Lord, save me...!"

MARY: Yes, in those days, the sick — or at least, those among them who could be there where Jesus was passing by — they were all healed, cleansed, sanctified. Not a one of them returned home empty handed...

Jesus, very much alive, restored them; He gave them new life. The "Prince of Life," the new and true Moses, brought them back from all their afflictions, from their sins...

SALOME: And, it was then that my relatives and the others began to grasp just what the Good News was all about ... how it was given to afford a new joy, a deeper peace to so many, to each one who would listen and really hear ... wherever they might find themselves on the face of this earth...

Yesterday ... what was it? hundreds? thousands of the "infirm" were healed and purified, saved and sanctified by the all Holy God, by the Immortal, the Almighty!

And ... that "yesterday" doesn't end! The miracles of love, Jesus repeats them over and over, in each generation, until He returns, surrounded by the angels of heaven, in all His splendor and glory...

Jesus' story — his Passing-Over from this world to the Father through His Cross and the Victory at Passover — that story goes on and on. Who could enumerate the times or the ways in which Jesus showed Himself at work in the lives of those who'd been baptized...?

MARY: And, you know, Salome, I can just imagine you talking with them, and telling them that through our Baptism, we are gradually "taken-up" into the full reality of Jesus, just as the sick and ailing were "taken" to Jesus to be healed...

We can't allow ourselves to forget the fact that — in our Baptism — it is Jesus who comes to us, and not the other way around! He who is more powerful, certainly, than John the Baptizer, He whose love is so overpowering, He empowers those waters to cleanse us from our sinfulness...

SALOME: And who among us doesn't recognize that — were we to remain submerged in those waters for any significant length of time — we'd drown! It all happens in so brief a moment... yet, it marks us for an eternity!

MARY: In the waters of our Baptism, it is Jesus Himself who puts to death all of our sinfulness, all that which distances us from God. He Who is Life itself, Who radiates the very glory of the Father, He catches us up into His own awesome triumph over death, and — with Him — grants us our places at the right hand of the Father...

SALOME: A deeper Exodus, a very real going forth from enslavement ... that's what Jesus accomplishes within us in our Baptism. We need only call to mind that "...of all Pharaoh's army, not one survived! The depths engulfed them all. They were all swallowed up by the depths, just like so many stones..."

MARY: ...with all our sins ... that's what Jesus accomplishes in and through His own death!

All those yokes which put us under the power of the Enemy, all the darkness which overshadowed our lives, all of our half-heartedness in seeking to live in complete harmony with God's laws ... it is all of this that Jesus crucified when He accompanied us to our true home, that of our God and Father in heaven.

SALOME: And, really, we are so very much like that prodigal son, caught up in the embrace of his father...

MARY: Jesus takes our hand in His, and allows us to share in His own triumph, His own joy and peace. By our Baptism, He engulfs our hearts in His Spirit of holiness and righteousness. He shares His very life with us as beloved children of God...

SALOME: And, when I'd explained this tremendous Mystery, all of them — family, relatives, acquaintances — all of them could only shout out that which our ancestors themselves had said: "Every Jew ought to think of himself or herself as one of those delivered from the hand of Pharaoh!" We rightly believe that by our Baptism, God Himself, our Father looks upon us in the very same way that He looks upon Him Who is the first-born of many brothers and sisters...

Through our Baptism, the Father says to each one of us: "Clothe yourself in your most resplendent garments! Put a ring on your finger, and sandals on your feet. We are going to have ... we have to have a great celebration!"

MARY: So, at that time, what did you do? What happened?

SALOME: Two young men from our village went down to Jerusalem and — soon thereafter — the apostle Peter came. On that first Lord's Day, those in my own family and a sizeable number of our neighbors were baptized; and together we celebrated by "breaking Bread" together.

And there was a deep, pervasive peace among us. As I recall now, a joy seemed to radiate from all of them. There were those who told me personally how they felt that Jesus Himself had placed a new heart within them, just as God has promised through the prophet, Ezechiel. Today, Jesus brought to fulfillment that promise, for us and among us, right here in this tiny, insignificant little village! As they said, "I just want you to know, Salome, that I feel that this is the happiest day of my whole life...!"

And another quietly told me about how she remembered the way that Jesus had come among them, and how He had healed the maimed and the infirm. But today, He'd accomplished even more; He'd led us from this world into His Kingdom of light and splendor ... from now on, we live with Him, in the House of His and our Father! Alleluia!!

One of the old-timers in our village told me something that he'd come to realize: "Remember, Salome, how God has spoken to us today in exactly the way He first spoke to His Son on the banks of the Jordan, and again on Mount Tabor: "You are my dearly beloved child, one whom I myself have chosen!" I'm an old man now, a grandfather ... and from now on, I'm as His dearly loved child! All of us have been given a new identity; we're no longer just citizens of Israel; we are citizens in His Kingdom. Yes, we remain in this world, but we've received the assurance of something more ... much more: the promise of that glory and magnificence that Jesus has received from the Father! One day — for some of us, sooner; for others, not that soon! — that inheritance will be ours! Thanks and praise be to God!"

And, someone else said simply: "You know, I don't have anything more in my purse today than I had yesterday. But, by my Baptism today, Jesus has come once more to be with us, among us! And, He has handed us riches beyond counting! He Himself is our treasure; it is now He whom we possess deep in our hearts! Thanks be to Him, we possess greater riches than the great Caesar, or Alexander ... or any ... or all of the kings combined, with all their gold and precious stones. His love is of so much more value than all the gold you can imagine! Alleluia!!"

So many of them came up to me and expressed their deep happiness! In my whole life, I've never known so many who were so effervescently joyous as on that day! One thing that no one would dare deny: that day, for all of us there, the Kingdom of God was right there, among us! ... Heaven was already in our midst!!

MARY: As I was listening to you, Salome, there's one word that kept coming up: today! I have no doubt but that you remember that day as the most blessed of all; Jesus Himself had again come among you... But, when we say "today" ... that means every single day that we live on this earth, one day following another! Every "today," Jesus lives on in the hearts of those who continue to "live" the awesome and tremendous experience of that Easter morning. From that moment on, He IS their Lord, and He will watch over each of them patiently. watchfully, and tirelessly! His Spirit will be with them, infusing new life, new strength, new courage ... sustaining them as they walk with their God, their Father, in His love!

SALOME: And that's our Hymn of Thanksgiving! (Salome quietly begins to sing of her own joy at having entered into the House of the Father.) "How my heart found joy as I said: let us go to the House of the Lord..." (Ps 122)

MARY: (...she has joined into the chant of that Psalm, right along with Salome ...) "...how deep, how great is my joy as I reflect yet again: How good it is to go to the House of the Lord."

St. Paul MN
November 5, 1996

Walking in Their Footsteps

18

Like and Aqueduct

*In the major trading and commercial center of Ephesus,
about the year 67, Timothy, one of Paul's co-workers, had
instructed Alexander in the faith and had baptized him.
Alexander was married, with a family of his own and he
was also a budding musician. Every Sunday, he, with his
children, shared in the "Lord's Supper," listening, on those
occasions, to Timothy's stirring sermons, which seemed
almost always to center on "the Breaking of the Bread,"
that remembrance of the Lord Jesus' death and his triumph over the prince of darkness.*

*Over the years, Paul's Letters to the various Churches
had been received, and circulated also in the Church at
Ephesus; and, quickly enough, those who followed "The
Way" in Ephesus made copies of them before sending them
along to the other Churches in the neighboring towns.*

*Just recently, from his prison in Rome, Paul had writ-
ten two letters to his beloved Timothy, who, in turn, had
shown them to Alexander. On one Lord's Day, later in the
afternoon, Alexander went to visit Timothy at his house,
seeking to come to a deeper and better understanding of
something he'd read in those letters.*

Perhaps, their conversation went something like this...

ALEXANDER: Those letters which you received from Paul...
which you shared with me... From what I can understand, Paul

thinks of you as an indispensable help to him on his earlier journeys (cfr. Acts 19:22). He really radically trusted you! In fact, from what I can tell, he entrusted some very special ministries to you. I'm thinking of what Paul wrote to the brothers in Thessalonica: "I've sent our Brother Timothy to you, a man whom God has chosen to work with us in the ministry of spreading the Gospel, to deepen and solidify your faith, and to keep you steadfast in the midst of your present difficulties and troubles... He is now back with me, and has told me of your faith and of your deep, enduring love, reporting that you continually remember us with joy, and that you're awaiting another visit from us, just as we ourselves are looking forward to another visit with you!" (cfr. 1 Thes 3:2-6)

TIMOTHY: ...and, it seems that he has not only a great deal of confidence, there's also a deep caring. I'm thinking of what he had written earlier to the Church members in Corinth: "If Timothy comes, demonstrate to him that there is nothing to fear there! Like me, he's doing the work of the Lord!" (cfr. 1 Cor 16:10) And, there's that other time when he wrote: "I've sent Timothy, my dearly beloved and ever faithful son in the Lord..." (1 Cor 4:17).

Paul certainly trusts me; it seems that he considers himself, in some way, as my father. Knowing his love gives me a great deal of assurance, as you can imagine.

ALEXANDER: And, there's something else that strikes me: Paul seems to know your own family too.

TIMOTHY: Yes... he wrote those words that really touched me: "I recall your tears, and how I long to be with you again so as to complete my own happiness. Continually, I remember your deep faith, which I first saw in your grandmother, Lois, and in your mother, Eunice. And I haven't the slightest doubt but that that is — deeply and solidly — your faith too!" (cfr. 2 Tim 1:4f).

ALEXANDER: Yes, I remember how you've reminisced with us about how it is that Paul went about writing his letters. Weren't you pretty close to him at that time?

TIMOTHY: His letters are full of faith, and of enthusiasm ... each of them, the one to the Church at Rome, to the Colossians, to the Churches at Philippi and in Thessalonica. Just remember, Alexander, Paul never sat down to write those letters.

ALEXANDER: Oh ...?

TIMOTHY: No, Paul had a scribe, a secretary who carefully and patiently wrote down Paul's thoughts and words. Paul would pace back and forth, his arms behind his back, completely focused on the Word of God which the secretary would write down. There are some things deeply imprinted on my mind and heart, words I'll never be able to forget: "It is with deep sincerity, it's in God's Name, before His very face, that we speak to you, in Christ! It is Christ speaking in me..." (cfr. 2 Cor 2:17; ib. 13:3)

And, you mustn't forget: when Paul writes, it is God himself who speaks, challenging us and leading us to Himself ... about this, I haven't a shadow of a doubt!

ALEXANDER: But, you'd have to admit: in some of his more recent letters, there are some things that are pretty difficult to understand, some things that are — well, to put it mildly — rather hard to understand.

TIMOTHY: Do you have something specific in mind...?

ALEXANDER: Yes! To cite just one example: "I remind you to re-awaken within yourself the gift that God has given you when I laid my hands on you. God's gift is not a Spirit of timidity, but the Spirit of power, of love, of self-discipline... Depend on God's power...in the faith and love that are in Christ, Jesus. You've been entrusted with the very Gospel! With the strength of the Holy Spirit, who is alive and operative in us, guard it! (II Tim 1:6; 1:14)
I'd be the first to acknowledge, I don't really understand just what Paul is saying!

TIMOTHY: Well, he begins by saying: "Re-awaken within yourself the gift that God gave you!" Let me put it this way. Paul demands that I not neglect God's gift, that I should not let it stagnate within me. Rather, like a rich, productive soil, I should allow God's gift to produce all the good fruits which God would like to draw forth from me.

...that I should trust in the choice which God had made, and remain convinced that God has "chosen me," selected me ... that I should never grow accustomed to this ... that I never take it for granted!

ALEXANDER: ...and that you must always remain deeply grateful!

TIMOTHY: Yes, you know: I'm still young, barely thirty years old. And still, God, from sheer goodness and His abundant bounty, has filled my heart with the Gospel of Salvation...

"God our Savior, wants everyone to be saved and come to the knowledge of the Truth. There is only one God, and one Mediator between God and humankind, Himself a human-being, Christ-Jesus, who sacrificed Himself for the salvation of us all! I thank Jesus, our Lord, who has strengthened me, and who has judged me faithful enough to have called me into His service!" (cfr. 1 Tim 2:3ff; 1:12)

ALEXANDER: Twice, you underline that "gift" of God: "Reawaken in yourself the gift that God gave you..." and "The Lord has given me strength..."

TIMOTHY: Yes, and only because each of us, all of us, needs to be reminded. Think of that other phrase: "Do not neglect God's gift which you possess, the gift you received when the prophets spoke and the body of elders imposed hands on you..." (1 Tim 4:14)

ALEXANDER: Which brings up a question that's been on my mind for quite some time now. You received the gift of God's Holy Spirit "when the prophets spoke and the body of elders imposed hands on you." Could you explain just how "our Fathers in faith, the Jews" were accustomed to beseeching God's gifts, which established the leadership in that community of believers? Did they too "impose hands" upon those who were to be their leaders?

TIMOTHY: Exactly! Recall this: God gave an order to Moses: "Among the sons of Israel you will separate the Levites from the remainder of the Israelites. They are to be mine. They are to be given to me, truly given to me, among all the children of Israel." (cfr. Nm 8:5-16).

Then, Moses laid his hands on those Levites. Which means that is was God's initiative to set-apart the Levites. Through their prayers and supplications on behalf of the people, they are constituted as representatives before God in a particular, a special way. Their presence and activities in the Temple would serve almost like a "filter" between the Lord God and His people. Without them, the people would never have made it...

ALEXANDER: Is this what you're saying? God provided the people of Israel with men whom they needed, with men who would intercede on their behalf. Certainly, in this way, God provided for His people ... and He continues to provide for them, even now, in our own times.

TIMOTHY: And, you must remember Moses and those who led the people of Israel after his death ...

ALEXANDER: Was Moses commanded to "impose hands" on his successor?

TIMOTHY: This is what we find in the divine Scriptures: "God said to Moses: take Joshua, the son of Nun, aside, set him apart. Impose your hands on him to demonstrate that he is the one who is to succeed you. In so doing, you will appoint the leader of Israel...!" (Nm 27.18ff) And, because of this, Joshua was filled with the Spirit of wisdom, because Moses himself had "laid hands" on him. And, as you'd anticipate, the people of Israel did, in fact, follow Joshua, listening to him, obeying the command that the Lord God had given to Moses. (cfr. Deut 34:9)

And, like Moses before him, Joshua led the Israelites. God relied on him to watch over His house and family, His people. And that continued, until our own times; and it will continue too on the house and family which Christ Jesus established among His disciples. It goes without saying...

ALEXANDER: How does God continue to lead the people of Israel, even now...?

TIMOTHY: Remember! "Moses had established preachers in each town, among each of the settlements (cfr. Acts 15:21). "They read Moses aloud in their Synagogues each Sabbath..." not only what Moses himself proclaimed on God's behalf, but also all that which is found in the Prophets and the Writings. Which indicates that Moses continued to teach and preach each Sabbath-day...

(Timothy is silent for some time, and then continues...)

Tell me, Alexander, in each of the Synagogues, that chair where the Leader sits, what do they call it? ... how do they refer to it...?

ALEXANDER: Everybody knows that it's called "the Chair of Moses." And we all know too that Moses is not there, physically. Never had been! He's been in the land of our forefathers for more than a millennium. We don't see him, nor hear his voice. Still ...

TIMOTHY: ...and still, that "same Spirit of Wisdom" who spoke through the mouth of Moses continues to encourage and to exhort believers. It is thus that our faith in the living and true God remains a "living faith." When preachers exhort us, it is God speaking to us, encouraging and strengthening us in our faith. God uses whomsoever He chooses to lead us, to seek us out, like the Good Shepherd.

And, we know this from so many "teachings" which are there in the Psalms and in all of the Scriptures. As just one example, in Psalm 138 we find: "...the Lord will do great things for me, because of His unfailing love. He will never despise the work of His own hands..."

[Timothy is silent for some moments], and then adds: "And then, for us who are living this New Covenant..."

ALEXANDER: Each of us ... all of us in our family of faithful followers of Christ, we too need to hear the Gospel; and not only us, but all those of future generations who will walk after us until the Lord's return in glory.

That word, preached with such strength by Jesus must be proclaimed "to the ends of the earth!" It was destined not only for those who heard Him during those three short years ...

TIMOTHY: Yes, during those brief months, Jesus rose up as the Great Prophet, recognized and acknowledged as such by those who heard His preaching and witnessed the signs He accomplished in the sight of God and of all the people (cfr. Lk 24:19). His words encompassed all, like the Sun "which crosses from the east to the west, and nothing escapes its radiance..." (cfr. Ps 19:6).

ALEXANDER: And those three years continue to be repeated over and over again, so that faith in the one, true God might spring forth, and put down deep roots in the hearts of people throughout the world. As the prophet Isaiah foretold in so striking a way: "Rain and snow fall from the heavens; and they do not return without having provided moisture to the earth which produces seeds and grain. Thus it is with my word: it will not return to me without having accomplished that for which it was given..." (cfr. Is 55:10f).

TIMOTHY: Think of it this way: here in Ephesus, and really, among people all over the world, the Gospel has to be proclaimed. Some — chosen by God, set-aside for Himself — will be consecrated completely to Him to go forth to proclaim, to lead other believers and to nourish their faith ...

ALEXANDER: That's so true! Will we ever have an adequate number of "Pauls" ... ten years, a hundred, a thousand years from now? Each one, in his time and place, will speak those haunting words of Paul himself: "It is with deep sincerity, it is in God's Name, before His very face, that we speak to you, in Christ. It is Christ speaking in me!" (cfr. 2 Cor 2:17, 13:3)

TIMOTHY: ...and that is what is happening to you, right now, day by day...

ALEXANDER: I'm not following you now, Timothy ...

TIMOTHY: Which brings up yet again what Paul wrote, which came up just a moment ago: "Do not neglect the gift which you possess. Re-awaken within yourself those gifts of God given through the words of the prophets when the Elders imposed hands on you

...You received a Spirit of power, of love, of self-discipline...!"
Think about that, Alexander ... that Spirit, that power of God, it is...

ALEXANDER: It is the very Spirit of Jesus. It is His Holy Spirit, the Spirit that guided and guarded Peter, that guides and guards Paul himself, and all of the others...

(Alexander is silently reflective for a moment...)

And then, right here, in our own gatherings, in our community... you are "sent," you are a second Paul! You have become the messenger of Christ, His envoy. It is Christ who speaks in and through you. He places His own word into your mouth! (cfr. Jer 1:6ff)

You, young as you are, you're empowered by the Spirit of the Savior Himself! Unbelievably awesome!

TIMOTHY: Yes, it is awesome! But, be careful: what really matters isn't that...

ALEXANDER: For Paul, for you, and for each of those who comes after you, the recognition and the acknowledgment that you are but clay in the hands of the master Potter, of the Savior Himself, and sent... How can you avoid recognizing the honor this confers?

TIMOTHY: What we most need to recognize, Alexander, is this: "We have never sought any special honor or status from others. Instead..."

ALEXANDER: Yes, "...instead we are unassuming. Like a mother, feeding and caring for her children, we've felt protective and supportive of each of you; we'd come to love each of you deeply, ready and eager to give you not only the Good News of Jesus, but our very lives too..." (cfr. 1 Thes 2:4ff)

TIMOTHY: I've come to realize: "...it is God's own Spirit, the Spirit of the living and true God, who supports and strengthens me day after day. Wherever I go, wherever — and whenever — I live, I feel empowered by Christ's love, which must radiate from me, because I myself have first been loved. The Spirit makes me a channel, an aqueduct through which the Savior's love passes unimpeded to those who hear that word..."

ALEXANDER: ...a canal ... or an aqueduct! You know as well as I do how long and with what determination the Romans worked to build the aqueducts, both in Rome, and elsewhere, throughout the Empire ... the impressive bridges, the tunnels, the channels. Here in Ephesus, we'd certainly be very thirsty if it weren't for the aqueduct which brings the fresh mountain waters to us...

TIMOTHY: You know, Alexander, the very word "aqueduct" means to "bring water." Stones and the mortar are brought together, to carry the water from the distant mountains to the city. Those miles and miles of masonry, all that construction, has just one purpose: to bring water to the people of the city. And now, you're comparing me to one of those aqueducts! And, how right, how just that is! I just can't find words to express my gratitude to Christ, the Savior. He chose to need poor human beings, men like myself! In His hands, I, like so many others, am just the canal, an aqueduct. My mouth, my hands, my soul and my heart, all of this is like the stones: Jesus uses me, uses each of us so that the life-giving water of His word might be carried to His sisters and brothers here in Ephesus.

ALEXANDER: So, right here, among us, as I see it, you stand in the place of Jesus Himself!

TIMOTHY: Now, wait a minute there! Never would I presume to say, or even to think that I am taking Jesus' place here among you!

ALEXANDER: Why not?

TIMOTHY: Remember Rome ... it must be about a dozen or so years ago ... who was then the Emperor?

ALEXANDER: Claudius! And, Nero has now taken his place!

TIMOTHY: When Claudius died, Nero succeeded him, he took over, in his place. And me ... do you think that I'd presume to say that I've "taken Jesus' place?" ...that I succeeded Him? If I said that, I'd be saying that Jesus was dead, gone...

ALEXANDER: ...and had not risen from the tomb!

TIMOTHY: Yeah! That Gospel — in which we've found such deep, lasting joy and peace — is simple enough: Jesus is alive! Today ... for all time, He is Lord, Master! "Alive now and forever, He intercedes before the Father for all who turn to Him!" (cfr. Heb 7:25) Forever at the right hand of the Father in glory, He intercedes for us while we continue on our earthly pilgrimage.

And here, Jesus — the new, the true Moses — who loved me, who chose me, and who elected the likes of me to serve as His spokesman ... He...!

Never forget, Alexander, I am only His spokesman; in no way do I replace, much less displace Him! It is His choice to use human persons like myself to proclaim His Word, so that His divine life might take root in the hearts of those who believe. I'm sure that you understand my joy, don't you?

ALEXANDER: And ... and isn't this the source of the deep joy of every true Israelite? Call to mind Psalm 144, "How is it that we poor humans mean anything to You, Lord? We disappear like a breath; we last no longer than a passing shadow. But You, Lord, watch over us; You trust us, You love us!"

Whether today or yesterday, or ten, or a hundred years ago, God made use of the Levites and the Rabbis; today, here in Ephesus, that Word which sanctifies is still being proclaimed. And that is what happens each Lord's Day when we gather to hear His word and to "Break Bread" and then to receive the very special gift of the Savior, His very Body and Blood!

TIMOTHY: Like you've just said, Alexander — and as each of us knows deep down! — each Lord's Day when we gather, whom do they "see" when I preside and proclaim the Word, and break the Bread? who it is that they see?

ALEXANDER: ...what we see is a man, flesh and bones just like ourselves! And, that's it! Still...

TIMOTHY: ...still, deep in your hearts lies that deeper faith: when I speak in the Name of Jesus, the Christ, when I pronounce those

Sacred Words, "...take it, and eat it, this is My Body given for you! Take and drink from it: this is the cup of My Blood, the Blood of the new and everlasting Covenant... Do this and remember me!..."

Tell me, at that moment, what do you see? What is it that the believers acknowledge?

ALEXANDER: It's a human being, one like anyone else, who speaks those words... Still...

TIMOTHY: ...still, through faith, they've come to that unshakable assurance: first and foremost, right there in the midst of their gathering, it is Christ Himself who speaks words of everlasting life, that Word which continually renews and refreshes, and which presents that world yet again to the Father in an offering of love...

ALEXANDER: Timothy, what you've said ... that I believe wholeheartedly, without a shadow of a doubt. Yet, I don't understand! It is just too good to be true! It's beyond me ... I ... I can't say just why...!

TIMOTHY: Don't worry about that Alexander! Words fail me too! This closeness to Jesus — so impenetrable a mystery — this presence of Jesus, the eternal Son of God, the Savior, present still, here and now, among His disciples ... all of this, I find it difficult to speak about, to explain it adequately too! It's something higher, and deeper than human words...!

ALEXANDER: Is there an explanation? Can it be explained? I haven't the slightest doubt about its realness! And still, what's beyond our understanding, is it real?

TIMOTHY: Alexander, when Christ speaks those words, what does God expect of us? How are we to respond? to understand? What're we supposed to do? Maybe, just accept the fact: He is "all Mighty!" We need not ask ourselves the question: how can He make Himself human, present as we are, how can He be present there in our midst? Can the Eternal God come down, to be with us mere humans? Is that possible?

ALEXANDER: Well, I'd really have to admit: there've been those times when that has certainly been a question for me...!

TIMOTHY: Each of us ... all of us, we have to walk in the pathways trod by Moses and Isaiah, by Jeremiah, and by the Prophet Amos ... and so many others ... we have to walk faithfully, steadily, persistently ... We've got to accept, too, that we are merely human beings, ... limited searchers, seekers...

It isn't for us to set limits for God, to tell Him what He can and cannot do, ... or say! Standing before God, walking faithfully with our God, it just isn't for us to judge Him! We're not here to be the arbiters ... Who would we claim to be, telling God what He can and must do? As if His actions and His ways to bring about the world's salvation should be measured by our human ways of thinking, and doing. Who are we pretending to be anyhow?

ALEXANDER: So, if we don't understand fully just what is happening, what can we do? where can we turn?

TIMOTHY: Oh, there's so much for us to do, long pathways for us to walk. The first, perhaps, is simply to acknowledge that we are mere humans, creatures. And we must humbly live the Truth, deeper reverencing our God!

ALEXANDER: ...but, that seems complicated...

TIMOTHY: But, it isn't, Alexander. Remember that Sabbath day, when Jesus rose in the Synagogue? There, He spoke to the people...

ALEXANDER: ...and He really made quite an impression, because as we read in the texts, "He spoke with authority, not like the other Scribes always seemed to do..."

TIMOTHY: And, present that day, in that Synagogue, there was that man possessed by an evil spirit. He looked, stared intently at Jesus; do you recall the dialogue that followed this?

ALEXANDER: At the top of his voice he shouted out: "Heh! What do you want of us, Jesus of Nazareth? Are you here to destroy us? I know who you are: the Holy One of God!" And, in reply, Jesus sharply said to him: "Be quiet! Come out of him!" And then, the devil threw the man down, right there in that gathering, and right then and there, came out of the man, not even hurting him at all, in any way.

TIMOTHY: And, just remember the concluding phrases of that Gospel story: "A deep fear came over them all. To one another, they kept repeating: 'Who is this? What kind of teaching is this? He commands — authoritatively! — and even the unclean spirits abandon their victims.' And, this reputation about Jesus spread quickly throughout that region." (cfr Lk 4:31ff)

ALEXANDER: In that story, there were a couple of things that struck me. The first: "What do you want from us...?" What's happening here...?

TIMOTHY: As I've reflected on those words, what I understand is this: "What business do you have here anyway? This is our dwelling place, within this man! It is no business of yours! What do we have in common? Go where you will ... get out! and the sooner the better...!"
    Or perhaps: "Your presence here is neither needed, nor wanted! You've come into a place where you're not welcome! Just get out, leave the Synagogue ... leave us alone!"
    You said "a couple of things..." What's the other?

ALEXANDER: It's when they said: "We know who you are! You are the Holy One of God!"

TIMOTHY: Just notice, Alexander, that particular phrase ... can you remember it occurring anywhere else in the Gospels!

ALEXANDER: Let me think... (and here, he pauses reflectively for a few moments...)
    As a matter of fact, when I think back to John's Gospel, when Jesus had finished delivering that long discourse on the Bread of Life, referring, obviously, to the Eucharist, there were many who'd been walking with Him who simply responded by saying: "All of

this, it's just beyond us ... more than we're willing to hear! It's just too much!" And, so they chose to walk with Him no longer. And then, turning to the chosen Twelve, Jesus asked: "What about you? Would you also leave?" And instantly, Simon Peter replied: "Lord, where would we go? You have the words of eternal life. Each of us, we believe wholeheartedly that you are the Holy One of God!" (cfr. Jn 6:60ff)

TIMOTHY: And, remember, too, what the Apostle, Peter, said after the crippled man had been healed! As I recall the scene, this is what was said: "The God of Abraham, Isaac and Jacob, the God of our ancestors, has glorified his servant Jesus. This is the same Jesus that you handed over and disowned before Pontius Pilate, after Pilate himself had decided to release Him ... He, the Holy One, the Just One, the Prince of life ... you killed Him. But God raised Him from the dead; and we are witnesses to that fact!" (cfr. Acts 3:13ff)

ALEXANDER: Those same words ... "the Holy One of God" ... what do they mean? That man had been possessed by an evil spirit. Did He suddenly recognize Jesus' greatness, His power?

TIMOTHY: All he saw was a man, flesh and bones not unlike himself, just like any other who happened to be there that day. But, now he sees more ... so much more than what his eyes perceive! He cried out: "You are the Holy One of God!" It's almost as if he were affirming that ... somehow, deep-down inside ... there was someone greater than what his eyes were seeing. "Deep inside, the glory and the majesty, the splendor of God is there! There, the beauty and the holiness of the Almighty!"

Somehow, in some unfathomable way, that man who was possessed by the unclean spirit — in his fright — recognized that in Jesus dwelt the very power of God Himself!

ALEXANDER: ...and he was not alone! Many of those in the Synagogue that day, they too ... [And, Alexander was quiet and reflective for a moment ... and then went on ...] Nowadays, here in Ephesus, that miracle as well as many another that we know from the Gospels ... are they just "stories"? ... really, little other than folk-stories? unreal?

TIMOTHY: Most certainly not! Those miracles, all of those healings must be announced and repeated to each succeeding generation ... repeated by those whom the Lord Jesus had chosen, set aside, and sent out to proclaim the Good News of salvation!

ALEXANDER: Then, when the hour had come for Jesus to pass over from this world to the Father, He Himself undertook to commission His disciples with the responsibility of continuing His work. As He said at the time...

TIMOTHY: "...As the Father sent me, so am I sending you!" [cfr. Jn 20:21]. And so it is that I, the last and least of the disciples, I too am empowered to speak those words of forgiveness in His Name! Whenever I do, I am deeply and thoroughly convinced that it is Jesus Himself speaking in me, and through me. And, you can construe for yourself the peace and the joy that I experience ... as well as the awe ... not really so different from the awe of those gathered in that Synagogue who had witnessed the sign which Jesus worked.

ALEXANDER: "... the awe..." and somehow a deep gratitude too, I'd imagine!

TIMOTHY: Assuredly! As Paul said it: "It is with the fear of the Lord that we speak! It is Christ's Name that we speak! We are ambassadors for Christ!..." [cfr. 2 Cor 5:11, 20]. And there is that other phrase that I mentioned just a moment ago: "It is with deep sincerity, it is in God's Name, before His very face that we speak to you, in Christ. It is Christ speaking in me!..." (cfr. 2 Cor 2:17; 13:3)

ALEXANDER: Caught up by the very Spirit of God, you represent, you continue to do, in new and different times and places, what Jesus did. It's renewing the living presence of Christ over and over again... You give the living Christ to us, over and over again, don't you!

TIMOTHY: Now hold on a minute there, Alexander! On Sundays, when we gather to hear the Word and to break the Bread, it is I who speak the words that Jesus spoke. Here, and I know that I'm repeating myself, but I think that we both recognize and acknowledge that I do not "replace" Jesus; I simply represent Him. I do not simply "repeat" what He said and did, but in that act, He becomes present: through me, He repeats those words, He it is who transforms the bread into His very Body...

Each Sunday, the Lord Jesus — Him Whom we do not, can not see, nor hear — stands there among us. To His right and to His left, we — each of us, all of us — we are Peter and Andrew, James and John, and all the others...

Each Sunday, we are "displaced" to Jerusalem, to that "large upper room furnished with couches, all prepared..." [cfr. Mk 14:15]. We come as His guests. And He offers that final Meal ... here, today and each time we gather, to us and with us. Each time we're reliving, and re-enlivening Jesus' own words: "No one takes my life from me! I lay it down freely, of my own will!" (cfr. Jn 10:18) ...What am I doing? Simply being the "mouth-piece" for Jesus who again repeatedly speaks those words: "Take this all of you, and eat it! This is my Body, which will be given, for you!"

And, what Jesus asks of me at that moment is simply to take a back seat, not to make mine what is not mine. It is in Him that my faith is focused. And this ... not only do I do this, but each of us, all of us there, we recognize that it is Jesus who has invited us, who has brought us together, and who leads us, laying His life down for us.

It is Jesus again, sharing His very life with us. He grants me the privilege of pronouncing His words with Him and in Him and through Him. We are His guests, He "hosts" that final meal. And realizing this, we have every reason to proclaim wholeheartedly: "How magnificent this Mystery of our Faith!" (cfr Eph 5:32).

ALEXANDER: Oh ... that's it then! When we come together each Lord's Day, it isn't a reenactment, not a "second Supper" that we celebrate, but the very same Supper that we represent! And you, leading us, you are the ambassador of Christ. You represent Him. Really, Timothy, I stand in awe at the ministry that is yours ... think of it: to be an instrument in the hands of the Savior! Is there a more sublime, and more exalted service than to be an instrument in the hands of the Savior?

TIMOTHY: Keep in mind, Alexander, that word that Paul wrote to us... "You must reawaken the gift that God gave you when I laid hands upon you!" [2 Tim 1:6]. For my part, I am continually, acutely conscious of those words.

[And then, reflectively...] To be chosen by God ... made to be an instrument in His service! I'd find no words adequate to express the awe, the gratitude that I feel when I contemplate the ministry that He has entrusted into these poor hands ... and which will endure as long as I live! Alexander, it's awesome!

ALEXANDER: For my part, let me simply say "Thank you!" ... Thank you so very much for bringing me to a new, a deeper understanding...

Those words that Paul wrote in his Letter to the Church in Corinth come to mind: "I never finish thanking God for the graces which are yours in Christ Jesus! I continue to thank Him for the multifaceted enrichment that is yours, especially for your gift of teaching, of explaining, of enlightening! It is the Lord Jesus, Himself, who will continue to guide you, and to strengthen you, to keep you blameless until that final day, the Day of the Lord Jesus. Our God is faithful! It is He who has called you to live in unceasing communion with His Son, Jesus the Christ! [1 Cor 1:4f, 9]

St. Paul MN
July, 28 1997

Walking in Their Footsteps

19

A Lyre, a Lute, and a Zither

Several weeks after their earlier conversation, Alexander went to visit Timothy again. After the initial pleasantries, Alexander went on...

ALEXANDER: Timothy, I've been running into something lately ... something I'd never run into before ... or even thought about until now! It's this: I am finding a problem in knowing how to deal with those who'd ridicule, or, for that matter, even with those who are simply inquiring about the Faith. Some openly and forthrightly say that it doesn't make sense, that it's stupid thinking, it's ridiculous. Depending only on their human reason as they do, they just can't make any sense out of it at all!

Time and time again, I hear them saying: "What you're saying, it's just too contrary to everything that we've always known; it contradicts what we've always heard ... and held!" And, their conclusion: if we were to acquiesce in what you're proposing, we'd be accused of being crazy ... or stupid ... ourselves! We're just afraid that until you can come up with something that is more reasonable than what you're proposing ... well, don't bother us!

Timothy, how can I speak with them ... and convince them? What can I ... what should I be saying so that they will see that the Gospel is "worthy of faith?" What ... or how should I be approaching them so that the Word of God will be received? [cfr. 1 Tim 4:9]

And, in asking the question, I'm thinking not alone of those I'm talking with here in Ephesus, but all those too from Achaia, ... really, to the very ends of the Roman Empire!

TIMOTHY: You know, Alexander, in the Gospels there are a number of things that go well beyond what "reason" can ascertain.

This is just one thing that you're finding troublesome right now, in dealing with these people!

ALEXANDER: Well, as I read and reread the letters of the great Apostle, Paul, the whole idea of "eternal life" recurs time and time again. He comes back repeatedly to address that life which God gives us: "God's grace has been revealed by the appearing of our Savior, Jesus, the Christ, Who abolished death and proclaimed new life and immortality through the Good News..." [cfr. 2 Tim 1:9]. His enthusiastic affirmation of our life "in Christ, Jesus," of our having been reconciled to God..." ...well, you know as well as I do that there are any number of people "out there" who are simply unable to buy into that! It's just something that's beyond them! On the other hand...

TIMOTHY: ...on the other hand... Let me interrupt right there! You're considering something that they are simply unable or unwilling to consider...

ALEXANDER: For sure! Persistently, Paul speaks knowingly and with such conviction of the resurrection of our mortal bodies. Not only repeatedly, but eloquently and without a shadow of a doubt! "We are citizens of heaven! We await the coming of our Lord, Jesus, the Christ, Who will transform these poor, mortal bodies of ours into echoes of His own glorious Body. And He will accomplish this through the power which He has over all creation...!" [cfr. Phil 3:21]

You see, the resurrection of our mortal bodies ... they just can't ... and won't accept it! The very idea is more than they'll even consider, much less accept. For some it's just too good to be true, and they reject it; for others, death is the end of it all, there's just nothing more. What they're saying is just this: resign yourself, accept the fact!

TIMOTHY: ...and still ... what an awesome, what an unimaginable thing it is that God has given us in the realness of our bodily resurrection! What Paul wrote to his beloved Corinthians comes to mind: "This is what we teach those who have come to believe, and who have really "grown up" in their faith: it's what no eye has seen nor ear heard. What we teach surpasses all of man's fondest imaginings, that which God has prepared for those who love Him ..." [1 Cor 2:6ff]

Also, Alexander, let's not overlook the simple fact that "...only God's Spirit can, one day, open their hearts in faith!" [1 Cor 2:10-13]

ALEXANDER: Yes, I remember that. For anyone to believe that one day God will revivify our mortal bodies, that demands deep faith! Of ourselves, even the most learned, the wisest among us, we will never be able to conceive of, to posit such a gift ... or even imagine that it could be given to us!

To recognize and acknowledge the limits of our human minds, we have to submit to One Who can accomplish such marvelous things, to One whose power so far exceeds ours!

To take God's love seriously, and welcome His overwhelming power ... to accept something that simply exceeds our own capacities, God's own Spirit has to intervene ... God — He alone! — can support and sustain us in our humanness, and lead us to go beyond that...

There's no question about it! Here, I'm with you all the way, Timothy!

TIMOTHY: What you're saying really strikes me, Alexander! It is only because of our faith that we can accept our human limitations. We "let" God be God in **our** lives! We recognize and accept a power that simply transcends all of our human capacities. It's to say that we simply "surrender" to God. It's just that simple! That's just the way it is!

The most difficult thing for us humans is to walk like Moses in this ... with humility [cfr.. Nm 12:3]. Moses, of course, and Jesus, our Lord and Savior, whose own humility is reflected and replicated in each of us...

This kind of humility, perhaps the greatest and most demanding of all human qualities, is given to some... and not to others!

So often in the course of his long voyages, Paul ran into this, he experienced it all first-hand. And still, he never lost courage! His determination...

ALEXANDER: And, I think back too to all that he underwent for it ... like when he was rejected at Athens — which was, and still is! — thought of as the intellectual center, the "think-tank" of the whole world, the model of all the other "cultured cities," the home of the philosophers...

It was when Paul was there, in Athens, that their idolatry overwhelmed him. All the statues and temples of all of their gods, all in glistening marble ... and often enough sheathed in gold, too. It was there that Paul spoke to them about faith in the one true God, and the Good News of Jesus' death and resurrection. Paul was, himself, so caught-up in that Gospel that wherever he went in Athens, he announced anew "The Way" as Jesus had taught it, that pathway to salvation, our hope of everlasting life.

And when he was there, he didn't limit himself to preaching only in the Synagogues, on the Sabbath. He preached that Gospel of liberation even in the central squares of Athens, where such vast crowds gathered for business, or even just for conversations and discussions. They'd come there to settle their legal disputes, and it is there too, under the proticos, that they talked with one another ... and to anyone who would listen ... about their philosophical "findings," about their diverse and varied theories and findings. That's how they'd proselytize.

TIMOTHY: You know, Alexander, I was there in Athens with Paul and some of the other disciples. Paul never passed up an opportunity to announce Jesus' death and resurrection. The days were full, one more so than the last! And from morning until evening, Paul spoke of that which literally consumed him ... whether he was welcomed and received by the Athenians or not. His forthrightness and boldness caught some of them by surprise.

Those who were preaching about their own diverse gods found him quite bothersome! For one thing, they were afraid that Paul would draw some of their adherents and some of those that they themselves were proselytizing ... that their "converts" would turn from them to the God of Paul ... and then, they'd lose the offerings that the people gave so generously in their temples ... and which they "dipped into" as a matter of course. That was their game!

ALEXANDER: To one another they were saying that Paul seemed to be nothing more than a magpie, crying out and shrilling, fluttering here and there through field and garden, plundering all the grain and seed that he could find.

Then, one day, they grabbed hold of Paul, to take him off and denounce him to the civil authorities. On their way, they talked with Paul, saying that some of that which he'd been preaching shocked even them, but that they'd really be willing, interested in hearing more about all of this. "What is this new teaching you're proposing anyhow?"

TIMOTHY: So, Paul found himself there, under the Porticos of the Areopagus, before the Elders, the Judicial Council of Athens. And, very cleverly Paul gained a hearing even among them. Remember how he did it? "Leaders of Athens: in wandering through your city, I've come to know that you and your fellow-citizens are the most "religious" of all the peoples I've ever known!" And then, quickly and subtly, he moved on to speak to them of the one, true God, the Savior, Who was the Creator of all that exists. "Him, you seem not to know! It is for this that I've come among you, that you might know and believe. Open your hearts to Him! There is need for you to do something without further delay. In fact, He has established the time when the whole world is to be judged, judged in righteousness; and Jesus has assumed His place from among the dead!" [cfr. Act 17:16ff]. And you certainly remember what happened then!

ALEXANDER: How could I ever forget? The mere mention of "resurrection of the dead" incited them to smirk, to laugh and to ridicule. "We'll listen to you on this subject some other time!" A none-too-polite way of telling Paul that they weren't even remotely interested! Smarting under this rebuff, Paul determined to leave Athens...

TIMOTHY: You know: in city after city, throughout the whole world, those Athenians are known and acknowledged as very noteworthy philosophers, the most profound thinkers. There, human reasoning is considered to have approached its zenith. From one end of the Roman Empire to the other, they have that kind of respect. Did you ever know any of them, or anything about any of them?

ALEXANDER: Well, I don't remember whether it was something I read, or something I heard somewhere, but what comes to mind is something that I think was attributed to a certain Celsus. He purportedly said something to the effect that God can do nothing which would contradict the nature of what He had created. He could, readily enough, create the human spirit to be immortal, but — here Celsus was quoting Heraclitus — the mortal body is and becomes as so much refuse once the soul has departed. It becomes something unmentionable, just garbage. God will not, because He cannot make it immortal because that would contradict the nature He had created. Since He created everything that is, to do something that would be so blatantly contradictory would be to do something that would be contrary to His very Being. It just wouldn't make sense!

TIMOTHY: Yes, it seems to me that, for a philosopher, Celsus does have a surprisingly high regard for God. It's easy to note that he has thought and reflected much about God. And, he has also thought a lot about the capabilities and the limits of human reason. Yet, I still have to disagree with him when he affirms that it is totally inconceivable that God could call a mortal, a human-being, back to life!

ALEXANDER: ...Which reminds me of the renowned Greek poet, Cleo. We all know him with more than just a passing knowledge ...

TIMOTHY: Yes, especially since it would seem that he knew about Paul's conversation with the public figures there at the Areopagus...

ALEXANDER: Yes, I'm quite convinced that he'd heard about that conversation. As a matter of fact, the people of Athens had — in those days after Paul's conversation — discussed it quite openly, and quite freely. And, a couple of weeks later, Cleo wrote to his friend Protus: "Here, we've all heard of Paul, one of those Jews, really something of a rustic! His ideas about a "resurrection of our human bodies" will never obtain a hearing. No one in his right-mind would ever buy into something as absurd as that! And you, Protus, what makes you inquire about one such as Paul, anyway? Even your mere interest seems to me to be something of an insult to our most refined thinkers ... and their thinking!"

TIMOTHY: It goes without saying that Cleo writes well. But, he seems too convinced that his fellow Athenians have some sort of corner on the truth. He seems so unquestioningly convinced that no sane person would ... or could! ... ever accept anyone, or any-thing that would suggest the resurrection of our mortal bodies ...

ALEXANDER: And, the way he envisions Paul! For him, Paul is nothing other than one more "barbarian," one who has never pen-etrated the inscrutable precincts of the "thinkers of Athens," or of any other that their venerable Greece had produced! He certainly says just what he's thinking ... and I'd be tempted to say, rather presumptuously!

TIMOTHY: Yes, how well I remember that day: I was standing right alongside of Paul. And I can assure you that Paul was terribly disappointed afterwards ... to see learned men, real thinkers, who seemed to be so narrow-minded, so presumptuous and so arrogant...

ALEXANDER: ...and that's undoubtedly because they had become so completely dependent on their own systems, their own reasoning processes. For them, that is the only way to come to any kind of real and deep understanding. They're simply locked into that ... almost as if they were locked into a deep, dark cave. It's as proof of what Paul wrote when he said that we can make no sense from our logic alone, and that then we end up with darkened minds. [cfr. Rom 1:21]

It's as if Isaiah, the prophet, were thinking and speaking di-rectly about them when he wrote: "They can only grope their way along, like blind men. They stumble along in noon day brightness as blind men would!" [Is 59:11]

What they seem to need ...

TIMOTHY: ...what they really need is that shining light that comes to us from God, through His Word!

> *"Your word is a light enlightening me on my journey..."* [Ps 119:105]
> *"You, Lord God, brighten my lamp, turning my darkness into light ..."* [Ps 18:28]
> *"The Lord's light is clear, it gladdens our hearts!"* [Ps 19:9]
> *"You, Lord, are my light and my salvation. Of whom should I be afraid? Teach me the way I should walk, lead me along the right path. Despite the efforts of those who seek me, I will come to see the blessings of the Lord in the land of the living..."* [Ps 27:1, 13]
> *"You, Lord, have shown me the path to life, and your closeness gladdens my heart. I shall always find my joy at your right hand!"* [Ps 16:11]

ALEXANDER: Yes, we have God's Word there, to enlighten and to focus our faith; and those who journey with us are those whose lives are enlightened and strengthened by God's Word as they make their journey back to God.

For such as these, all the philosophers and ideologies of this world, solid as they may appear, are as dust on the balance of the scale in comparison to the infinite Wisdom of God.

For such as these, the blessing "God has prepared for those who love Him" [1 Cor 2:9], simply and overwhelmingly surpasses everything any mere mortals would ever imagine. [cfr. Eph 3:20]

These men of faith, each one of them, have simply gone beyond any merely human insights and perceptions!

TIMOTHY: That's true enough. All those who've gone before us in faith have allowed God's Word to be the rule of their lives; they've built their lives on the solid rock of God's Word rather than on the blowing sands of all human reasoning powers...! [cfr. Mt 7:24ff]

Through faith, they've surrendered; they walk simply before their God! [Mi 6:8]

ALEXANDER: In this, I think again of the example of Moses! I see him as one of the most humble men who've ever lived. And too, there's Job, and the seven brothers whose stalwart faith serves as such an unforgettable example. As one of them said: "It is better to die at the hands of men and to hope in God, and in Him find a new and better life, resurrection! [cfr. 2 Mc 7:14]

TIMOTHY: Yes, those seven brothers... and their mother who encouraged and sustained them in their desire to be faithful to the faith of their forefathers. Just recall what the Scriptures tell us of her: "Now, their mother was admired beyond all measure, and worthy to be remembered by all good men who beheld her seven sons, all slain in a single day. She bore it with great courage, because her hope was in God. She, filled with wisdom and courage from above, exhorted them in their own language, each of them. An unshakable 'man's heart' was truly joined to that woman's thoughts, as she spoke out and said: 'I know not how you were formed in my womb; I neither gave you breath nor soul, nor life. Neither did I form your limbs. It was the Creator of the world who formed you, He the source of all that is. He will again restore you, because He is merciful. You will find breath, and life again, just as truly as you are not despised because of His commands!" [2 Mc 7:20ff]

That woman of heroic faith ... and with her, all our forefathers in faith are sources of our strength. They are there, showing us the way God would have us walk...

And, in this vast assembly of people of faith, there's one who stands out among all the others, our "father in faith..."

ALEXANDER: You're undoubtedly thinking back to Abraham!

TIMOTHY: Yes! How often Paul reminds us to find in him an example for ourselves, in our own times. He does not go on at any great length, but what power, what forcefulness he puts into what he wrote! Those words are quite literally worth their weight in gold!

ALEXANDER: And, over these past months ... years! ... I've learned those phrases by heart! "The faith of Abraham, our common father, we make that faith our own! He put his faith in God,

Who restores life to those who have died, just as He calls into being what had not previously existed! By overcoming all motives for losing hope — so common among so many! Abraham believed with a total trustfulness. Even knowing that he was well past the age of becoming a father — he was about one hundred years old at the time! — and that his wife, Sarah, was well beyond the age of child-bearing, still his faith did not falter. Since God had made the promise, Abraham would neither deny nor doubt it. He found strength in his faith, and gave glory to God. He was completely convinced that God would accomplish everything just as he had promised!" [cfr. Rom 4:16ff]

TIMOTHY: Yes, at 99, Abraham — and his wife was 90, and sterile — knew that his kinsfolk were already thinking ahead to his death and burial. Still, when he received that promise from God: "Look up to the sky, count the stars if you can! And your descendants will be as numerous as these...!" [cfr. Gn 15:9] Immediately he was in a realm well beyond mere human calculations, he was convinced that God through His supreme power would accomplish what He had promised. [cfr. Mk 12:18ff]

Abraham believed that his offspring would be more numerous than the stars in the skies, or the grains of sand on the shores of the seas.

He believed ... not because he saw his son and heir, Isaac. No, he was not yet born, ... or even conceived. Yet, he was unshakably convinced that he would one day cradle a child of his own in his arms.

And, he couldn't have understood how all of this ... any of this, would happen! There was only one thing on his mind, and that was the Word spoken by God, the promise he had heard, spoken by God. One day, it would become real. And that was that!

ALEXANDER: Overcoming any feelings of desperation, so common among other men his age, he believed God who gives life to those who have died, and calls into being what does not yet exist. As the great Apostle Paul puts it: "He is the father to all of us!" [Rom 4:16-21]. His descendants have but to walk in his footsteps.

Here in Ephesus, all of us, children of Abraham, and disciples of the Prince of Life, Jesus our Lord ...

TIMOTHY: You know, Alexander, our challenge and our task is to overcome all those systems, those philosophical systems that men concoct, those philosophers and poets, like Celsus, or Cleo, despite their brilliance and eloquence. We must root ourselves in the conviction that all the lights of such singularly outstanding minds are like the flicker of distant stars on a dark night.

We look to Abraham and to the example he left us. We may never be able to figure out just how it is that our mortal bodies will return to life, how death will loosen its grip on us, but we can find a deep inner joy in the fact that one day, our Savior, Jesus, the Lord, will transform these mortal bodies of ours into images of His own glorious body. And He will accomplish this through the power which is His, and which dominates over all creation!

ALEXANDER: For us who truly believe, rather than walking with those well-known philosophers and poets which Athens offers, we have that deep, serene conviction that stems — not from what our own thinking can attain — but from that which is rooted in God's Word.

In the depth of our hearts, we know that the Spirit of Truth dwells within us, teaches us the awesome truth about that "life after life.' The Holy Spirit enlightens and guides us to that "last Word," God's Truth: "Jesus is mighty Lord!" [1 Cor 12:3]

In the depth of our hearts, the living and life-giving Spirit of God bears witness, confirms that which the pagans — into whose world we're placed — deny the priceless glory of the great mystery: "Christ is with us, among us, our hope of glory!" [cfr. Col 1:27]

TIMOTHY: To look at it in another way, what we cling to, what is posited as "the bottom line" of our lives is this: that Christ is "the first-born of all creation, the first to be reborn from among the dead!" [cfr. Col 1:15, 18]

He it is who has run the race, who has won the crown of glory, the first born of all creation. In dazzling glory and power, it is He who will share with us that which is already His. What He received from the eternal Father, that awesome splendor, one day will be ours too. [cfr. Phil 3:13ff]

ALEXANDER: And this is what we proclaim each time we come together at the Table of the Lord: "For the Kingdom, the Power, and the Glory are Yours, now and forever!" We rejoice not alone because Jesus has attained His place in glory, but we also profess our faith in that destiny that will, one day, be ours too!

Each Day of the Lord, the roots of our hope go deeper in the good soil of our hearts, that hope that "where Jesus is, one day, we will be too!" [cfr. Jn 14:3]

TIMOTHY: Yes! In my own heart and in my life, I find that that brief section of Paul's Letter to the Christians at Rome sheds abundant light ... it sustains my hope and nurtures my faith. You too, undoubtedly, remember it well: "The Spirit of Him Who raised Jesus from the dead lives within you. And, one day, He who raised Jesus will restore life to your mortal bodies, through His Spirit, alive in you!" [Rom 8:11]

Any of us ... all of us are saddened when one of us dies. Yet, sustained by our faith, "we do not grieve like those who have no faith, nor hope..." We know that "the day is close at hand when we too will be with the Lord!" [cfr. 1 Thes 4:13ff]

ALEXANDER: Somewhere deep within us, the Spirit of the living God glows brightly, like the sun, guiding and enlightening us as we make our way on our earthly pilgrimage. [*He pauses for some brief moments* ...] But, Timothy, I oftentimes wonder just how things are going to be in heaven ... This, I'd really like to know, even now!

TIMOTHY: So would I! But, it hasn't been given to us to see ... not yet, not now!

ALEXANDER: Still and all, it would reinforce and sustain our faith...!

TIMOTHY: And yet, it's just not given to us. Somehow, I feel that it is better this way!

ALEXANDER: How can you say that "it's better this way"?

TIMOTHY: Try to put it all together, Alexander! Through our Baptism, we've become children of God, our Father. And when we reflect on this: in our everyday ways of living and acting, there are so many things — big or small — that could hardly be seen as guided by God's Spirit. I say "we" ... well, at least, I find this only too true for myself!

ALEXANDER: And, I do too! My faith, my hope, my love of God and for the brethren is far from being what I'd want or hope it would be...

TIMOTHY: And that's just the way it is! God — in His inexhaustible mercy! — affords us the time after our Baptism and before our "passing-over" — when we'll go to "inherit the Kingdom of the saints, in light!" [cfr. Col 1:12] He affords us the opportunity to continue to strive to overcome these failings, these shortcomings...

ALEXANDER: Yes, that makes eminently "good sense"! God gives us the time for our faith to become more deeply rooted, for our hope to go beyond our doubts and hesitations, and for our love to burn away all that doesn't yet belong to God... It's the Lord Jesus Himself asking us and empowering us to accomplish what lies in us so that our lives may be on the same wave length, closer to the same rhythms as His own...!

TIMOTHY: ...that His heart and ours may beat in one same rhythm...

ALEXANDER: You don't have to insist on that! I see just what you mean! In our little community here in Ephesus, as you certainly know! I often accompany our singing with one or the other of the instruments that I play ... the lyre, the zither, the lute ... the harp! And, I'd hope that you've heard ... I don't know, maybe even remember? ...one or the other of the hymns that we've put together...

TIMOTHY: Tell me, Alexander! Isn't it a continual process to tune, and re-tune those instruments of yours? Don't they often times get "out-of-tune?"

ALEXANDER: Of course! As a matter of fact, even the changes of the seasons, with the changes in humidity, the heat and the cold ... the strings are "off-key," either too tight or too loose ... So, I have to tune them, to make the necessary adjustments. And, if I'd fail to do this ... well, the whole community would do well to close their ears!

TIMOTHY: And that's how it is! We're as those musical instruments, in the hands of the Lord. The chords of the lyre, the lute or the harp, these are our hearts, our faith, our hope and our love. Jesus wants to make us, to make of each one of us such that His own voice and ours might be "in tune." Each day, Jesus wants us to make those adjustments, to "tune" us ... just as you tune your instruments before you are able to use them...

We are already Christians, undeniably, irrevocably! But, we have to allow the Lord Jesus to "tune" our faith, our hope, our love, so that the melody becomes what He wills...

ALEXANDER: Yes, Timothy, I agree with what you're saying, with all of it. I guess that it is better that we don't know all the "particulars" of that life we will share in God's presence for all eternity.

Still, hasn't God left us at least some "hints," some "clues"?

TIMOTHY: That makes sense! There are some ... some "clues" as you've termed them! God has given some indicators about what He has prepared from all eternity ...

ALEXANDER: So, what, for instance...?

TIMOTHY: Well, when we read the Gospels carefully...

ALEXANDER: ...for instance!

TIMOTHY: Well, there was that occasion when Jesus took Peter, James and John with Him up onto that high mountain. There, before their very eyes, He was transfigured ... His clothes shone brilliantly, just glowed so much brighter than any bleach could ever obtain... [cfr. Mk 9:2ff]

And, Peter and his companions saw the Lord Jesus in the brilliance of His splendor [cfr. 2 Pt 1:16]. In this, they saw something of the glory that God had prepared for each of us when that day dawns, when Jesus comes to take us to Himself...

ALEXANDER: And, it's not only for the three of them, but for each of us too! ... for every one who follows Him. That brightness, that radiance which we find so splendid, that holiness which God alone can grant to those He has chosen and whom He loves so dearly ... and it is this that we can look forward to, when that day is finally at hand...

TIMOTHY: And, you surely remember what Cleopas and his friend told one another that day when their eyes were opened, when they'd recognized the Lord after they'd walked and listened to Him on the road to Emmaus...

ALEXANDER: Sure! Their story about how "their hearts were aflame within them" as He walked and spoke with them as they made their way along the road, when He was explaining the meaning of the Sacred Scriptures... [cfr Lk 24:13ff]

TIMOTHY: Well, it is in different Gospel stories such as these that we can come to some inkling of just what God has prepared for us. He will endlessly assist us to grasp an ever fuller meaning of His Word; for all time we will continue to discover the infinite tenderness, the gentle and persistent love God has for us ... it is without end! [cfr. Eph 3:18f]. We'll continually grow from one insight to another. And, our hearts, too, will be enflamed with and by Christ's love for the Father. It is thus, so that our own love for the Father will forever deepen and grow!

ALEXANDER: Yes, I see now that there are such "clues" if we'd only know how to look and find them. Are there others?

TIMOTHY: Well, yes, as a matter of fact. You recall what we've read so often in John's Gospel... "Towards evening on that same day — the first day of the week — while the doors were barred, because of the disciples' fear of the Jews..."

ALEXANDER: Yes... "Jesus came and stood there in their midst. He said: 'Peace be with you', and He showed them His hands and His side. Seeing Him, the disciples rejoiced heartily. And then, He repeated: 'Peace be with you!' And then, He breathed on them and said 'Receive the Holy Spirit'..." [cfr. Jn 20:19ff]

Through the power of God — which possessed Jesus in its fullness — He was there present among them. And seeing Him, they were exuberant!

TIMOTHY: And today — just as truly as in Jerusalem yesterday — Jesus is present to us, right here in Ephesus. And He continues to transfuse our hearts with His Holy Spirit, with a love that makes all things new... [cfr. Rom 5:5; Rev 21:3ff]

ALEXANDER: And on some tomorrow, when He returns surrounded by the Powers and Thrones of heaven, He will again renew us, re-energize us through the outpouring of His Spirit, so that the image to which we were created might be re-fashioned. [cfr. Col 3:10]

Then, we too will radiate a deep inner joy, when we see the Lord right there, among us ...

TIMOTHY: Right! As I read and re-read the Gospels, it is from pages such as these three which I've just suggested that we can catch some glimpse of what Paradise will be. We can sample, get some foretaste of what is in store for us! ...And our understanding will continue to expand ... if we dare speak of it in this way!

ALEXANDER: Timothy, I want to thank you! A very sincere thank you for reminding me of the splendor and the radiant glory that

God has prepared for us in and through Christ, Jesus. His Word is Light! It is a consuming fire! And, His very power will "dwell in us, in our very bodies..." [cfr. Col 2:9]

Each day we re-echo our own "Maranatha! Come, Lord Jesus!"

TIMOTHY: From the day He rose from the tomb and returned triumphantly to heaven, Christ is "the first born from among those who have died." He is the first in a long line of those "born again" of water and the Holy Spirit. And, one day, whenever it dawns, Jesus will gift us too with the glory that is already His!

Just as the father of the older brother of the prodigal son, He will repeat again and again to each of us: "You've always been with me. Everything that I have is yours!" [Lk 15:31ff] Everything that I have ... everything! And that means so much more than just "something...!"

ALEXANDER: So, when we affirm — each Lord's Day when we gather to break the Bread — that refrain: "For the Kingdom, the Power and the Glory are yours, now and forever..." we proclaim what will unquestionably come to be. With hearts overcome with joy, we affirm what we shall become. We are even now caught up in and tied into what shall be forever, with God, for all eternity!

TIMOTHY: Alexander, incessantly we need to call forth the Holy Spirit ... pleading that our hope might be solid as a rock. God is forever faithful to His promises. We have that deep, unshakable conviction that "one day, Jesus will transform these lowly bodies of ours into the image of His glorious body. And He will accomplish this through the power which He has over all creation...!" [Phil 3:21f]

ALEXANDER: We can just forget about those questions or concerns about the "how" of our own resurrection. We need only to repeat over and over: "To those who love Him, God has prepared wondrous things, unimaginable things! We cannot see now what that life of glory and splendor will be, nor can we hear the songs of praise that people of every time and every nation will be singing in

249

such a variety of languages. But of this we are sure: one day we will see, even as we are now seen by Him!" [cfr. 1 Cor 2:6ff]

We must continually try to make that astonishing hope which was Paul's become our own. And with him, we need to constantly repeat: "I desire to go, to be with Christ, which would be far superior to what is now ... For me, life IS Christ even now; but death will bring me so much more even than this!" [Phil 1:23, 21; 2 Cor 5:8]

TIMOTHY: And too, there's that which Paul wrote in his letter to the Colossians: "When Christ is revealed — and He is your very life — then you too will be revealed in all your glory, right along with Him!" [Col 3:4]

"Maranatha! Come Lord Jesus!" [Rev 22:20; 1 Cor 16:22]

St. Paul, MN
October, 1997